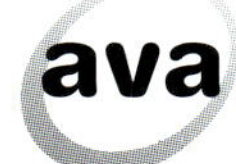

AVA Publishing SA
Switzerland

An AVA Book
Published by AVA Publishing SA
rue du Bugnon 7
CH-1299 Crans-près-Céligny
Switzerland
Tel: +41 786 005 109
Email: enquiries@avabooks.ch

Distributed by Thames and Hudson (ex-North America)
181a High Holborn
London WC1V 7QX
United Kingdom
Tel: +44 20 7845 5000
Fax: +44 20 7845 5055
Email: sales@thameshudson.co.uk
www.thamesandhudson.com

Distributed by Sterling Publishing Co., Inc.
in the USA
387 Park Avenue South
New York, NY 10016-8810
Tel: +1 212 532 7160
Fax: +1 212 213 2495
www.sterlingpub.com

in Canada
Sterling Publishing
c/o Canadian Manda Group
One Atlantic Avenue, Suite 105
Toronto, Ontario M6K 3E7

English Language Support Office
AVA Publishing (UK) Ltd.
Tel: +44 1903 204 455
Email: enquiries@avabooks.co.uk

ISBN 2-88479-027-6

10 9 8 7 6 5 4 3 2 1

Design and project coordination by Kate Stephens

Production and separations by
AVA Book Production Pte. Ltd., Singapore
Tel: +65 6334 8173
Fax: +65 6334 0752
Email: production@avabooks.com.sg

black & white

camera craft

william cheung

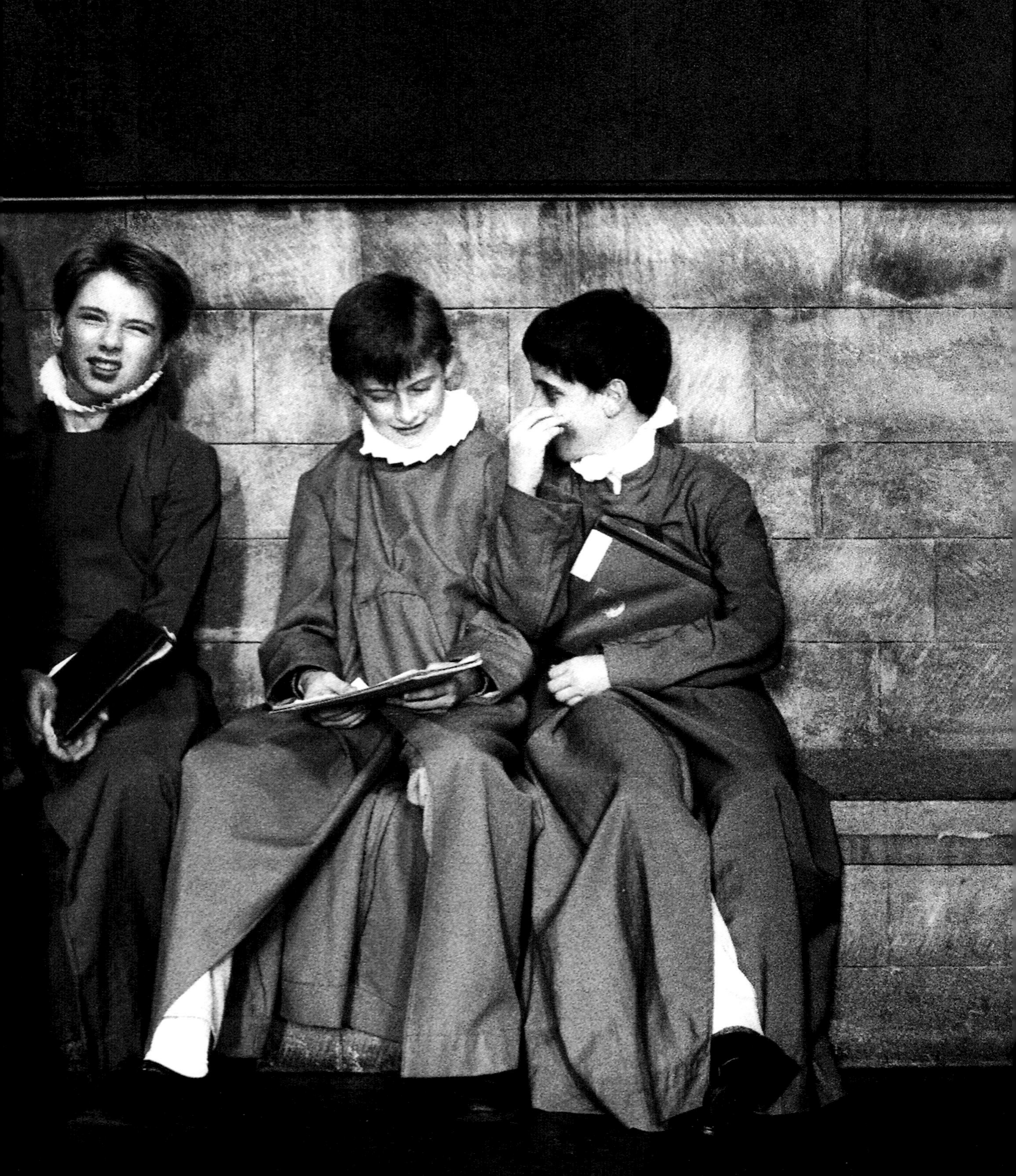

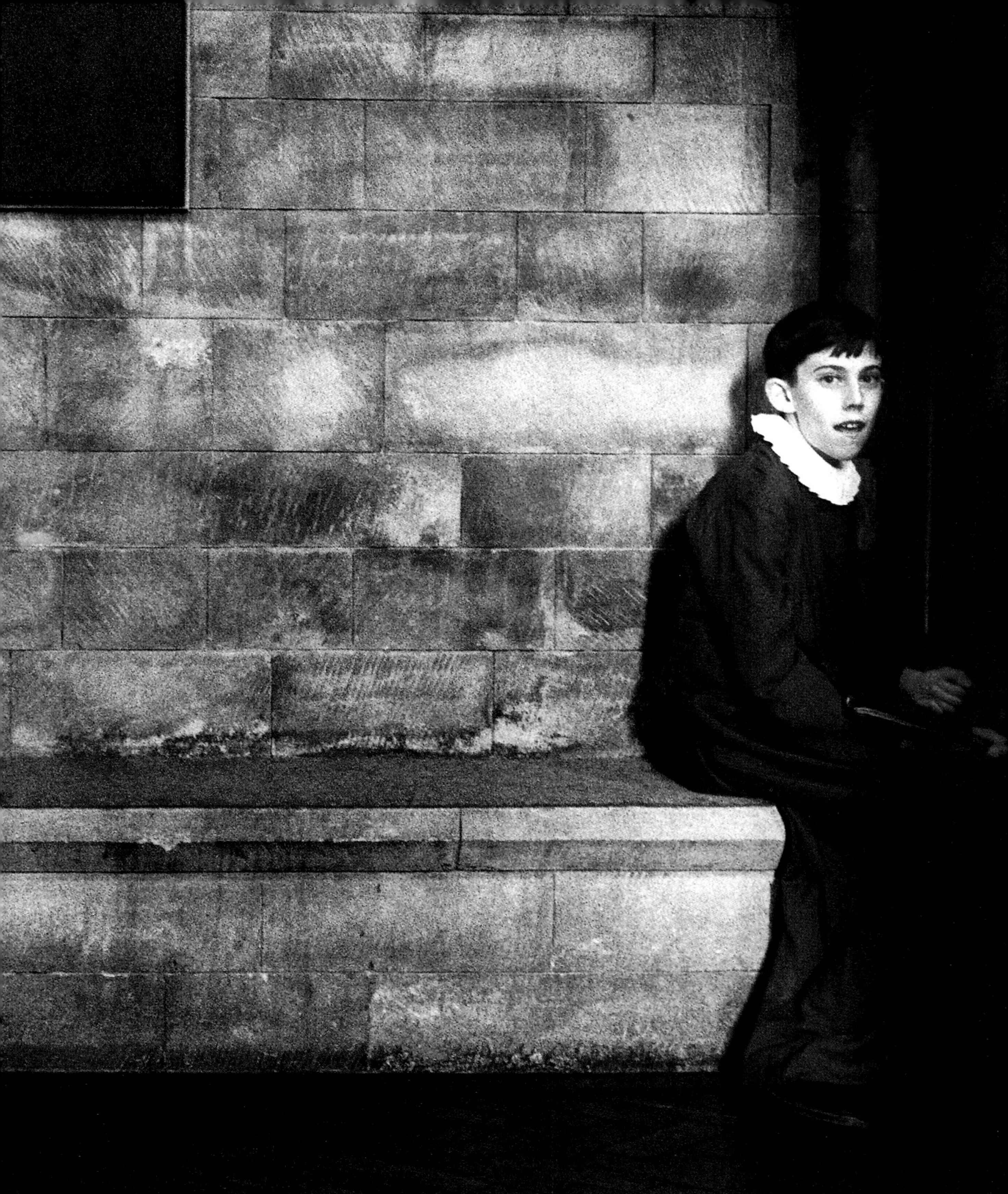

introduction

The world is an intensely and beautifully colourful place but I love photographing it in black and white. I have had a love affair with monochrome ever since I first picked up a camera 30 years ago, and it remains my medium of choice whenever I take pictures for my own pleasure.

A large part of this is because I feel I 'see' best in black and white. I look at scenes and think and visualise pictures in terms of shades of grey rather than vibrant colours. I have not been trained to do that, it just comes naturally which probably explains why I will always love black-and-white photography.

Another factor is that there is so much control that, as a photographer, I can exert over the image, from pre-visualising it in the first instance all the way through to making the final print. I have the destiny of the photograph, literally, in my own hands.

Despite the convenience of commercial processing and the simplicity of digital photography, I have a 'wet' darkroom in which I can lock myself away for hours and experiment with different papers, chemicals and toners. To me, what happens in the darkroom is intrinsic to the medium. Photographers who are in the same situation will understand exactly what I mean by this.

But this does not mean that you need a darkroom and years of experience to get involved in black and white. Far from it. Many of the latest black-and-white films are designed for convenient commercial processing and by choosing the appropriate one, you can have excellent quality black-and-white prints back in your hands in an hour.

It is the pure pleasure of this medium and how you can use its abstract nature to best effect that Camera Craft: Black & White is all about. With techniques from film choice all the way through to alternative processes and toning, it is an excellent starting point for your adventure into this most exhilarating medium.

I hope you find it as enjoyable and as fulfilling as I do. Good luck.

William Cheung

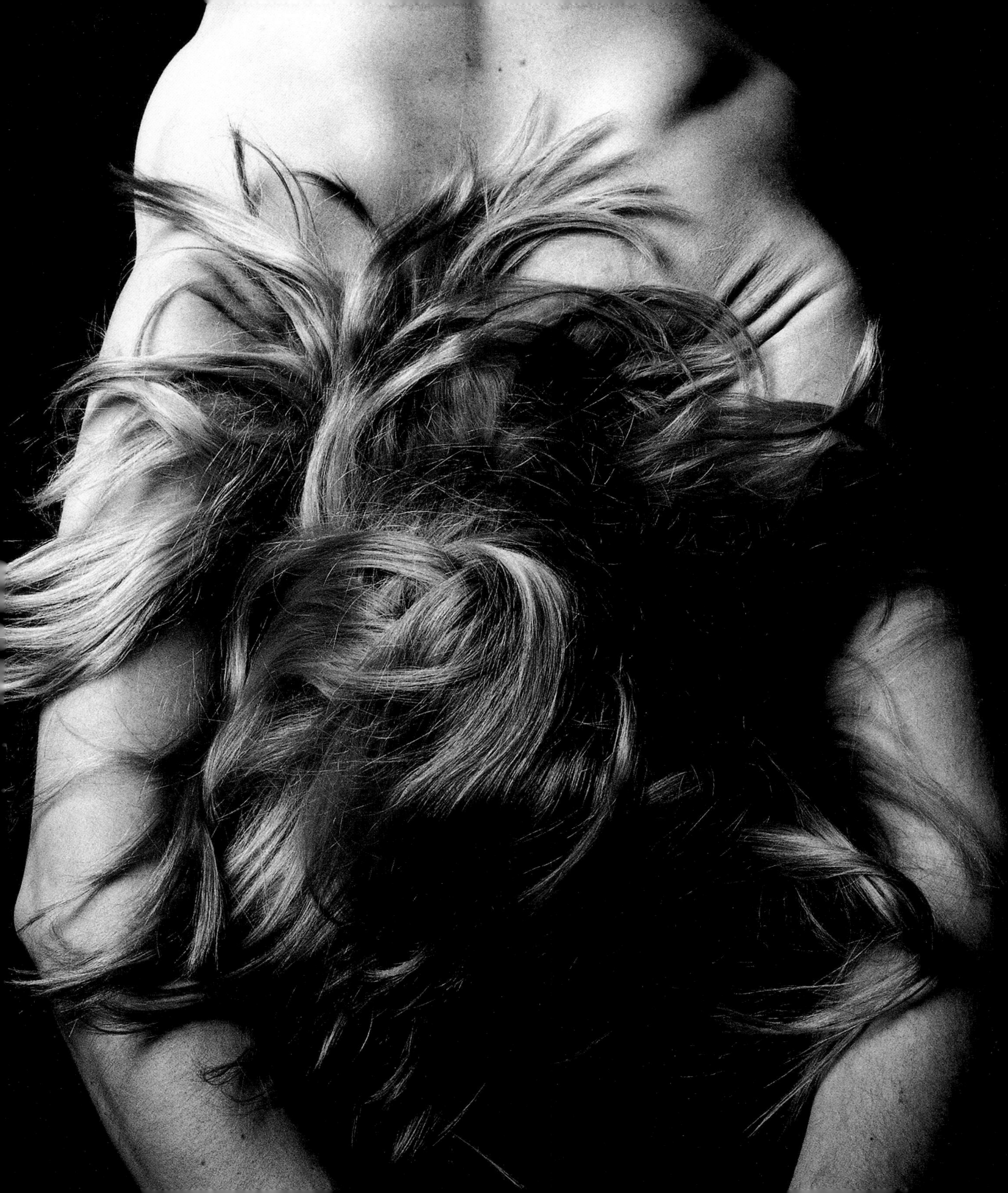

contents

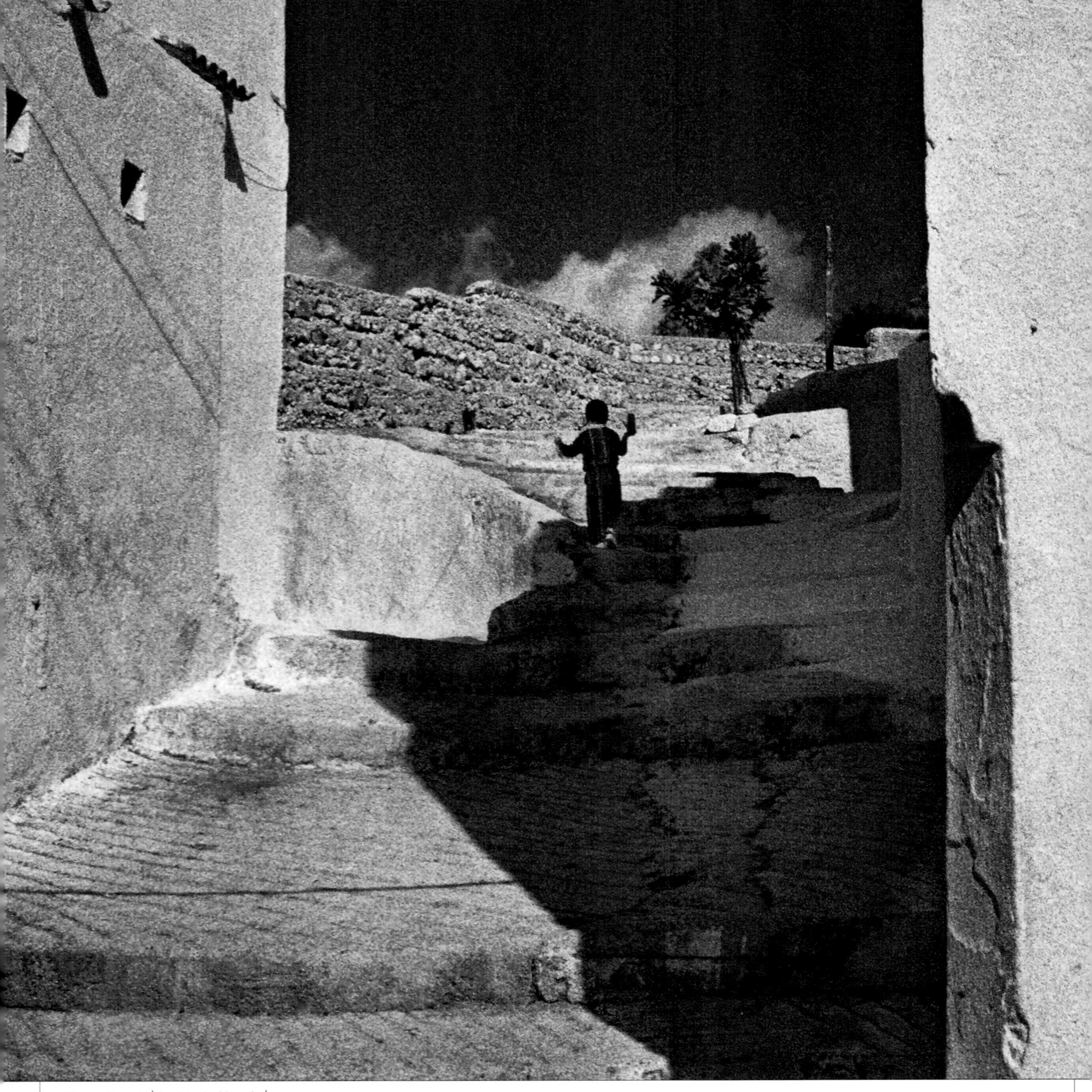

▲ Vince Bevan | Fatima's Hands |

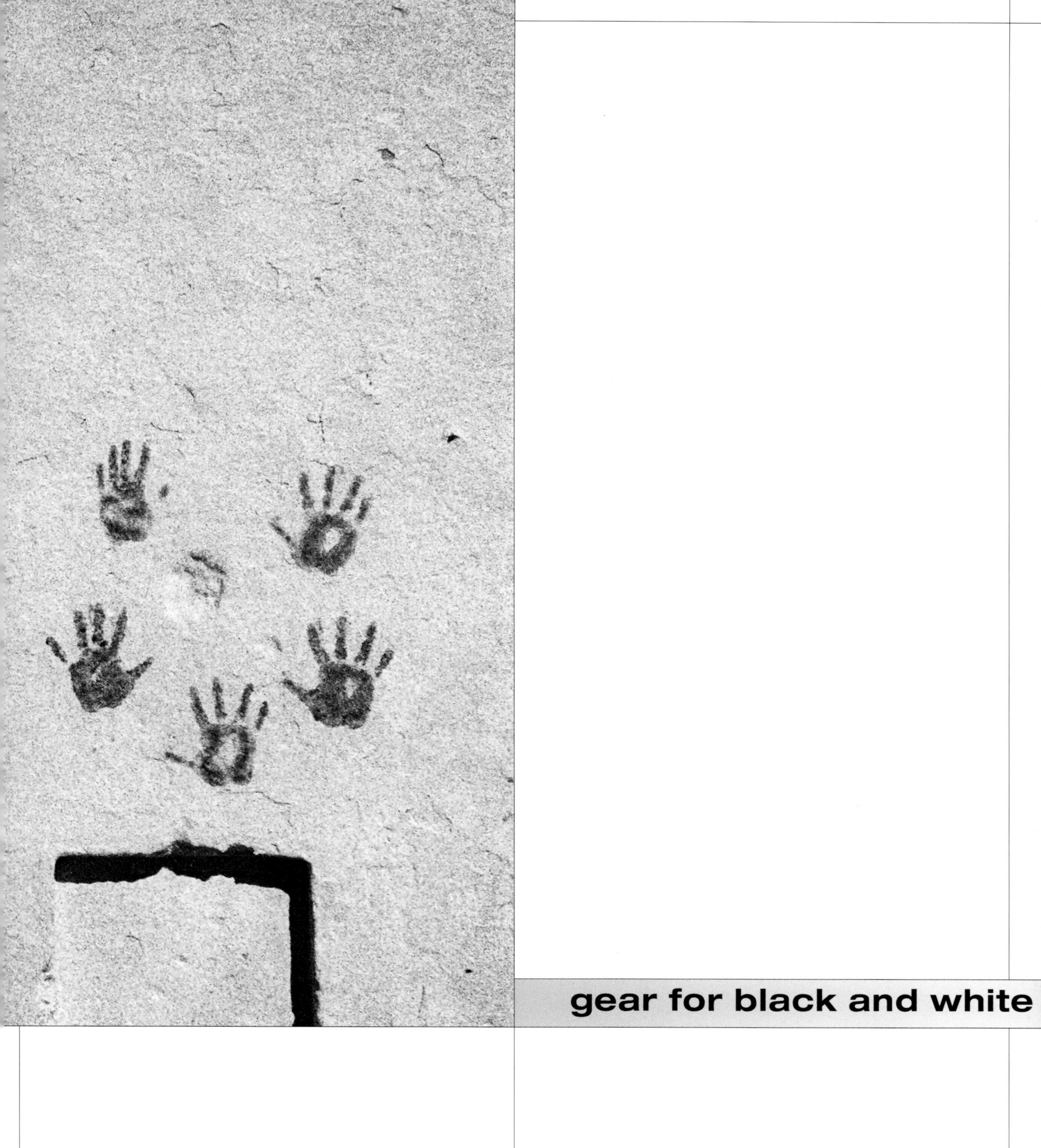

gear for black and white

Black-and-white film is available in all formats and speeds so every photographer can express themselves in this rewarding medium. Allied to this is the fact that digital technology makes it perfectly feasible to take colour pictures and transform them into black and white using the computer.

If taking pictures digitally appeals, many digital cameras have the option of black and white or sepia shooting modes. Photographers have never had so many choices when it comes to indulging their passion.

If you have a medium or large camera outfit, get a photo rucksack to carry your kit around. It would make walking more comfortable because the weight is distributed across your back and leaves both hands free. Photo rucksacks come in all shapes and sizes and to help you decide which is the best for you, take your outfit along to the shop to make sure your purchase will suit your needs.

gear for black and white the right camera

The 35mm format

For most photographers, the modern 35mm format single-lens reflex (SLR) camera is the perfect instrument. It is portable, quick handling and fully endowed with advanced features. Virtually every modern SLR is blessed with a sophisticated metering system backed up by exposure compensation facilities and most models have accurate autofocus so often the camera can be left to its own devices. Add convenience features such as automatic film transport, integral flash and a huge range of lens options, and there is every reason to use this format.

Its drawback, of course, is its size. The 35mm frame gives an image area measuring around 24x36mm so it is a small format. Modern films are excellent quality but if your aim is large, fine art prints with every nuance of a scene recorded, opting for a larger film format might be the better option.

Medium-format

There are several film formats available if you decide to base your photography on roll film. The film itself comes in 120 or 220 sizes. Both are the same width but 220 film is twice as long and there is no protective backing paper. It is worth noting that not all medium-format cameras will accept the 220 size and fewer film types are available.

Both film sizes give images of around 6cm in width but the length varies according to the camera. There are 6x4.5cm, 6x6cm, 6x7cm, 6x8cm, 6x9cm, 6x12cm and 6x17cm formats. Some models allow a choice of formats with the appropriate optional film back.

Of the formats on offer, the 6x4.5cm, 6x6cm and 6x7cm formats are the most widely used. They are relatively portable, have slick handling and many of the cameras are full-system models, which means that optional film-backs, metering prisms and lenses are available.

Large-format

Large-format cameras use 5x4inch, 7x5inch or 10x8inch sheets of film. The most popular sheet film format is 5x4inch but the large formats are on the wane, thanks to the advances in digital technology.

Sheet film formats give amazing image quality and if this is your ultimate aim then consider them. Obviously, the cameras are big and heavy and using them is a slow, contemplative process, which might suit your style. Running costs are also high which encourages disciplined metering and composition.

Of all the formats, 35mm is the most widely used.

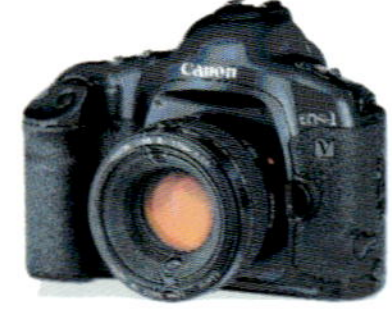

The 6x4.5cm format offers quick handling.

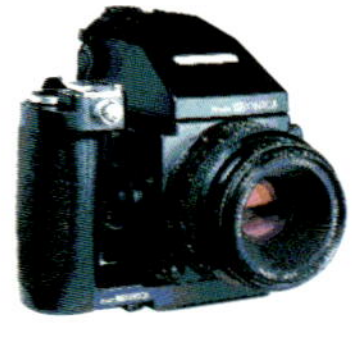

Large-format cameras are very versatile but slow to use.

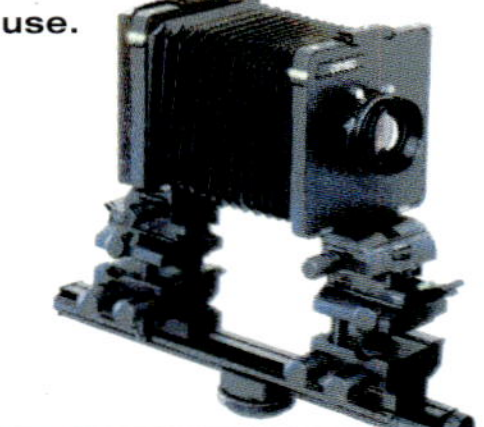

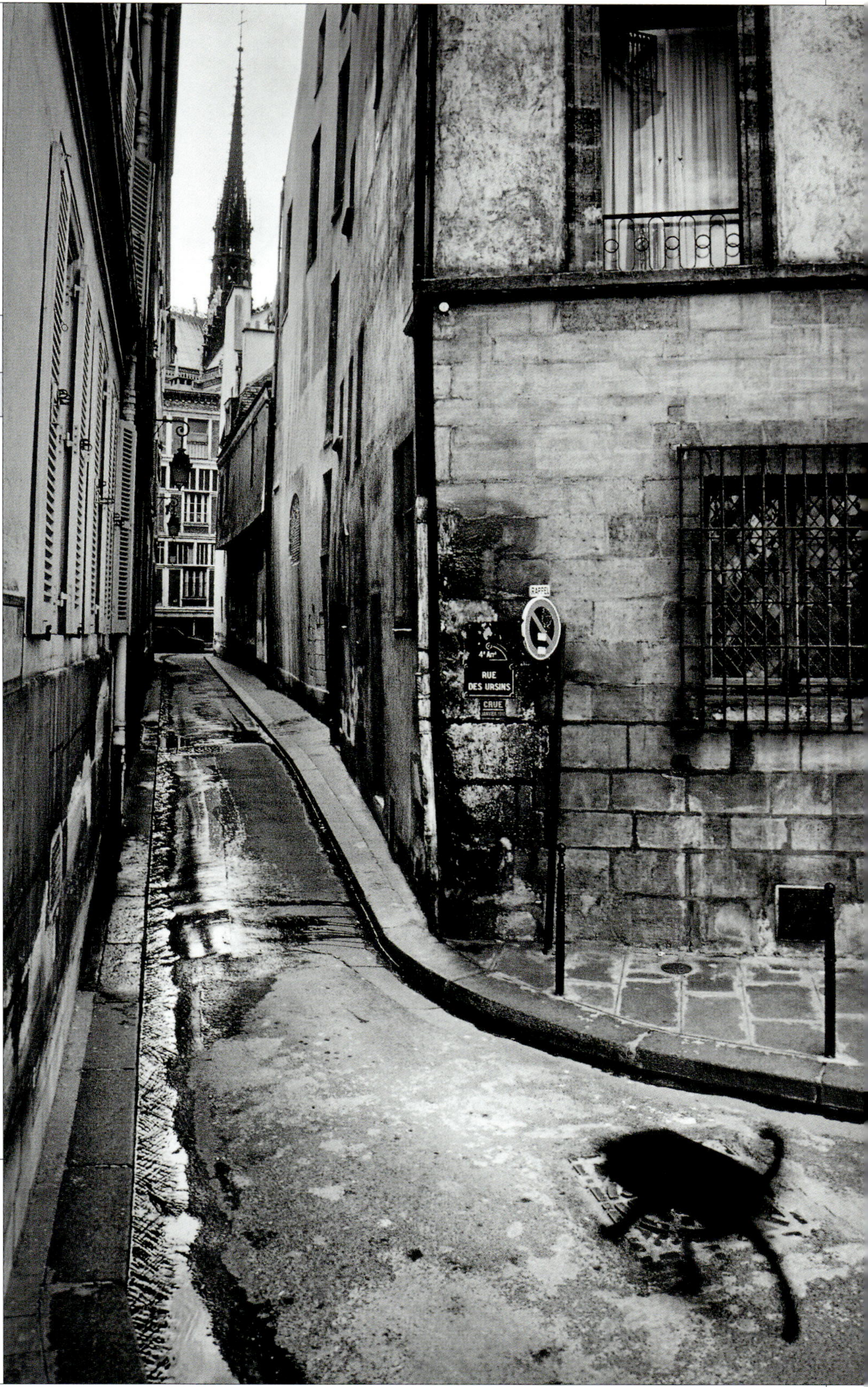

Digital

Filmless picture-taking is in its infancy but already the image quality possible is comparable with film, and getting better all the time. Digital capture and printing is a different craft compared with film photography but it still requires skill and the ability to visualise the image in the first instance.

Digital cameras come in different resolutions. The higher the resolution, the bigger the photographic quality print you can make and the current models that appeal to keen photographers are 3 megapixels or more. A 3 megapixel model will easily allow excellent quality 10x8inch or A4 (21x29.7cm) prints. Bigger prints are possible with minimal quality loss, especially if 'interpolated' in the computer's imaging software.

In terms of features, the typical advanced digital camera is broadly similar to its film equivalent. Autofocus, automatic exposure, built-in flash and zoom lens are all there, so there is plenty of creative control with most models.

Digital cameras behave just like film models.

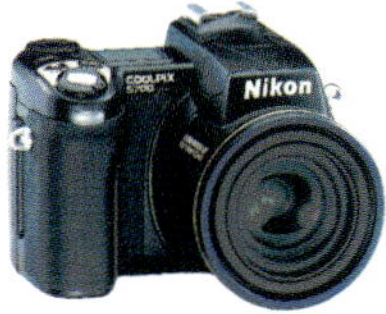

Every photographer has their own unique way of 'seeing' pictures hence lens choice is very personal. However, it makes sense to have a selection available to deal the widest range of picture opportunities.

Lenses from 28mm wide-angle through to 200mm telephoto will cope with the majority of situations and how you achieve this is up to you. An option is to use fixed-focal length lenses so a typical outfit would comprise 28mm, 35mm, 50mm, 100mm and 200mm lenses. But weight and space can be saved by going for a pair of zoom lenses, a 28–80mm and a 70–200mm.

It is possible to save even more weight and space, although there is a pay-off in terms of ultimate picture quality, by opting for a 28–200mm or even a 28–300mm so-called superzoom. The latest models are very good optically, but squeezing so much into one lens means that such models can suffer from distortion and flare.

▼ Rene de haan | Myrthe | A standard focal length lens (50mm for the 35mm format and 80mm for medium-format) is perfect for flattering people shots with good perspective.

gear for black and white lenses

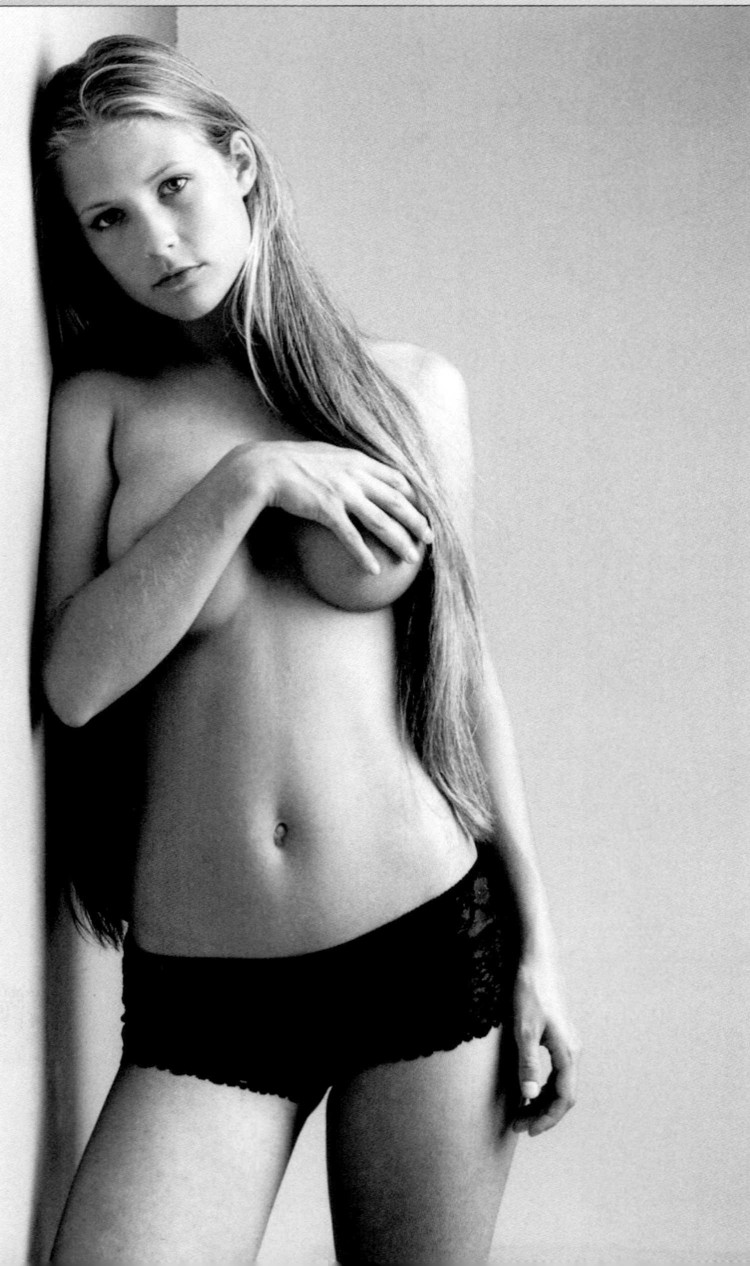

Camera tip

Buy a tripod if you want to get the very most out of your lenses. It will provide extra stability when you are shooting at fast shutter speeds and essential stability at slow shutter speeds. A tripod also gives the photographer complete freedom as regards camera settings. You may want a slow shutter speed to deliberately blur flowing water or a small aperture to ensure maximum sharpness in a scene. You need the heaviest, most stable tripod that you can comfortably carry around. Obviously, much depends on what you like shooting but if you are keen on scenic photography there is no point buying one that is so heavy it is always left at home. Often it is a compromise between stability and portability.

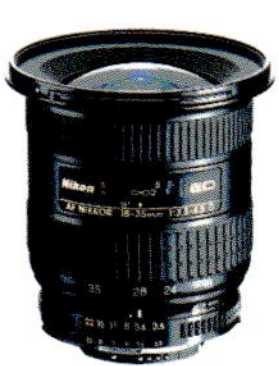

Wide-angle lenses are ideal for general use.

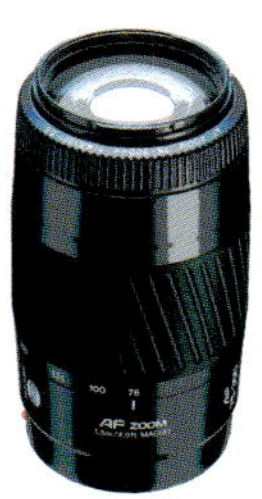

Modern telezoom lenses are compact.

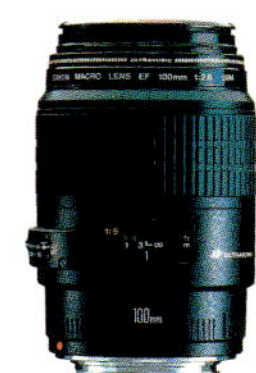

For close-up shooting a macro lens is essential.

Wide-angle lenses

Wide-angle lenses let you get more into the picture without having to move the camera position back from the subject. But that is being very simplistic because wide-angle lenses also let you be much more creative with composition; in particular, using foreground detail in a powerful way, to attract the viewer into the photograph. The wider the lens the more effective this technique can be.

In the 35mm format, a moderate wide-angle lens is a 24mm or 28mm focal length while an 18mm or a 20mm will be classed as an ultra-wide-angle lens.

Wide-angle lenses are perfect for scenes with sweeping lines and bold foreground shapes because the result will be a bold composition. Set a small lens aperture, i.e. f/16, so that everything from just in front of the camera to the far distance will be in sharp focus.

Standing too far from the subject or being timid in their use are the most common failings when it comes to using this lens type. Be brave and your pictures will benefit.

Telephoto lenses

Telephoto lenses 'pull in' distant detail so the subject appears larger in the camera viewfinder. Their magnifying effect is why telephotos are essential for sports and wildlife photography where the subjects are a long distance away.

In the 35mm format, focal lengths of 85mm and 100mm are called short telephotos and anything longer than 300mm is referred to as long telephotos. The most popular telezoom is 70–210mm which neatly covers the key telephoto settings.

Telephotos need good camera technique. Their greater magnification means that the slightest camera movement during the exposure will also be magnified. The risk of camera shake grows as focal length increases, so it is important to use a support such as a monopod or set fast shutter speeds to avoid it. As a guide, for a 200mm lens consider 1/250sec the minimum and 1/500sec for a 300mm lens.

Telephoto lenses give less apparent depth-of-field than wide-angles so focusing is more critical, but this can be used to advantage. When photographing a portrait, set a wide lens aperture such as f/4 and the background will be attractively out of focus.

Macro lenses

Macro lenses are designed to focus much closer than other lenses but the key thing is that they do so and deliver excellent optical performance at the same time. These lenses are deemed essential by nature and still-life photographers but they have general appeal too.

A true macro lens will focus close enough to give 1:1 or life-size magnification. This means the subject will be the same size on film as it is in reality. Less powerful macro lenses only allow 1:2 reproduction or half life-size magnification. Lenses that give 1:4 or one-quarter magnification are not true macro lenses.

Macro lenses usually have focal lengths of 50mm or 100mm although longer focal-lengths such as 180mm are also available. Longer focal length macro lenses are useful because they allow the photographer to work at a greater distance from the subject, while still allowing powerful close-up shots.

A huge selection of black-and-white film is available and each offers different characteristics.

Experimenting is important, especially so if you are new to shooting monochrome. This includes the choice of film developer, processor and printing paper as well as the film.

Films are available in a range of speeds. Scenic workers often prefer slow- or medium-speed films for the smallest grain and smoothest tonality while documentary photographers rely on faster films because they shoot in low light situations.

Most photographers carry a selection of film speeds so choice can be tailored to the shooting situation.

Camera tip

The manufacturer's speed rating is denoted as an ISO number. The higher the number, the more light-sensitive the film which means you can continue shooting as light levels fall without needing a tripod. However, generally speaking, faster films give less impressive image quality than slower films. For the optimum quality, slow- and medium-speed films are advised. They are capable of finer grain, superior tonality and higher sharpness.

gear for black and white general purpose films

Slow ISO 25 to 50	Medium ISO 100 to 200	Fast ISO 400

Slow ISO 25 to 50

Slow films are less popular than they used to be, which explains why there are so few of them to choose from. This is true in colour photography too. Their decline in popularity is partly due to the fact that slow films need longer exposure times with the accompanying risks of camera shake and subject movement. Another reason is that the huge advances in film emulsion technology means that comparable picture quality is possible with higher-speed films.

Example: Ilford Pan F Plus, Kodak Professional Technical Pan

Medium ISO 100 to 200

A typical ISO 100 or 200 film will produce very fine grain, high sharpness and excellent tonality. They are extremely popular because of their high image quality which is practical enough to cope with a wide-range of lighting situations. It is only in very dull light that you will need a tripod.

Newer mono films use advanced grain technology, such as Ilford Delta or Kodak T-Max grain, for optimum image quality. They handle slightly differently from older, conventional grained emulsions and the results can look different too. This might not always be evident with commercial processing but home printing will certainly reveal differences. Newer films exhibit finer grain and smoother tones which will suit those pursuing the ultimate in fine print quality.

Examples: (conventional films) Agfa Agfapan 100, Ilford FP4 Plus; (new technology) Fuji Acros 100, Ilford Delta 100, Kodak T-Max 100

Fast ISO 400

Films of this speed are well suited to less than perfect light. For example, shooting action on overcast days demands a fast film to allow fast enough shutter speeds to 'stop' any motion.

As with ISO 100–200 films, there is the option of newer, advanced grain films or conventional films. Grain at this speed of film is more noticeable particularly on big enlargements so the benefits of the advanced technology high speed films are worth considering.

There is another film type at this speed. These are black-and-white films based on colour film technology called 'chromogenics' and are discussed next.

Examples: (conventional films) Kodak Tri-X, Ilford HP5 Plus, Fuji Neopan 400; (new technology) Ilford Delta 400 Professional, Kodak T-Max 400

Slow films give the best image quality.

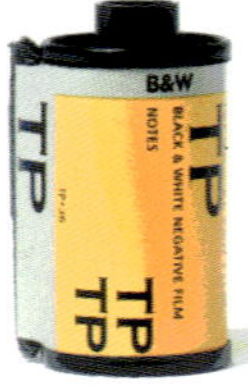

Medium speed films give a fine balance of image characteristics.

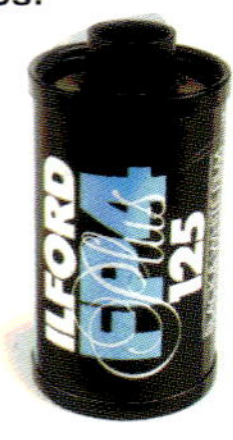

Fast films give coarser grain but the extra speed is useful.

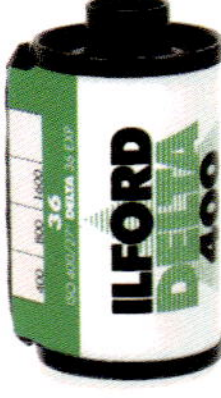

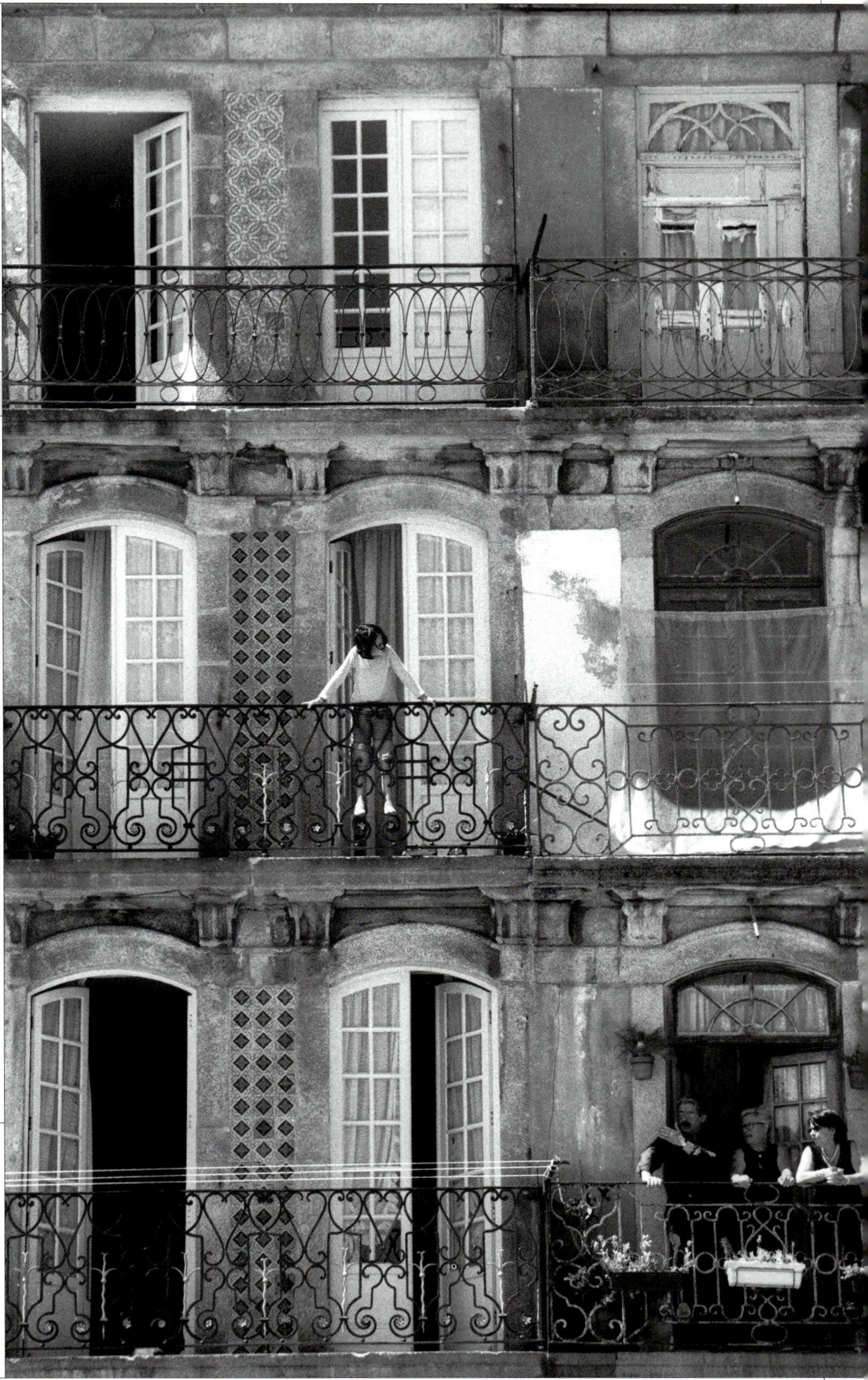

Chromogenic ISO 400

These films belong to the ISO 400 speed group but differ in the way they work.

These form the image with dyes rather than grains of silver and give picture quality comparable to slower film speeds. But not only that, they can be processed using the universal C-41 colour print film process and printed on colour paper (as well as mono papers) to give great-looking black-and-white prints. This film type also has great exposure latitude and slight overexposure actually gives smoother-looking grain.

With fast colour-processing widely available, this means you can shoot black and white conveniently and get prints in an hour.

Examples: Kodak Portra 400BW, Kodak T400CN, Ilford XP2 Super 400

Chromogenic mono films can be processed in colour chemistry.

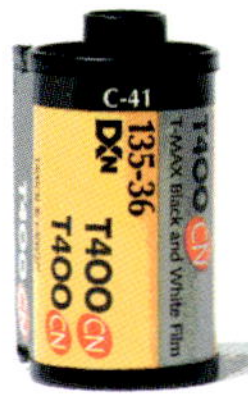

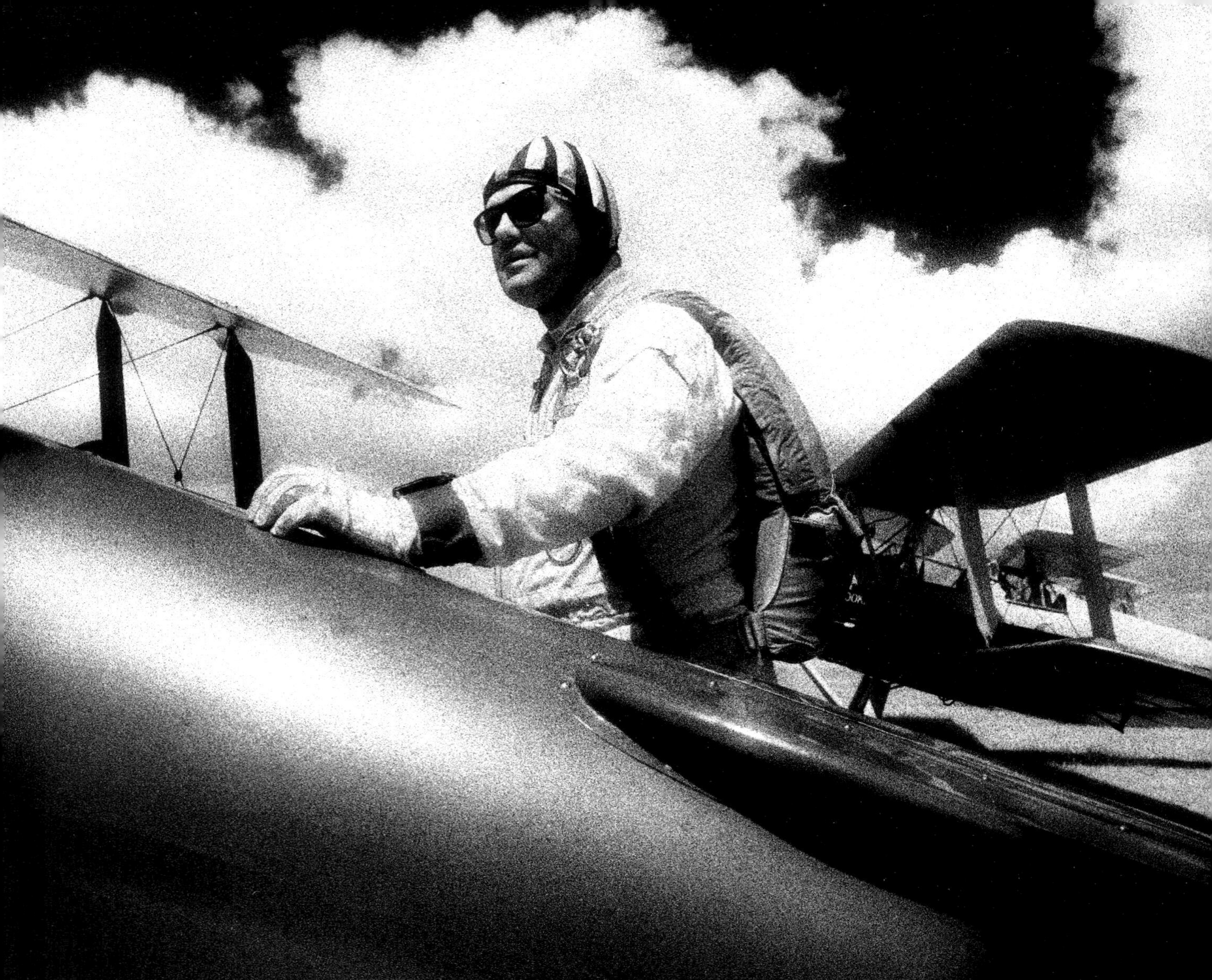

gear for black and white specialist films

Most photographers stick to the straight and narrow when it comes to film choice. Yet there is a huge collection of films out there to try and experiment with. It is fun too and you might find that using an unusual film leads to developing your own unique photographic style.

▲ William Cheung | Parachute man and clouds | Infrared film used on a bright sunny day gave the dramatic result here. This film type exposed through a red filter produced an almost black sky and the clouds stand out prominently against it.

Ultrafast ISO 1600 & over

Such high-speed films are reserved for very-low-light situations, such as dimly lit sports arenas, concert halls or dark interiors.

Generally, picture quality drops off as film speed increases. Resolving power is lower so the image seems less sharp with less detail, contrast can be poor and the grain is much more obvious. However, while all this sounds very negative that should not be the case because such high speed films let you shoot sharp pictures in the dimmest of lighting and getting a decent, sharp, grainy image is definitely better than getting none at all.

Examples: Fuji Neopan 1600, Ilford Delta 3200, Kodak T-Max 3200

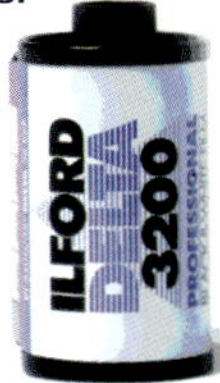

Ultra-fast films are fun to use and give individual-looking pictures.

Camera tip

Always carry around some self-adhesive labels and a pen so you can label film cassettes that need special treatment during processing. You can note the ISO rating you used, whether the film needs extended development to increase contrast, the date of use and anything that you consider of relevance.

Infrared film

Infrared film was devised for scientific use but it is now also used by pictorial photographers looking for an unusual look for everyday subjects. For example, vegetation reflects infrared radiation differently from visible light and appears light on prints while skies go very dark.

Infrared films are normal panochromatic films but with an extended red sensitivity into the infrared end of the light spectrum, the actual sensitivity depends on the film itself.

To get the best infrared effect a camera filter is needed to cut-out visible blue and green light. A deep red (Wratten 25) filter is very popular. This has a filter factor of 8x so there is a three stop light loss but it still transmits visible light so composition through an SLR camera viewfinder is possible.

Filters opaque to visible light but which transmit infrared wavelengths are available, such as Wratten 87, 88A and 89. With these, because you can't see a great deal through them, you will need to set the camera on a tripod, compose and then fit the filter. Metering is tricky too. Meters are not designed to cope with just infrared radiation you will have to bracket exposures and experiment with different ISO ratings.

The Kodak version is highly sensitive and must be loaded and unloaded into the camera in total darkness. For location shooting, this means that a lightproof changing bag is a vital accessory.

Examples: Konica 750nm, Kodak High Speed Infrared, Maco IR820C, Ilford SFX (extended red sensitivity)

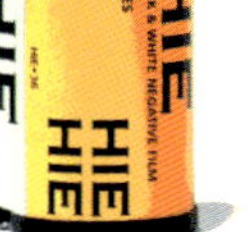

Infrared film needs careful handling for the best results.

Black-and-white slide

This is the perfect and convenient solution if you want to shoot black and white for projection or want to enjoy the medium without the expense of getting your images printed. Agfa Scala 200 is the only purpose-made mono slide film and has an ISO rating of 200. It gives fine grain slides with a slight warm tinge and the film can be push-processed for greater effective speed.

Some black-and-white negative films can be reversal processed to achieve slides. Kodak offers a processing kit specifically for their T-Max 100 and Technical Pan films.

Examples: Agfa Scala 200, Kodak T-Max 100 (with reversal processing kit)

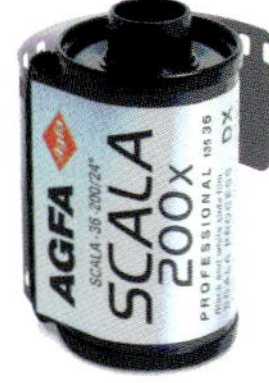

Agfa is the only company that makes a mono slide film.

Graphics art films

This category mainly includes films designed primarily for darkroom rather than in-camera use. Included are ortho copying and high-contrast lith and line films, which are blue-sensitive so they can be handled under darkroom red safe-lighting conditions. Some ortho films can be used in-camera but they are relatively insensitive.

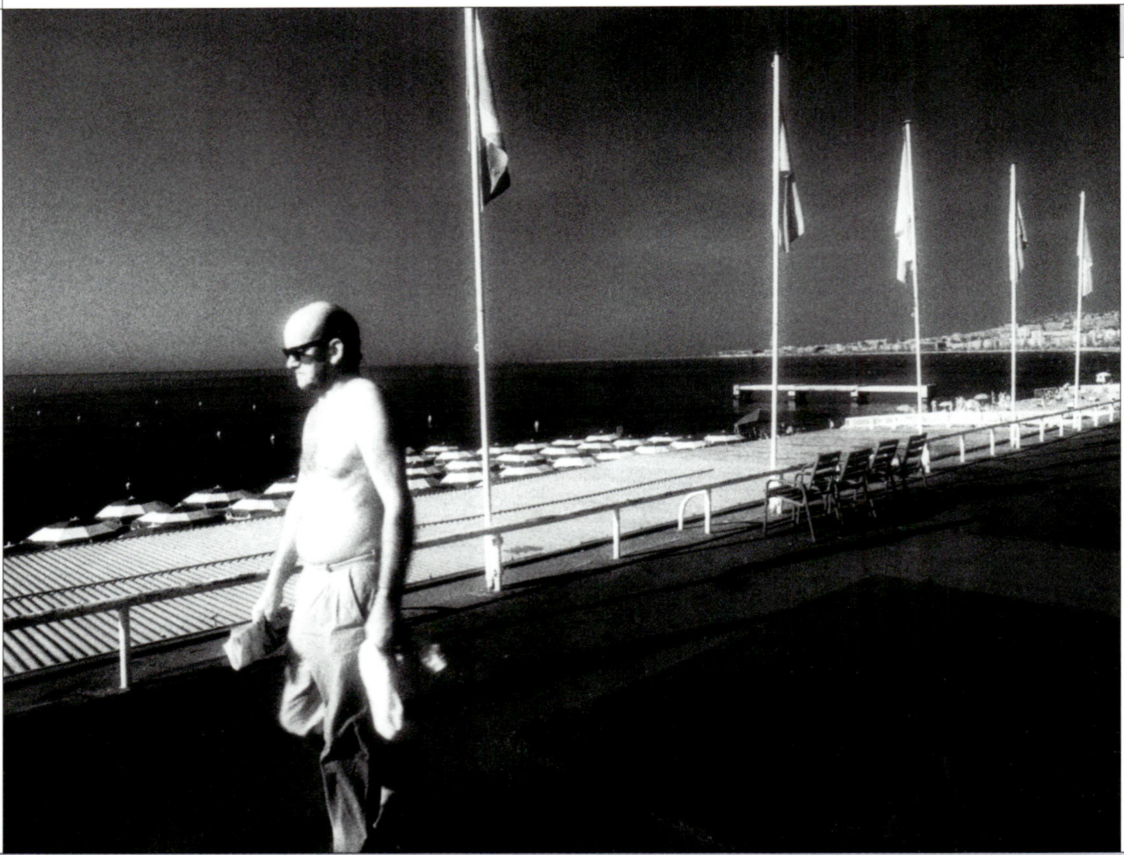

◀ William Cheung | Man at Nice | A red filter gives dramatic results. This was taken with infrared film, but a red filter can be equally powerful with normal black-and-white film.

gear for black and white camera filters

Camera filters let you modify how different colour subjects are recorded on black-and-white film. The tonal relationships between different colours and how they relate to each other on black-and-white film is an important aspect of monochrome photography.

Colour

Yellow

Filter factor x2, 1 stop
Mildly darkens blue skies and brings out white clouds.

Yellow-green

Filter factor x3, 1.5 stops
Similar to yellow but more so, and will lighten green vegetation too.

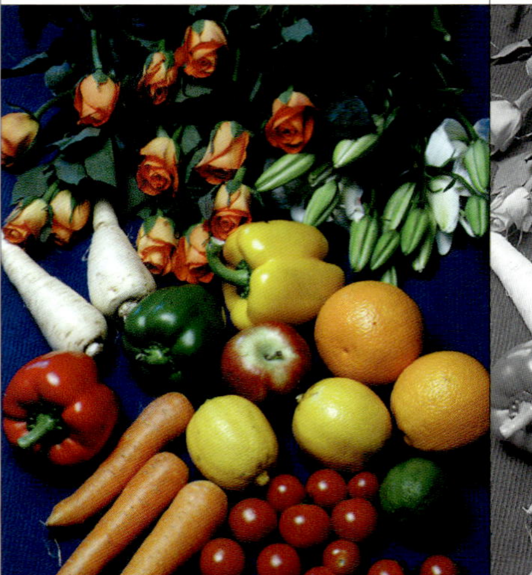
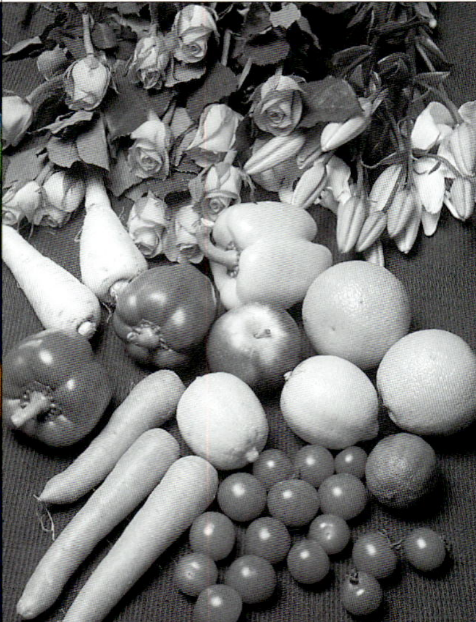

Set of five comparison pictures showing filter use.

Filter types

Filters come in two styles.

Screw-in filters – These attach directly into the lens' accessory thread. The filter's size will be indicated either on the lens itself or in its instructions. Failing that, just measure the lens' diameter in millimetres. Common sizes are 49mm, 52mm, 55mm, 58mm, 62mm, 67mm, 72mm and 77mm.

Names to look out for: B+W, Hoya, Tiffen

Buy the best filters you can afford.

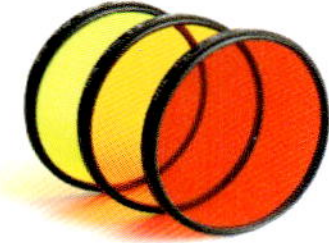

Creative filters are very versatile.

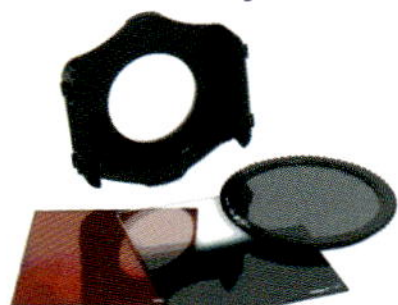

Creative filter system – The second type is the creative filter system. These filters fit into a grooved holder and this then attaches to an adaptor which is screwed onto the lens just like screw-in filters. This type of filter is immensely popular for many reasons. Here are some:

One, a set of filters and a holder can be used on all your lenses with the appropriate adaptor rings. Changing lenses or system no longer means a new set of filters. Two, creative filter systems have a huge selection to choose from. Three, the holders will accept two or more filters so very individual images can be produced.

There are many brands of creative filter system on the market. Few can be used interchangeably so make sure the filters you want to use are available.

Names to look out for include: Cokin, Cromatek, Lee Filters

Contrast filters

Colour filters – The most widely used filter type for black-and-white photography is plain colour filters. These transmit light of the same colour as the filter itself and block complementary colours. For example, a yellow filter will stop blue light passing through while transmitting red and green wavelengths which make up yellow light. A yellow filter will bring out detail in a blue sky, an orange is similar but the effect is stronger while red is more potent still and the sky can go very dark. If you want to lighten foliage try a green filter.

Green

Filter factor x4, 2 stops
Lightens vegetation more strongly and darkens blue skies.

Orange

Filter factor x4, 2 stops
Brings out blue skies even more, but also handy for photographing people with freckles.

Red

Filter factor x8, 3 stops
Has a dramatic effect on blue skies, making them very dark indeed. Also makes Caucasian skin tones appear very pale too.

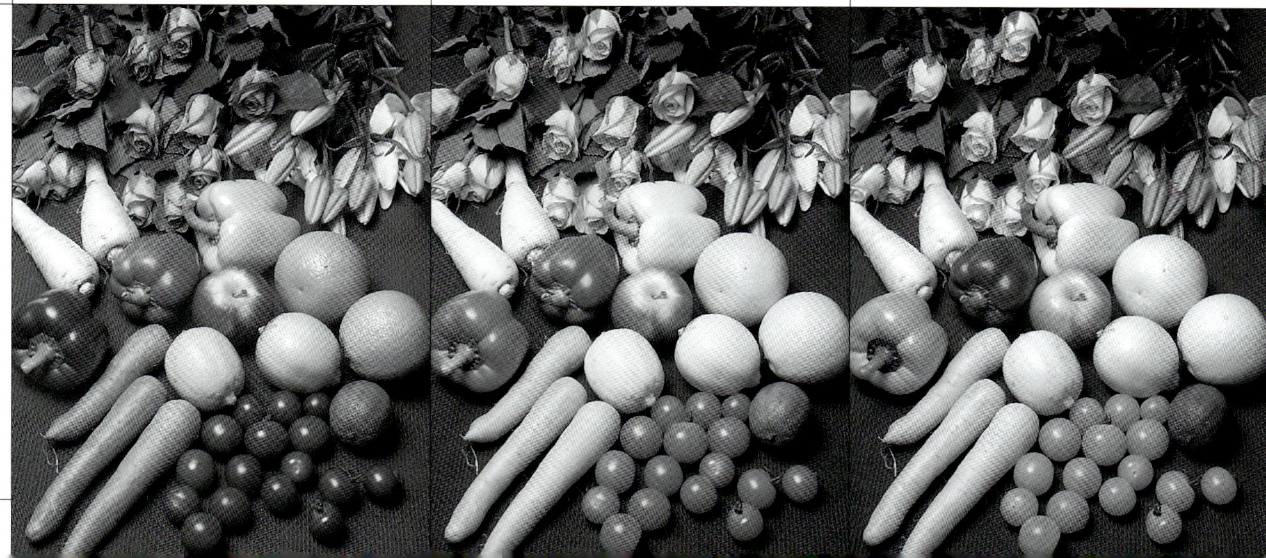

Graduate filters

In colour photography graduate filters are used to add colour and density to the sky or foreground. In black and white they balance the shadow and highlight areas.

The most useful is the neutral density (ND) or grey graduate filter. There are different strengths available, with 0.6 and 0.9 most useful for landscapes. This means the filter's densest area will cut down the amount of light passing through by two and three stops respectively. They can be used in combination for a stronger effect.

The effect of the graduate filter varies according to the set aperture. Wider apertures give a less-defined transition while with smaller apertures the effect is more pronounced. Check this with the camera's depth-of-field preview feature. It indicates the effect at different apertures, and helps with the filter's positioning so that the right area of the scene is being darkened.

Take an exposure reading before slipping the filter into place. The meter can be fooled by the dark area of the graduate filter into overexposing the unfiltered area. With autoexposure modes, use the exposure lock to memorise the reading before putting the filter in place.

The polariser

Colour photographers use the polariser to cut down glare and enhance saturation, kill reflections and enhance sky detail.

Obviously, in black and white cutting out glare will do nothing for colour reproduction but it will enrich tones. It is equally effective for eliminating reflections and enhancing blue skies, having an effect similar to that of a medium yellow or orange filter. The advantage, however, is that the polariser has no effect on other tonal relationships within the scene.

It is important to buy the correct polariser type for your camera. Check the camera's instructions, but broadly speaking, any SLR that is autofocus and/or has a spot meter facility needs what is known as a circular polariser. Manual focus, centre-weighted metering models are fine with linear polarisers.

Soft-focus

Diffusing the scene is a great way to add atmosphere to your pictures, although it is true to say that the effect will not suit every subject. Traditionally, portraits and social pictures have benefitted from the use of the diffuser or soft-focus filter but they work too with landscapes and street scenes.

All sorts of soft-focus and diffusion filters are available and in various strengths. The effect can vary according to the chosen aperture, with wider apertures giving a more diffused effect than smaller apertures. Check with the camera's depth-of-field preview feature.

Slight overexposure helps to enhance the mood of the image so set the exposure compensation with an extra one-half or one-third stop.

For more on how filters can be used to improve your black-and-white pictures see Chapter 4.

Camera tip

Putting a filter in front of
the lens degrades optical
performance so it makes
sense to buy the best
possible quality filters and
to keep them clean.
Creative filter systems
allow two, three or even
more filters to be held in
front of the lens. Clearly,
the more you use the
greater the potential effect
on the image even with
high-quality filters. This is
especially noticeable when
shooting into the light
when flare is a real hazard.
In short, try not to stack
too many filters in front of
the lens.

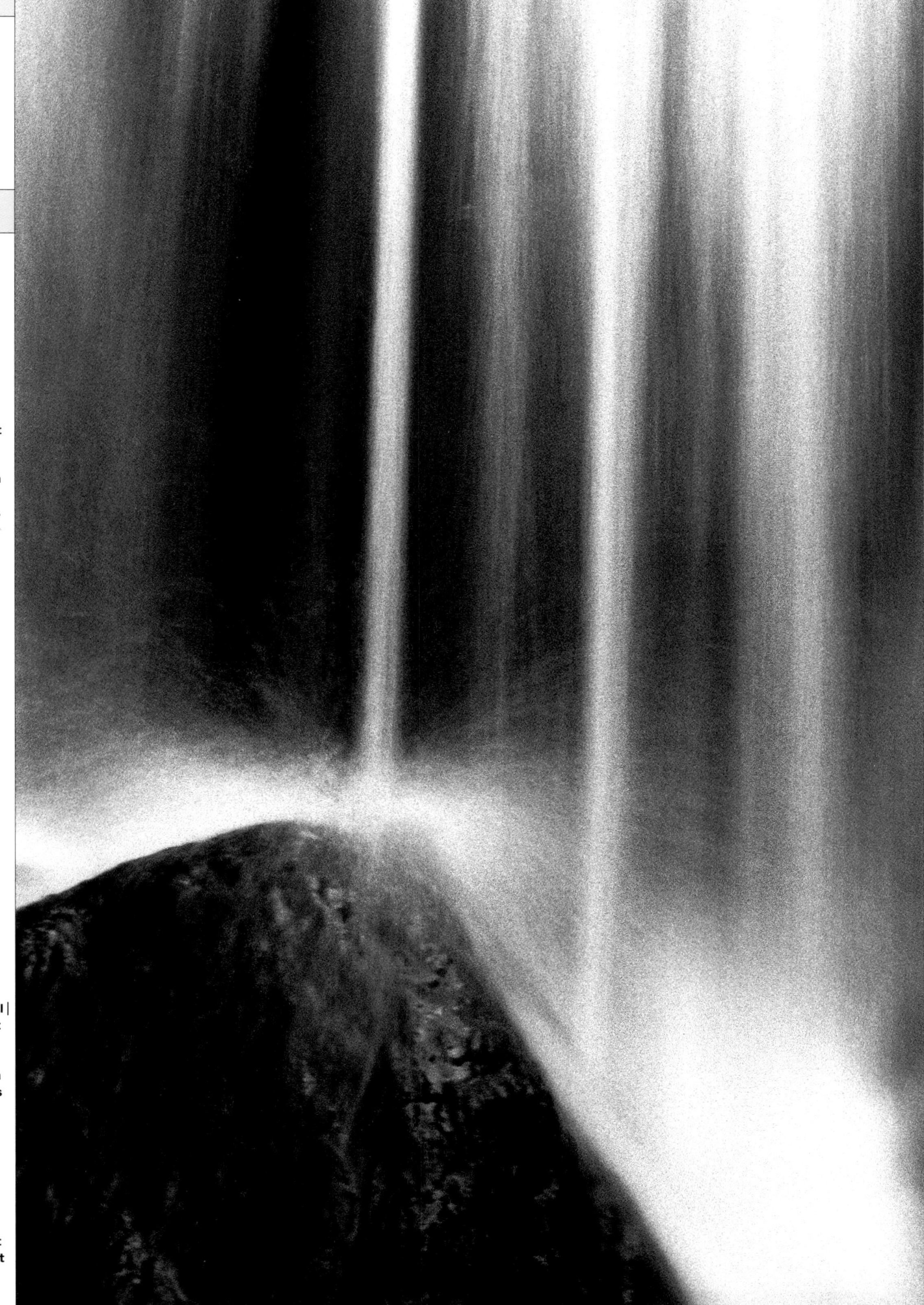

▶ William Cheung | Waterfall |
The polariser has no effect
on the tonal relationships
in black-and-white
photography, but it is still a
very useful filter. It doubles
as a neutral density filter
absorbing up to two stops
of light. Fit a polariser
when you want slower
shutter speeds for
deliberate blur effects. In
this instance, the shutter
speed, even at the lens'
minimum aperture, without
a polariser was 1/15sec but
a speed of 1/4sec was
possible with one.

Many photographers will prefer to let a processing laboratory look after their exposed films, but setting up a home darkroom gives the ultimate in creative freedom and the opportunity for the black-and-white photographer to take total control. Not only that, but there is huge satisfaction to be gained from making your own prints.

A home darkroom does not demand too much room. A small bedroom, a dry cellar or even the garden shed would be perfectly adequate. A permanent darkroom is obviously more convenient because you can leave it set up ready for use at short notice. If you do not have the space, a temporary darkroom is perfectly feasible provided that blacking-out the room is not too difficult. And contrary to popular belief, you do not need plumbed in running water so long as fresh water is within a short carrying distance.

gear for black and white the chemical darkroom

The enlarger

The enlarger is the centrepiece of the darkroom. Models are available in a wide range of prices and there is a thriving secondhand market, especially as many photographers are going digital.

An enlarger comprises of a light source, a negative holder stage and an enlarger lens and projects the image onto the sensitised printing paper. There are models available which are suitable for different film formats with more expensive versions accepting negatives from medium-format to 35mm. Such models are supplied with special masks or negative holders of different sizes to ensure film flatness.

More advanced enlargers have a built-in 'colourhead' for colour printing and for use with the popular variable-contrast printing papers.

The enlarger lens

The lens is the vital link in the printing chain and it is as important as the camera lens, so it is worth investing in a high-quality optic. A cheap enlarging lens will not do your beautiful negatives full justice.

As a guide, a 50mm focal length lens is for 35mm format use, while a 75mm or 80mm lens is fine for up to the 6x7cm medium-format.

Paper choice

Variable-contrast printing papers are designed to give a full range of contrast grades with different grades accessed by use of enlarger filtration. Yellow filtration gives low or soft contrast grades such as grade 0 and 1, purple for high or hard contrast grades such as 4 and 5 and a mix of the two for the in-between grades, namely 2 and 3. An enlarger colourhead makes using variable-contrast papers easy but you can use specially designed filters which fit above or below the enlarger lens.

A basic darkroom

To set up a basic darkroom you need:

For processing film
You may have neither the room nor the inclination to set up a darkroom, but you can still exercise control over a vital stage in the pathway to sparkling prints, namely that of film developing.

Film developing tank
Film spiral
Thermometer
Measuring graduates
Wash hose
Film developer
Stop bath
Fixer

For making prints
Enlarger
Enlarging lens
Printing easel
Processing trays
Thermometer
Measuring graduates
Blower brush or can
of compressed air
Contrast filters
Processing tongs
Wash hose
Safelight
Bucket
Print developer
Stop bath
Fixer
Electricity and water

To consider later
Enlarger timer
Four-blade enlarging easel
Grain focus finder
Compressed air duster
Print washer
Four-blade printing easel

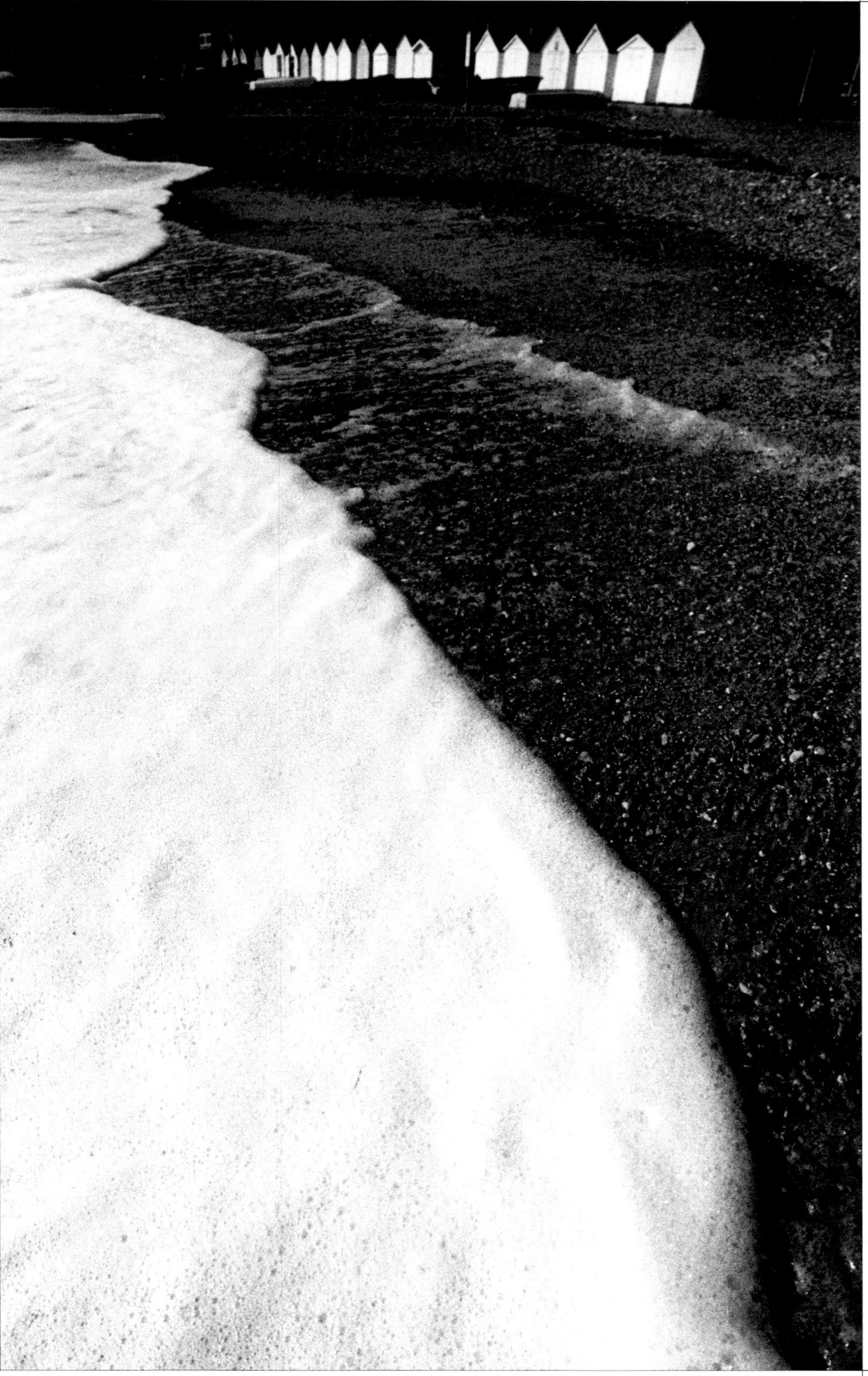

William Cheung | Tidal light | When a photographer previsualises a final image relaying that vision to a commercial processing laboratory is almost impossible. The advantage of having a home darkroom is that it is possible to realise the original visualisation.

Camera tip

Dust is the bane of many a home darkroom and the tiniest speck on the negative assumes monstrous proportions when enlarged. Prevention is better than cure so make sure that processed films are hung up to dry in a dust-free atmosphere if you can. A proper film dryer is ideal but even a room which has been left undisturbed with its windows shut for a few hours can do. And leave the hanging film undisturbed until fully dry. When you hang the wet film up, use a piece of new absorbent kitchen towel folded into a neat pad and gently wipe down the shiny side (not the emulsion side) of the film. This technique works really well with 35mm film to avoid drying marks. Gadgets called film squeegees are available to remove excess water but they are best avoided.

Stuff called wetting agent, which breaks down the surface tension of water, used in the final wash can also be used to promote even drying. It should be used very, very sparingly, and you only need a drop or two in the final wash.

Making black-and-white prints digitally has several advantages. The key one is there is no need for a light-proof area or room to set up the enlarger and chemical trays. Basically, it is possible to work anywhere where there is a power supply available.

gear for black and white the digital darkroom

Computer

The computer is at the heart of the digital workstation. The latest machines have fast processors, large amounts of RAM memory and plenty of storage space on the hard drive. They are perfect for digital imaging.

Computer technology is advancing at a rapid rate, especially with regards to the processor. If you are just setting up, it makes sense to buy the fastest computer you can afford but there is also much more to consider.

Images and files that you work on are saved to the hard drive and with image files being large documents a big hard drive is a plus point. However, it pays to keep your hard drive organised and write files to CD, DVD or to a separate hard drive when you can.

The other key specification you need to look at is the amount of built-in RAM. Again with big files and memory hungry software programs you will need as much RAM as possible, say 256Mb or more.

You will want to connect devices such as scanners and printers to the computer so do check the connections. The most popular currently are USB 2.0 and Firewire.

Scanner

Two types of scanner are available, the film scanner and the flatbed scanner.

Broadly speaking, the flatbed scanner digitises flat artwork, hard copy and prints.

Many modern flatbed scanners can now scan in negatives and transparencies with an optional accessory. While the latest flatbeds still lag behind dedicated film scanners in terms of resolution and are less suited to 35mm format use, they are perfect to suit medium- and large-format photographers because top-end scanners for these formats are very expensive.

For 35mm photographers, the dedicated film scanner is still probably the better option, unless you want one box fulfilling both functions and are happy with relatively modest enlargements.

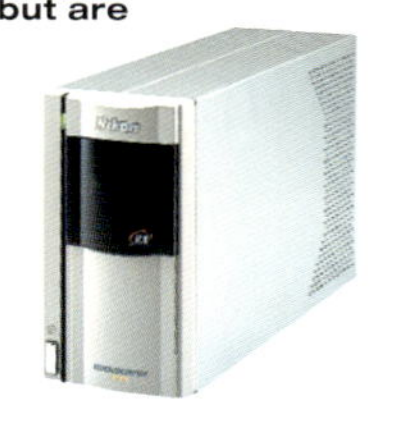

Film scanners give the highest resolution but are expensive.

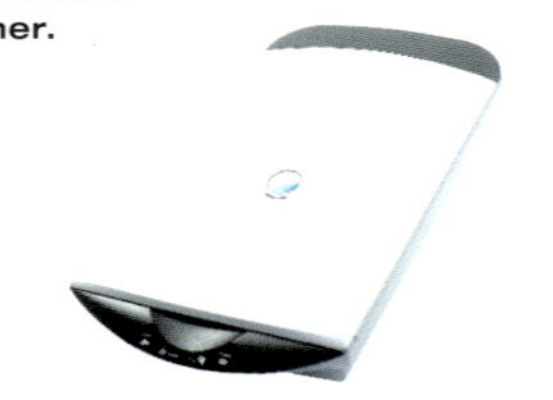

For scanning prints and flat artwork, you need a flatbed scanner.

Inkjet printer

The latest inkjet (or bubblejet) printers give genuine photographic print quality, giving a maximum resolution output of 1440dpi or 2880dpi (dots per inch) resolution. Printers for the enthusiast give either A4 (21x29.7cm) or A3 Super (32.9x48.3cm) prints on specially coated inkjet paper.

The light stability of inkjet prints depends on the inks, the media and how the prints are stored or displayed. If a high degree of permanence is required, it is suggested you buy a printer that uses pigment inks with very good lightfast characteristics. Not all do, and some printer/ink/paper combinations might give prints with a 10 year life or shorter.

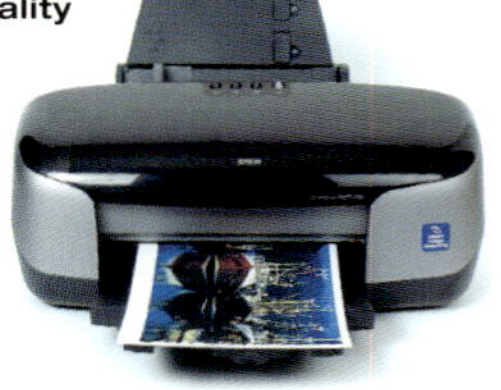

Photo quality printers are popular and give high quality results.

Inkjet media

Photographers are spoilt by a huge choice of different media for inkjet printing. Of course, there are the usual finishes that photographers are familiar with, such as glossy and satin. But there are also many textured papers available that means very individual results are possible. The right images printed onto textured watercolour-type papers can look fabulous.

Software

There are many programs available if you want to make more of your photography. At the bottom end of the market, packages will allow basic enhancement and have simple photo album features. At the top end of the market, all sorts of advanced manipulation are possible. For photographers, packages such as Adobe Photoshop, Ulead PhotoImpact and JASC Paint Shop Pro should be considered. Photoshop is the most widely used by imaging professionals.

Storage

High-resolution photo images are large files. The computer's hard drive may have a large capacity but it will soon be clogged up if you don't regularly archive your work. Anyway, it is sensible to regularly back up valuable files.

The ideal back-up is a separate, high-capacity hard drive connected to the computer via USB2.0 or Firewire. Models of 100Gb are more widely available and not prohibitively expensive, if you consider the peace of mind they provide.

Camera tip

CDs are not a failsafe method of storage so it is advised that you write two of each one if the files are valuable. One CD can also be kept off site so in the event of a domestic disaster you will always have a back up.
The actual quality of CDs is also variable so for archiving purposes, buy the best quality you can afford. Save the cheaper ones for sending images around.

▶ Rene de Haan | Myrthe |
The latest digital scanners and printing technology means that superb black-and-white prints can be produced without the need for a traditional chemical darkroom.

know the camera

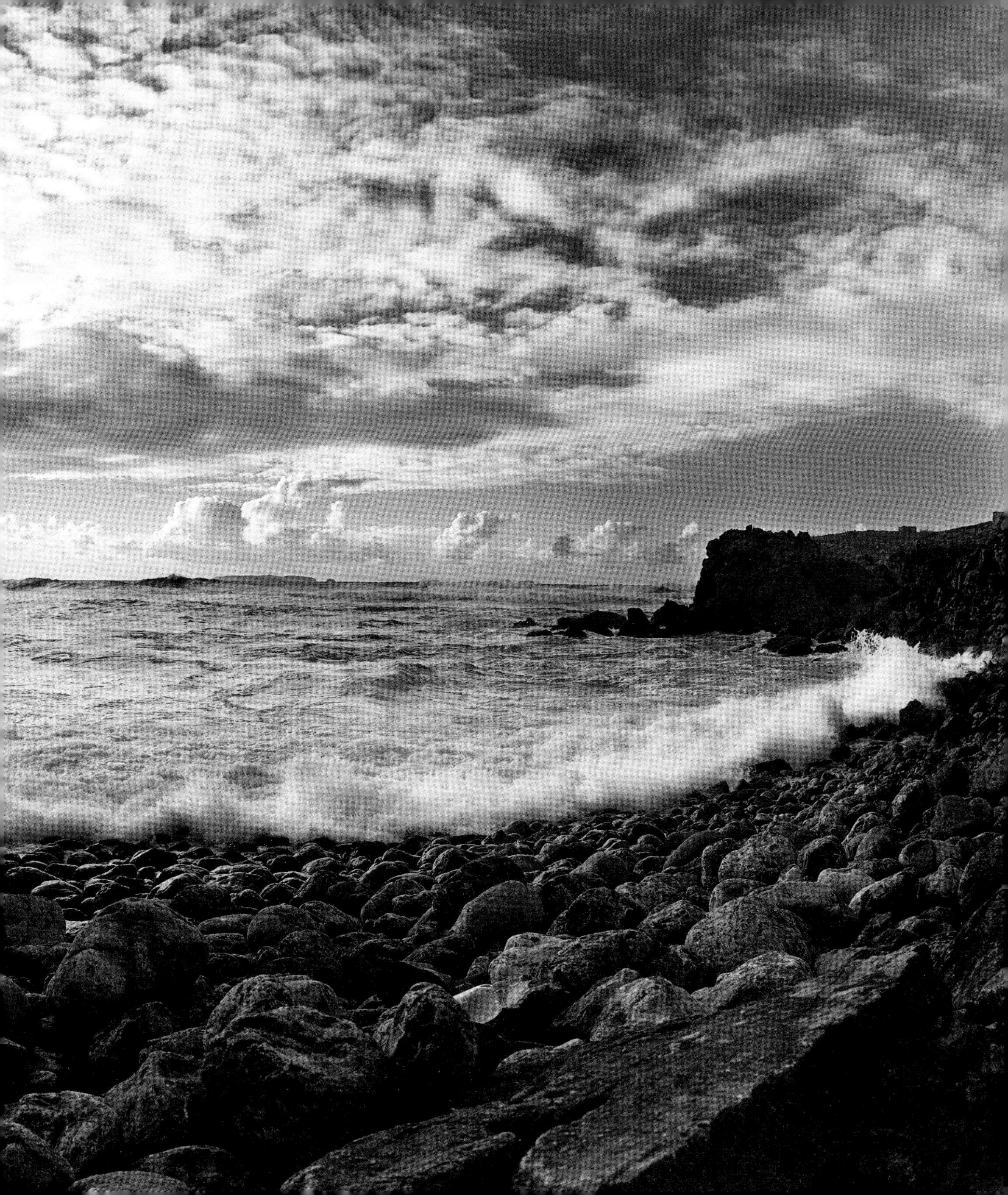

Fact file 1: White door and wall 1981, Fort Steele

Photographer: Lynn Radeka

Camera: Super Cambo 5x4inch on a tripod, lens: Schneider 210mm Symmar, film: Kodak Tri-X exposed at ISO 160, developer: Kodak HC-110, paper: Oriental Seagull, grade 2, toner: selenium

Camera tip

Buy a spirit level to slide onto the camera's accessory shoe. There is nothing as annoying as a horizon that is badly slanting. Of course, that is not to say an angled horizon is always a bad thing because it can actually be a useful composition tool, which works well with portrait or fashion work. For scenics a level horizon is a good thing and a camera-mounted spirit level can help you achieve this. Some tripods have spirit levels built in.

know the camera metering

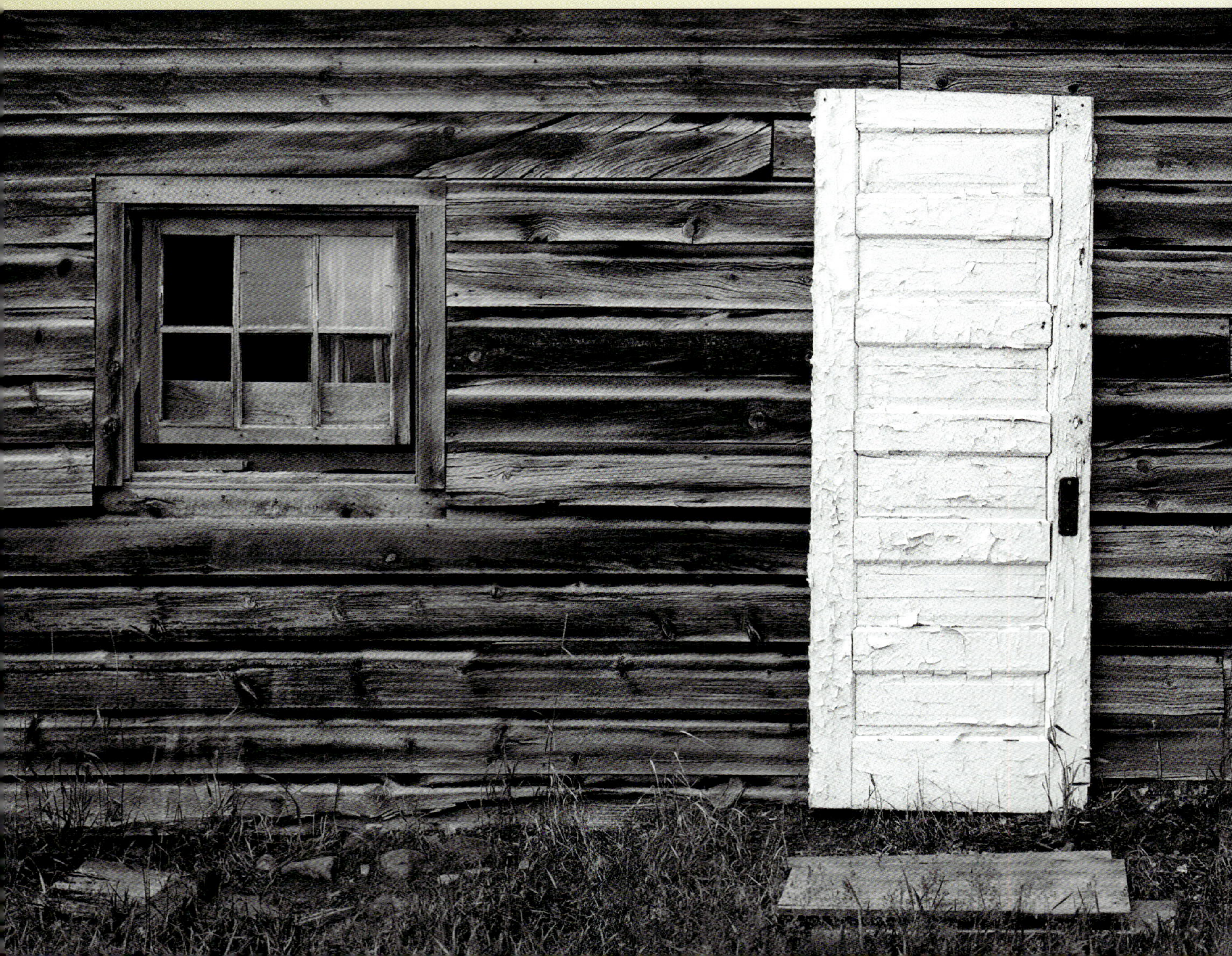

Concept

I noticed this scene while walking through the historic ghost town of Fort Steele in Canada. I responded to the various rectangular shapes and strong lines present throughout the image. Although the scene was in the shade, the luminosity of the cracked paint on the white door seemed to glow with an unusual brilliance.

Composition

Keeping the lines level was important to the success of the photograph. I set the Cambo 4x5inch camera on a tripod taking special care to make sure the horizontal and vertical lines were as square as possible. In other pictures I had taken in this ghost town, keeping everything square proved impossible because the buildings were leaning at unusual angles.

Technique

I made the exposure based on an average reading of the weathered wood, which I placed in Zone V. The door fell in Zone 8. The film was developed normally.

My first print seemed lacking. The overall values were appropriate but the white door did not have the brilliant luminance that I experienced at the time. The simplest solution would have been to use a higher contrast paper, which would have increased the overall contrast, especially in the weathered wood. The result would have been a harsh print lacking in subtlety. Instead I made a very thin highlight mask to 'touch' the door's white tones. This worked beautifully and gave the white door a crisp intensity against the soft neutral background.

▲ Fact file 2 | Lynn Radeka | Crosses | As is customary for me, I walked around the church looking for opportunities. Round the back of the church I saw this clothesline post in the shape of a cross. I recognised the interesting and ironic duplication of the tone and forms, with the dark foreground cross and its shadow set against a white wall and the white cross set against a deep coloured sky.

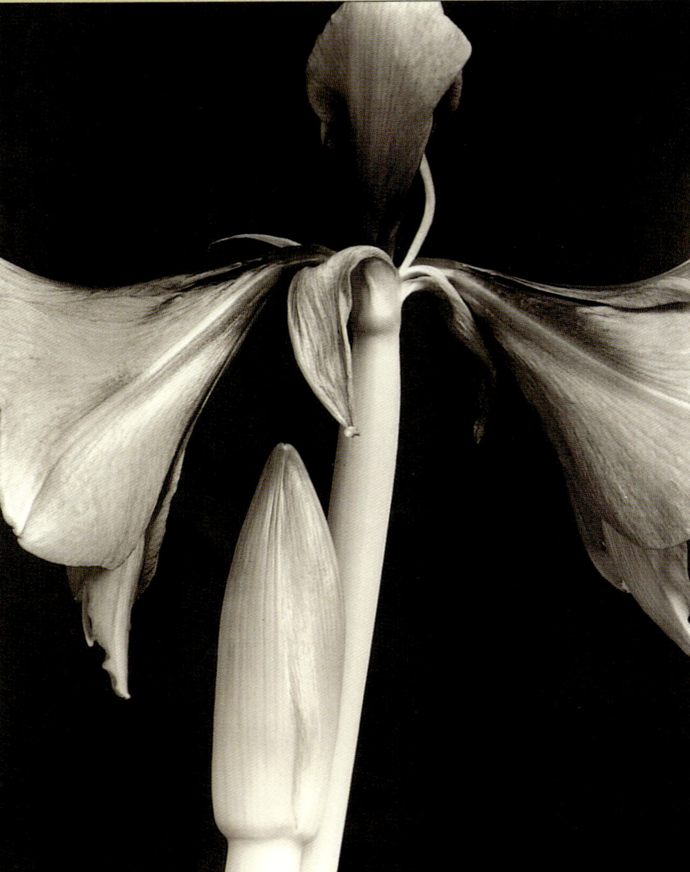

▲ Fact file 3 | Wynn White | Amaryllis | Scenes that are dominated by very light or very dark tones will fool the camera meter into underexposing or overexposing respectively. A spot meter was used for this picture with a reading taken from the highlights and then another taken from the background to ensure that it would come out dark enough.

Camera tip

Modern cameras have a choice of exposure modes and it is worth exploring what they have to offer. Program mode is fully automatic so it is perfect when you are just snapping away in fast-moving situations.

Aperture-priority AE means the photographer sets the lens aperture and the camera sets the shutter speed. This is the best mode when you want to control how much depth-of-field there is in the scene. A small aperture gives lots of depth-of-field and a wide aperture much less.

Shutter-priority AE lets the photographer set the shutter speed and the camera attends to the choice of aperture. This is an excellent mode for shooting action. You set a high shutter speed to ensure that the subject is as sharp as possible.

Manual metering lets you decide both aperture and shutter speed with the help of either the camera's meter or a separate hand-held model. This is the mode to use when you want to take control.

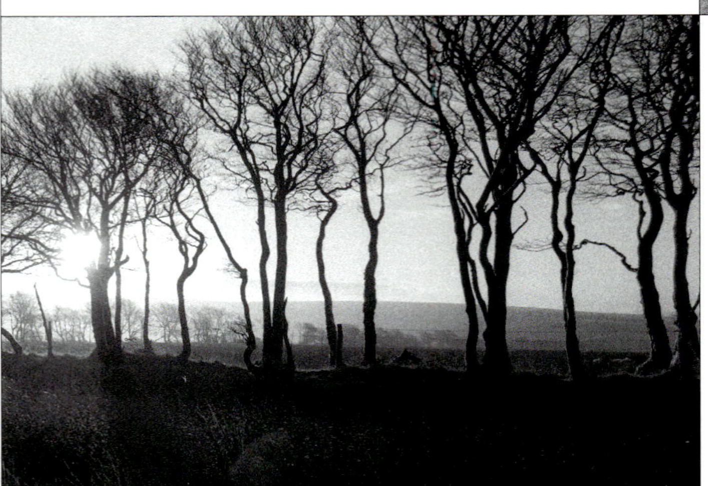

◀ Fact file 4 | William Cheung | Exmoor sunrise | In terms of contrast, it does not get more extreme than including the sun in the picture. But shooting directly into the light gives dramatic pictures which is why it is a technique worth trying. Shielding the sun's disk behind something like a tree is a great help in controlling contrast as well as keeping flare down to a minimum. For this picture, a meter reading was taken from an area of mid-toned sky to the right of the scene. This gave a semi-silhouette image.

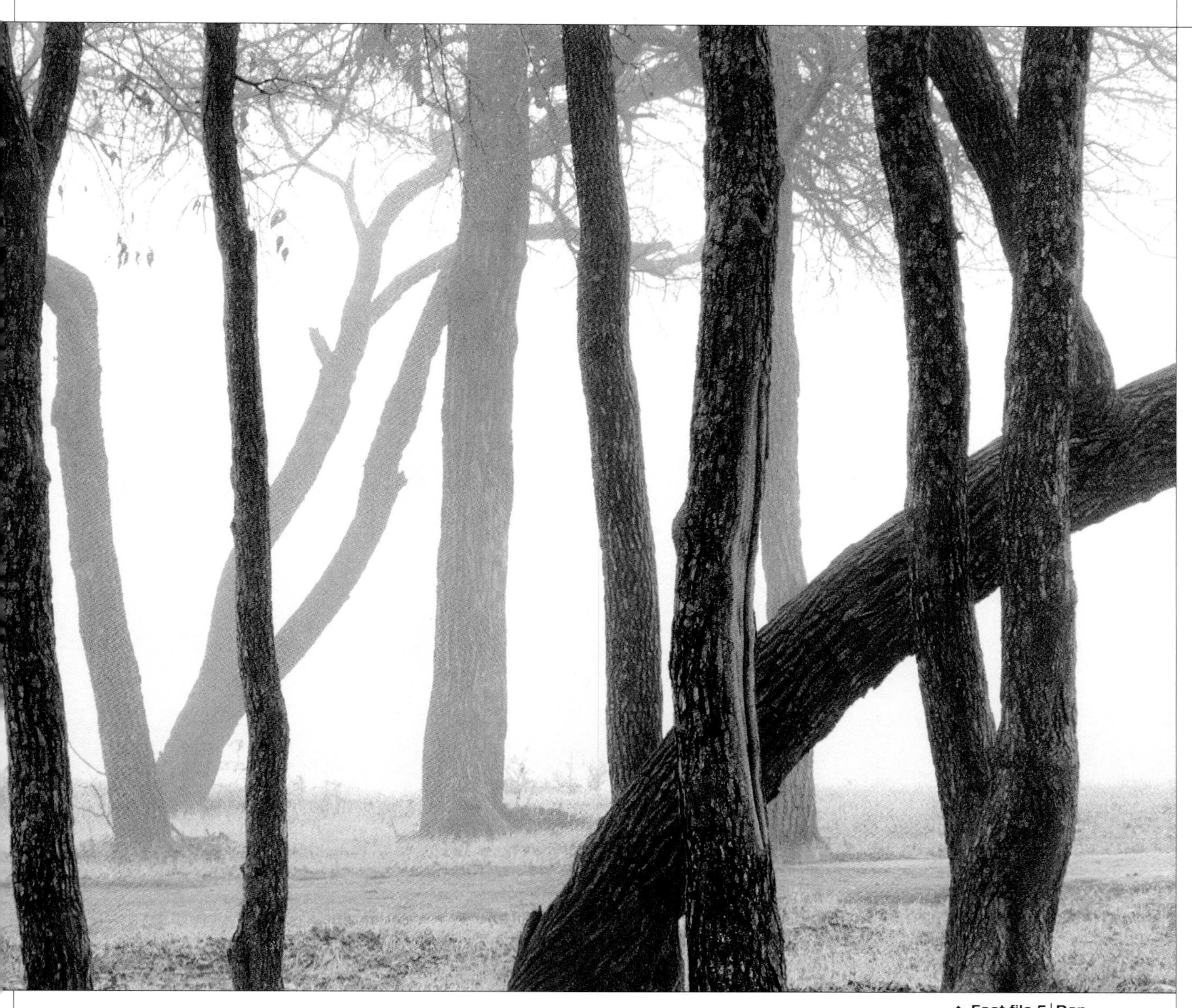

▲ Fact file 5 | Dan Burkholder | Path and trees in fog | I remember waking up to see this beautiful fog in south Texas, I hurried outside immediately before the fog started to lift. The fog gave a wonderful depth to the overlapping trees and helped with this simple but effective composition. Conditions like this can fool camera meters into underexposure but such scenes can benefit from marginal overexposure on the meter reading to retain an atmospheric feeling.

Fact file 1: Jolanda

Photographer: Rene de Haan

Camera: Hasselblad 500CM, lens: 80mm, film: Ilford Pan F, exposure: 1/250sec at f/5.6, developer: Kodak X-tol, paper: Agfa Multicontrast, grade 3

Concept

I have a whole series of photographs of this woman taken over a period of time, trying to catch her beauty and sensuality. I often work in this manner because it is the only way that a subject can truly be explored and understood. The feeling of familiarity also helps to get great-looking pictures where the model looks totally relaxed.

know your camera lens apertures

Composition

Composition in portraits is often an impulsive and natural thing, decided by the pose and the shape of the model. This portrait is typical. Her eyes are huge and very striking so they immediately attract the viewer but because of the way she was posed, I wanted to make more of her arms too. An important thing to watch with such pictures is the fingers. Bunched together, they look ungainly and tense so you need to ask the model to move around until you find a natural pose.

Technique

Lighting was provided by one studio flash unit fitted with a large softbox to give a lovely directional light. A small white reflector was placed on the model's right side to lighten any deep shadows.

I selected a fairly-wide lens aperture – f/5.6 – to make sure that the background was effectively thrown out of focus so that it did not clash with the model. Aperture choice is important to the success of portraits. Obviously, it is crucial that there is plenty of sharpness in the face and you do not want so much detail in the background that it distracts from the subject.

Camera tip

If your SLR camera has a motorwind or motordrive, leave it set to continuous shooting. Then, if the situation in front of you is unfolding rapidly you can just keep the shutter release pressed down and take a sequence of shots in very quick succession. Of course, in normal situations all you have to remember is not to keep your shutter finger pressed down otherwise you end up wasting film.

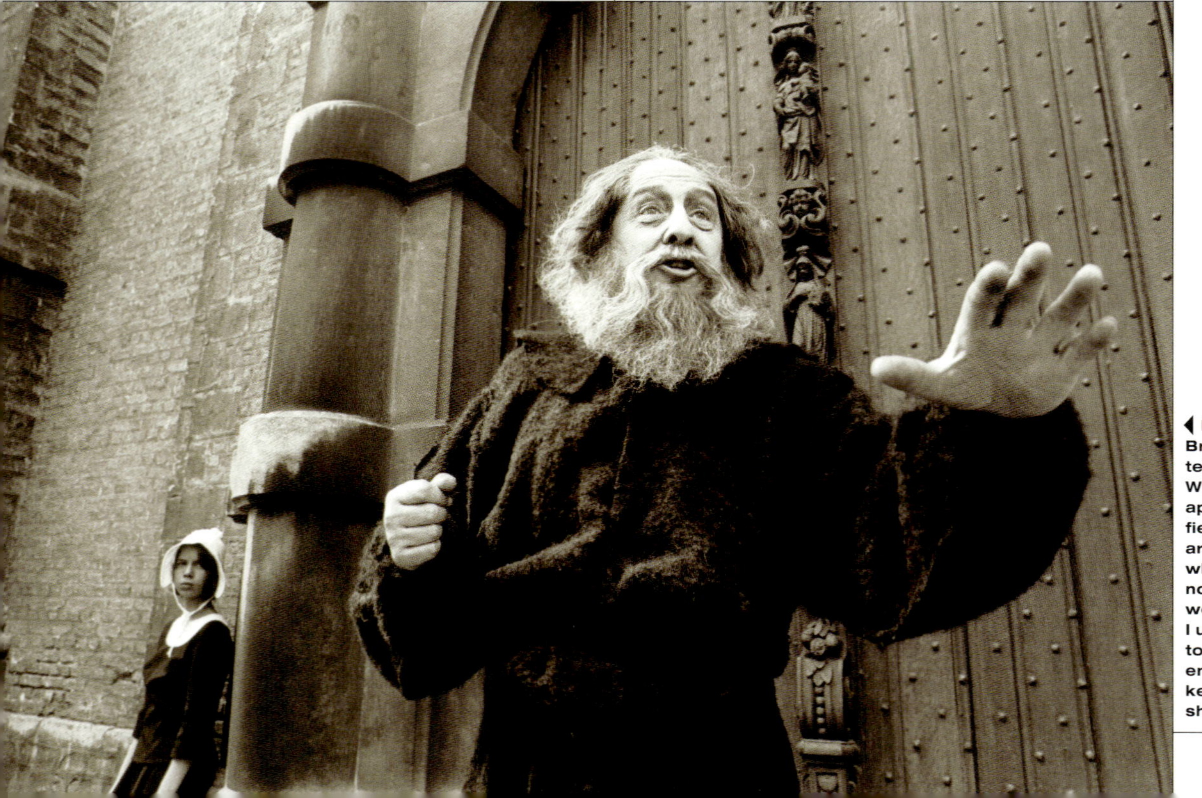

◀ Fact file 2 | John Braeckmans | I am only telling you once | Wide-angle lenses give, apparently, more depth-of-field than longer lenses so are ideal in situations where quick refocusing is not practical. Here people were constantly moving so I used a wide-angle lens set to an aperture of f/11 for enough depth-of-field to keep the key elements in sharp focus.

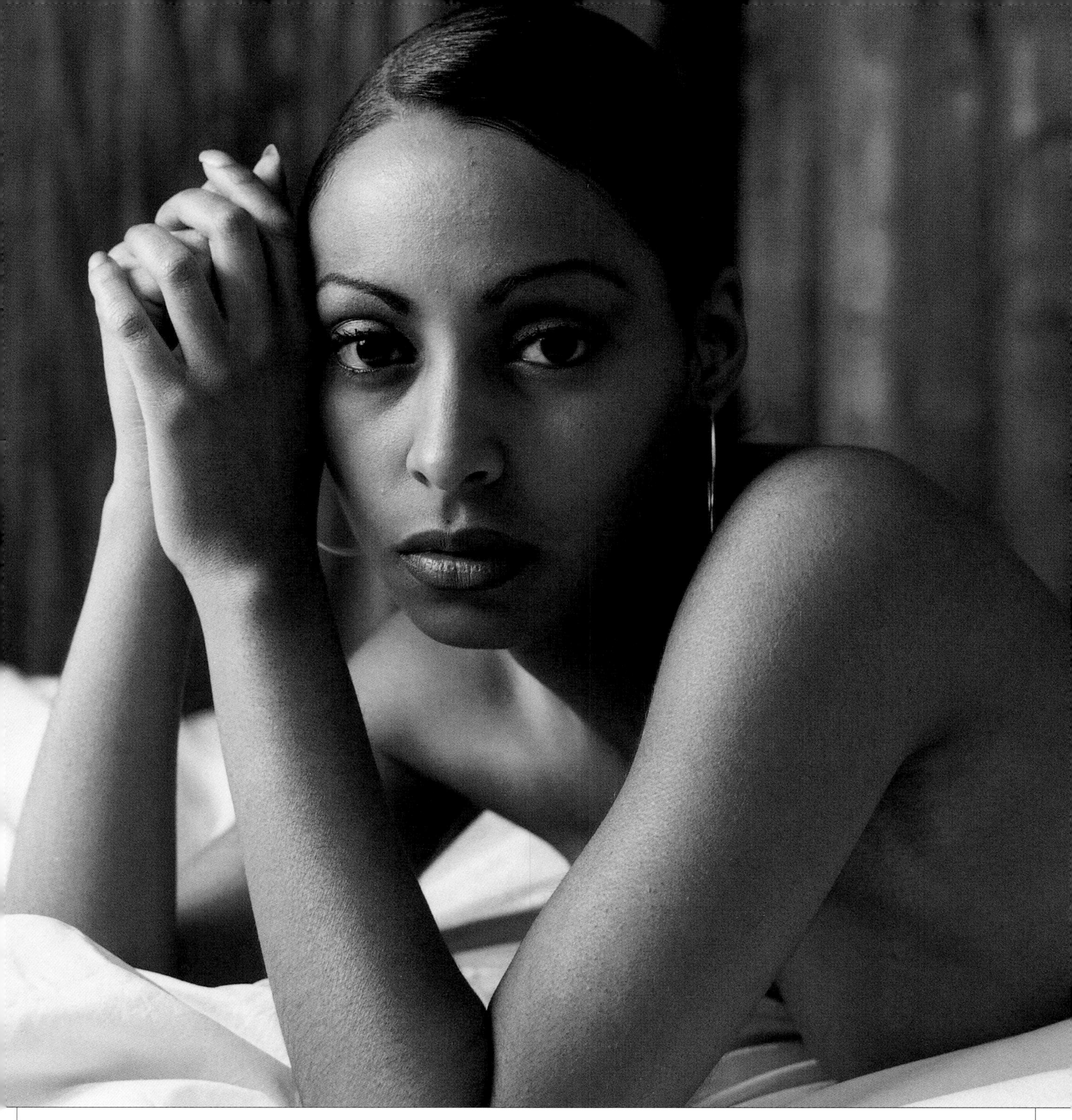

know your camera shutter speeds

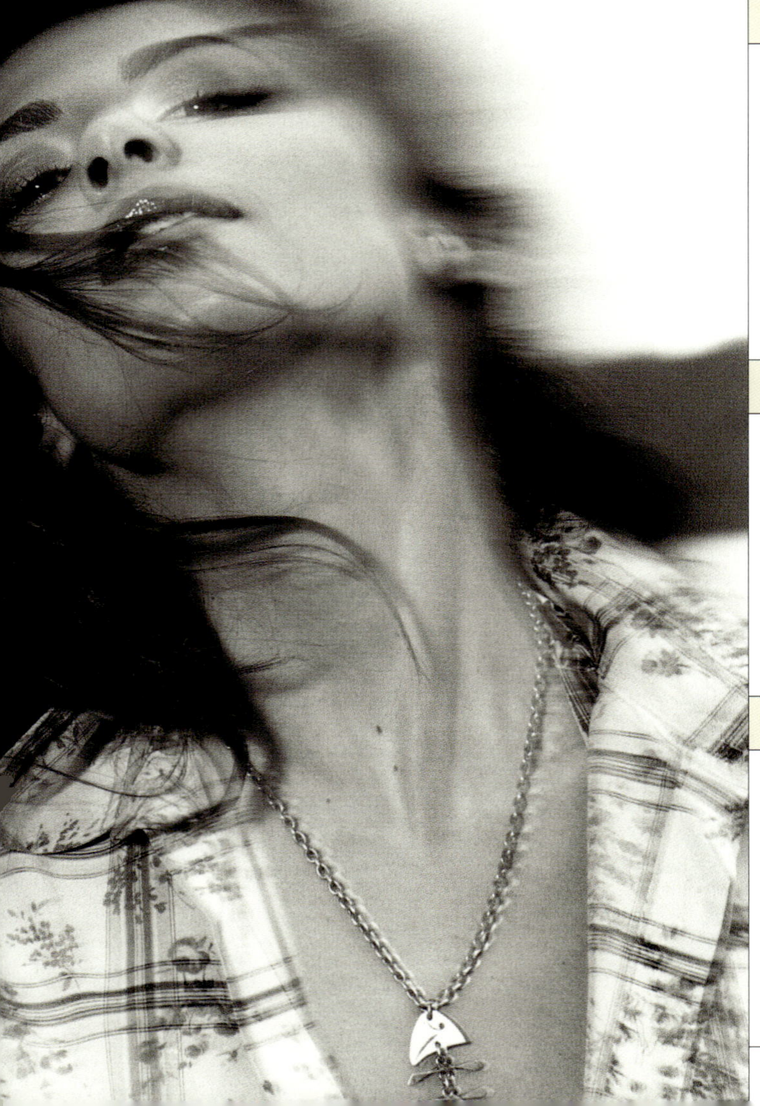

Concept

Water blurred through the use of slow shutter speeds looks good and that was the technique I wanted to show off here. How much blur is achieved depends on the actual shutter speed as well as the velocity of the flowing water. In this instance, the water was reasonably fast and I was close up so, from past experience, I knew that 1sec would work well.

Composition

This photograph is an exercise in tone and that was my main consideration when I composed it. It was important to get an attractive balance between dark and light tones. The sweeping lines of blurred water help bring the viewer's eye into the picture and hold it there.

Technique

This was a straightforward picture. I determined exposure with spot meter readings from the shadows and the highlights, while in the darkroom there was some burning in and dodging to get the right tonal balance. I also 'flashed' the highlights in the water so that they revealed more detail.

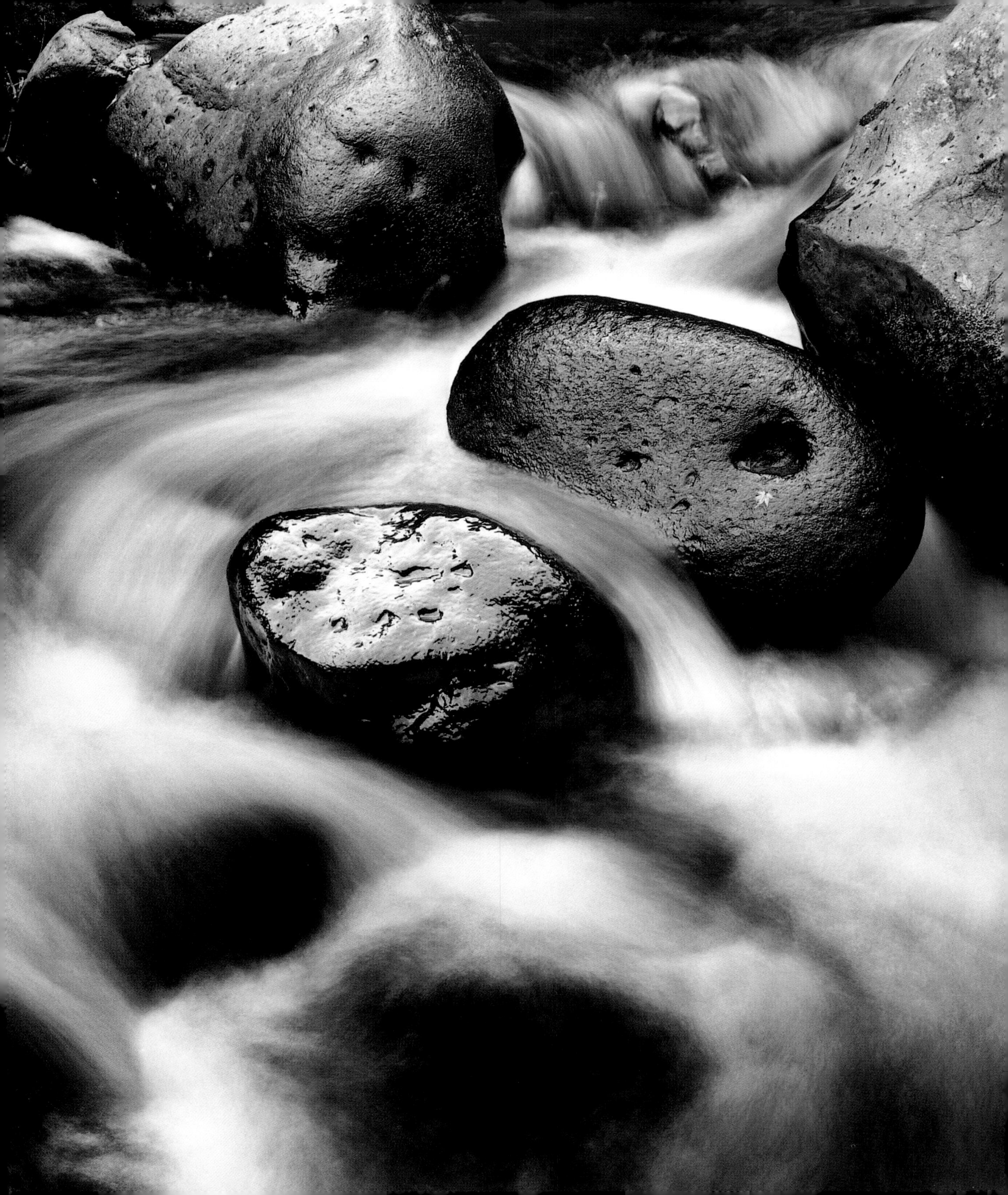

Fact file 1: Horse nuzzle

Photographer: Daniel Bayer

Camera: Nikon F5, lens: 80–200mm, film: Kodak Tri-X at ISO 400, exposure: 1/200sec at f/5.6

Concept

I wanted a tightly cropped picture of a girl happily greeting a familiar horse. I was surprised when she suddenly nuzzled the horse but I timed the exposure just right to capture the moment. Setting a relatively wide-lens aperture on a long focal length lens has helped to concentrate attention on the girl's face and thrown her hair attractively out of focus.

know your camera focusing

Technique

It was a dull overcast day and there was not much light around. I wanted limited depth-of-field so I set an aperture of f/5.6 which meant that I could set a reasonably fast shutter speed to avoid any subject movement. Of course, with such limited depth-of-field, focusing had to be critical but the camera's autofocus system did well and I used the focus lock to ensure I got sharpness in the girl's face.

Composition

With the telephoto zoom I composed very closely, giving an almost abstract look to the photograph. Excluding any distractions in the background by cropping in closely has helped too. The upright format works well especially the way the girl's long hair hangs down, adding some lovely curved lines.

Camera tip

Depth-of-field is the amount of front-to-back sharpness within the picture. It is affected by several factors: the set aperture, lens focal length and the subject-to-camera distance. For any given focal length, the wider lens apertures (f/2, f/2.8, f/4) give a shallower depth-of-field than smaller (f/11, f/16, f/22) apertures. Consequently, if you want selective focus, set wider apertures while if you want lots of front-to-back sharpness set smaller apertures.

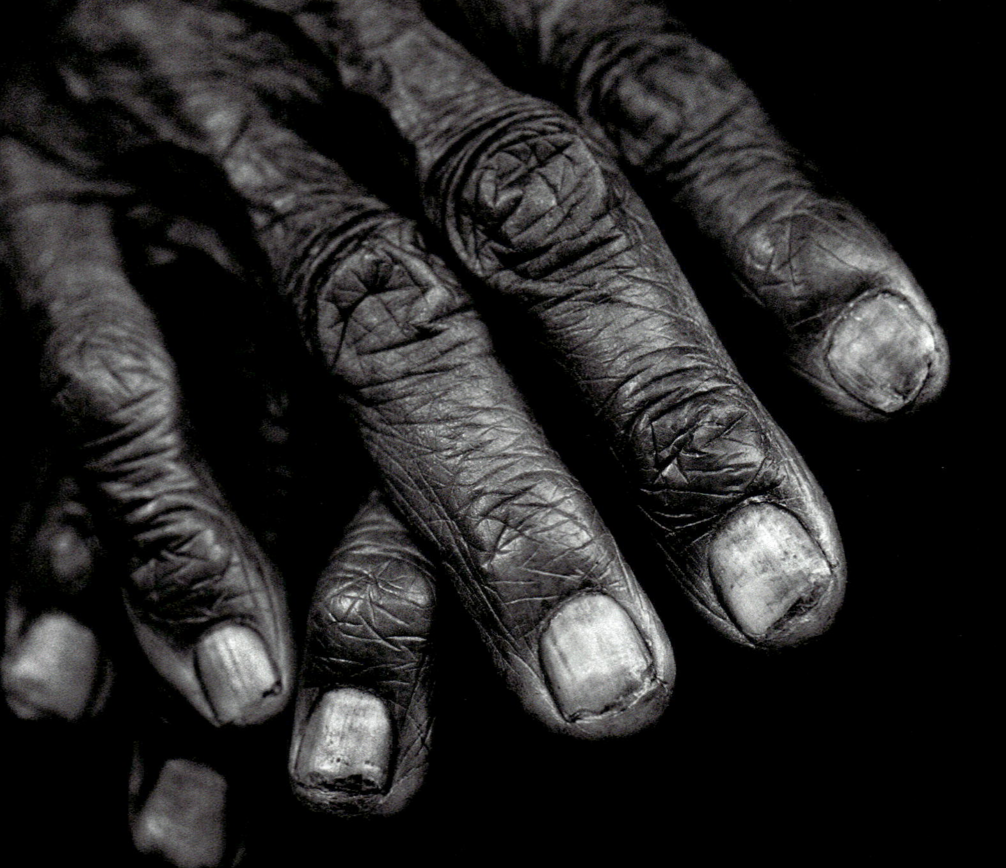

◀ Fact file 2 | Daniel Bayer | Hands of time | I did a story on Thailand's vanishing island culture and my aim here was to document the very telling hands of this 90-year-old lady. They had a rich texture which showed the woman's hard working lifestyle. By setting a lens aperture of f/11 I got as much depth-of-field into this close up study as I possibly could.

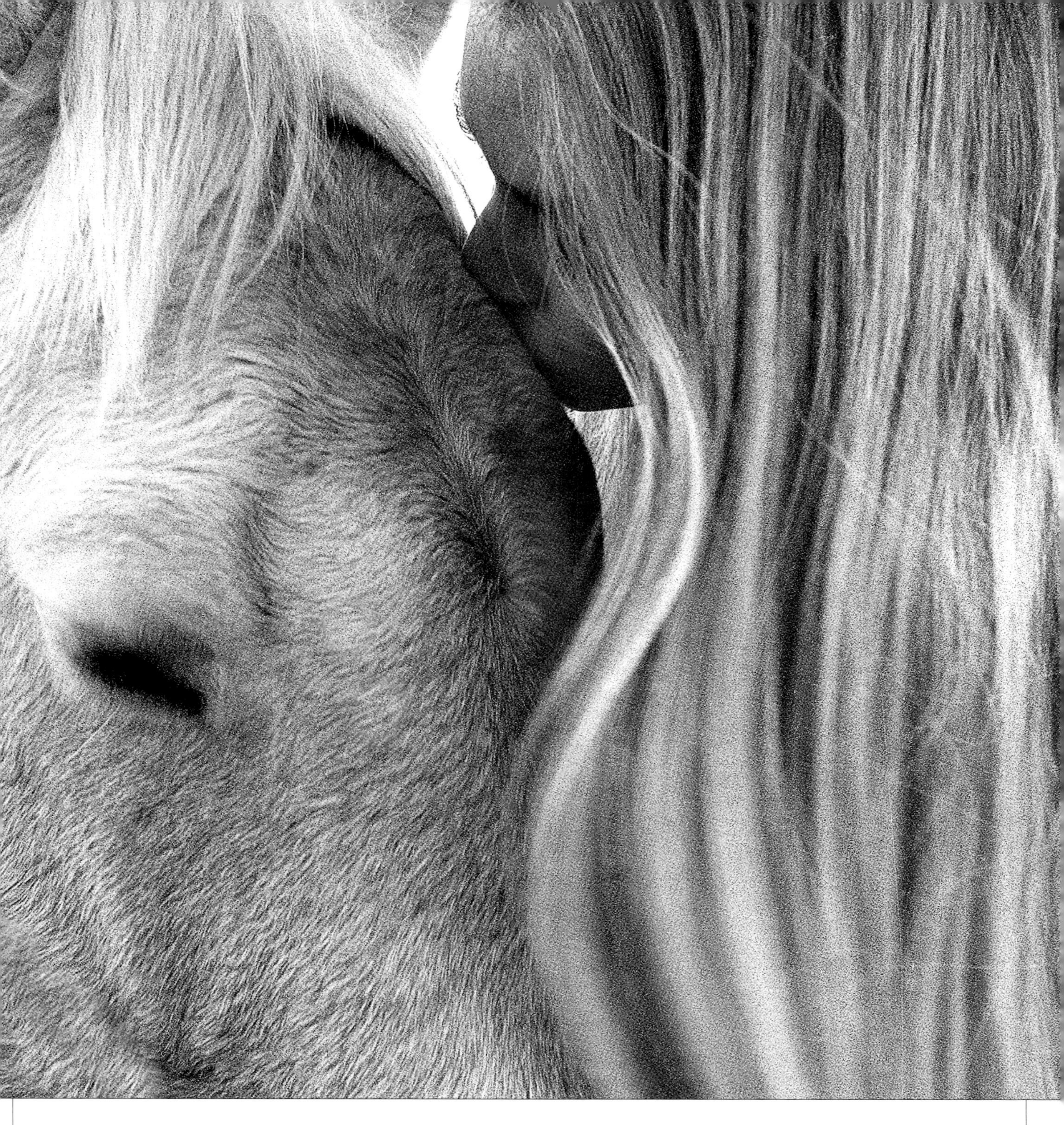

Fact file 1: Trees, near Cascade Pass 1982

Photographer: Lynn Radeka

Camera: 5x4inch Super Cambo, lens: 210mm telephoto, film: Kodak Tri-X rated at ISO 400, exposure: 1/60 at f/32, developer: Kodak HC-110, paper: Forte Polygrade, grade 3

Composition

The telephoto lens was needed because of the subject's position and its distance from me, but this also helped to flatten the perspective of the trees. This separation also meant that I could take a very formal approach to the composition, making sure the image was as symmetrical as possible.

Camera tip

Protect the camera lens. Fit an ultraviolet or skylight filter on each of your lenses to protect their front elements from dust, water and fingerprints. There is no light loss with these filters and they have no tonal impact on the image. Of course, keep the filters spotlessly clean to eliminate image degradation and any risk of lens flare when shooting into the light.

Concept

I was driving through the spectacular North Cascades National Park in the USA and noticed this clean stand of dead trees a short distance off the road. The way the scene was organised seemed like a pen-and-ink drawing. I set up my 5x4inch camera and used a 210mm telephoto lens and got the cleanest composition possible. The image works well as a small print because of its pen and ink quality.

Technique

Exposure was relatively fast as there was ample light around and depth-of-field was no problem either. My main concern was movement of the trees in the wind. This can be easily over-looked because the eye has a tendency to compensate for large objects like trees swaying in the wind. It was even more difficult in this case because there were no stationary objects to judge movement. I timed the exposure by using the foreground dirt and vegetation to detect swaying in the trees and made the exposure at a 'still' moment.

know your camera the right lens

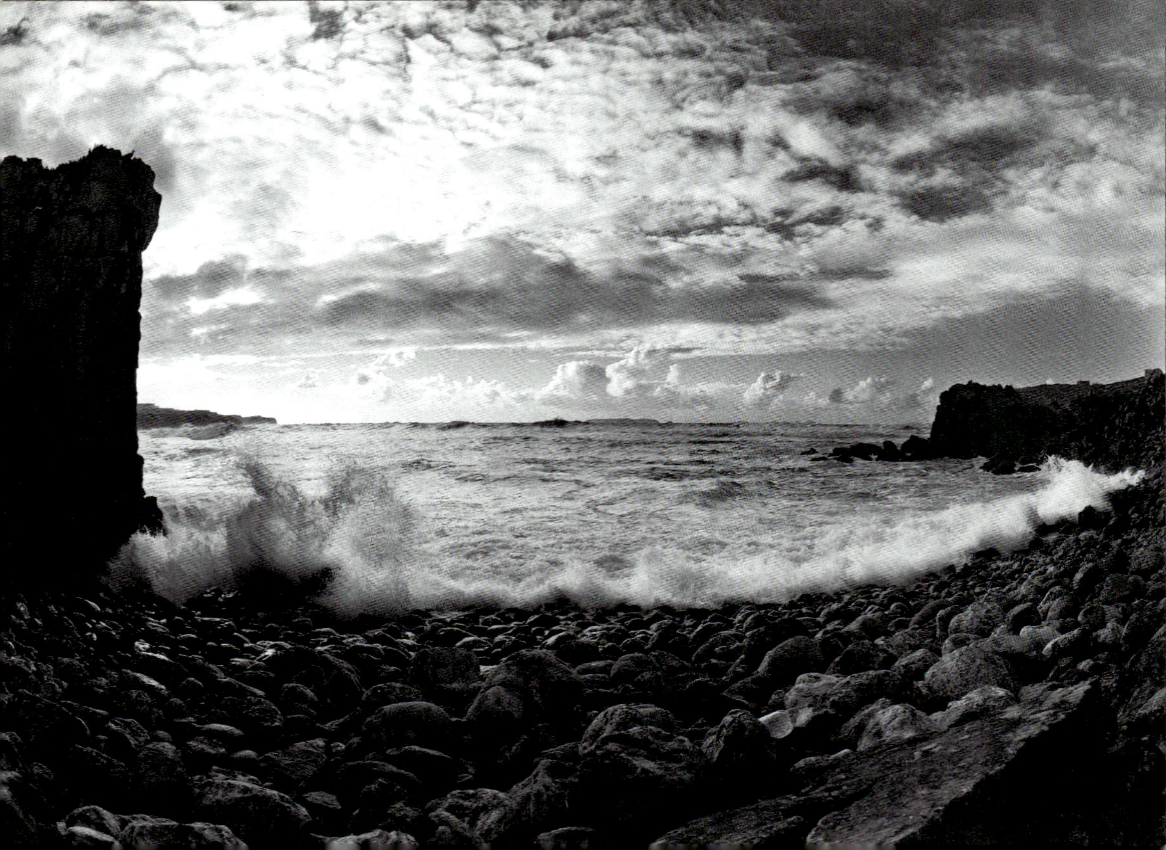

◀ **Fact file 2 | Nana Sousa Dias | Papoa |** An orange filter helped to bring out the cloud detail in the sky of this ultra wide-angle lens picture. Such lenses are ideal for exploiting eye-catching foreground and the low camera viewpoint has helped to make the most of the situation.

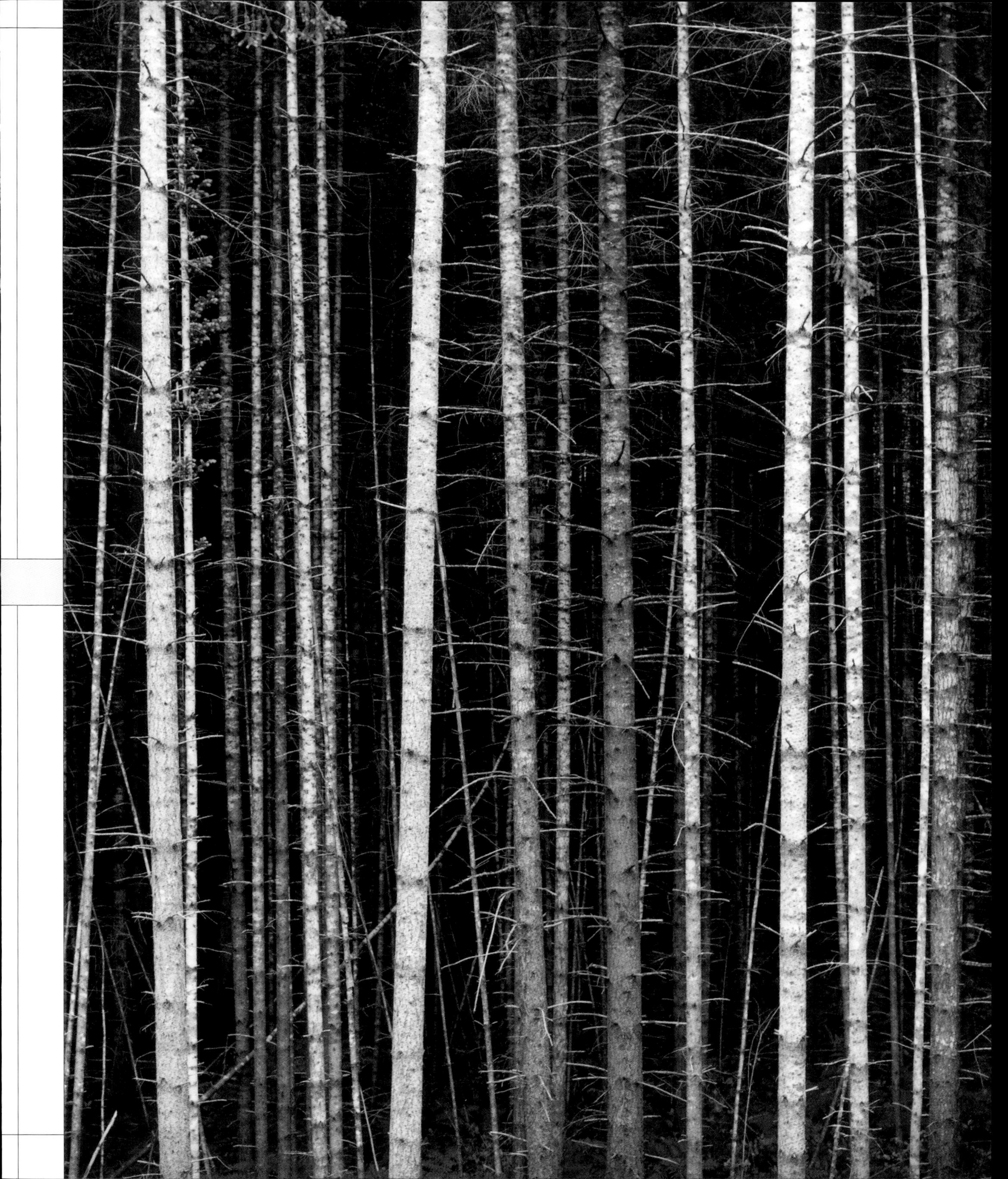

▼ Fact file 3 | Nana Sousa Dias | Dr No | I was doing a few experiments with a semi fish-eye lens on the camera when I saw this intriguing figure. I did not have any time to think, so I just quickly set a fast enough shutter speed to get a sharp image and shot. This is quite a selective crop because the lens was so wide that everything got included, but I would have missed the shot if I had decided to change to another lens.

▶ Fact file 4 | Bob Hudak | Sand patterns | Macro lenses are designed to let you focus much closer than normal lenses so they are ideally suited to abstract photography.
This photograph was taken on my first trip to Vilano Beach in Florida. In the afternoon I was just looking around the beach when I found this area that contained a mix of white-and-black sand. It was these patterns that caught my eye and was the reason I shot this picture. With no real sense of scale, I decided to include the small white shell in the lower half of the composition to give a clue to this abstraction.

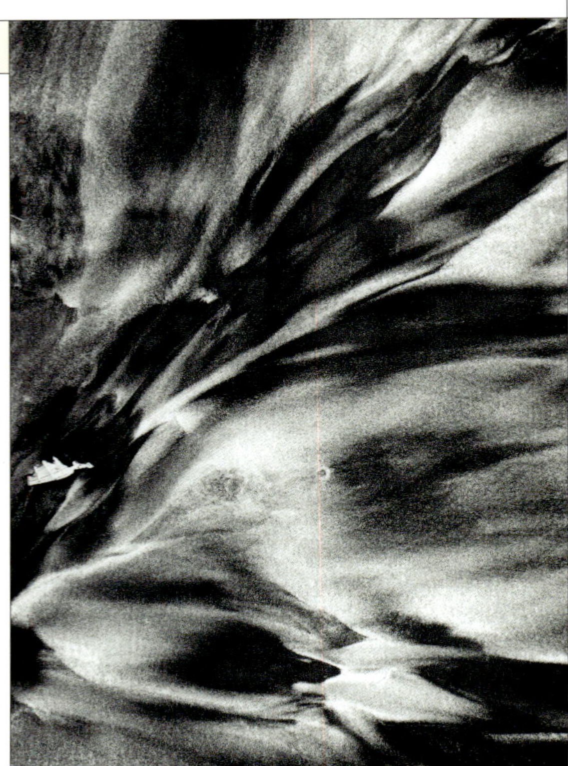

Camera tip

Tripods give ultimate camera stability but they are heavy, bulky things to lug around. A monopod is a worthwhile alternative because it is much easier to carry and provides a high degree of steadiness. With careful use, and bracing your own legs with the monopod it is possible to shoot at 1/8sec or slower. A derivative of the monopod is the lightweight walking pole which has a tripod bush so that a camera can be mounted. For walkers wanting to take pictures but without wanting to carry too much kit, this is the perfect solution.

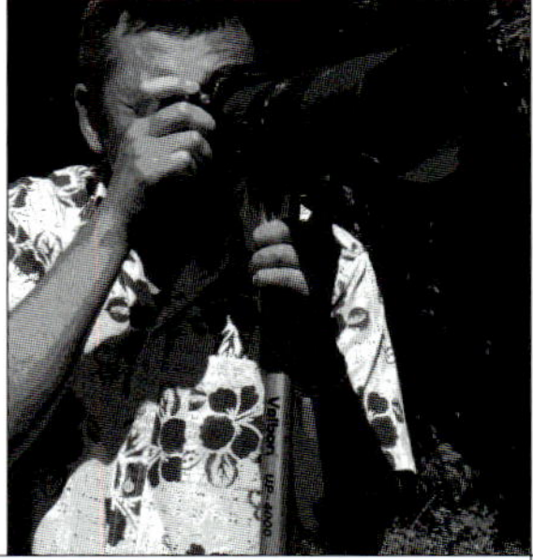

Fact file 5│Vince Bevan│Paris│This picture is part of a personal project on Paris. What appealed is that the scene seemed timeless and I felt it gave a flavour of the city. Although it was a busy street I knew that if I waited I would get a clean background. I wanted to direct most of the attention to the car, especially the wheel hub, and using a 24mm wide-angle lens has helped to do this. The wheel hub looks like an eye. Because I was using a wide-angle I was careful to position the camera to reduce any possible distortion, particularly with the straight lines of the background.

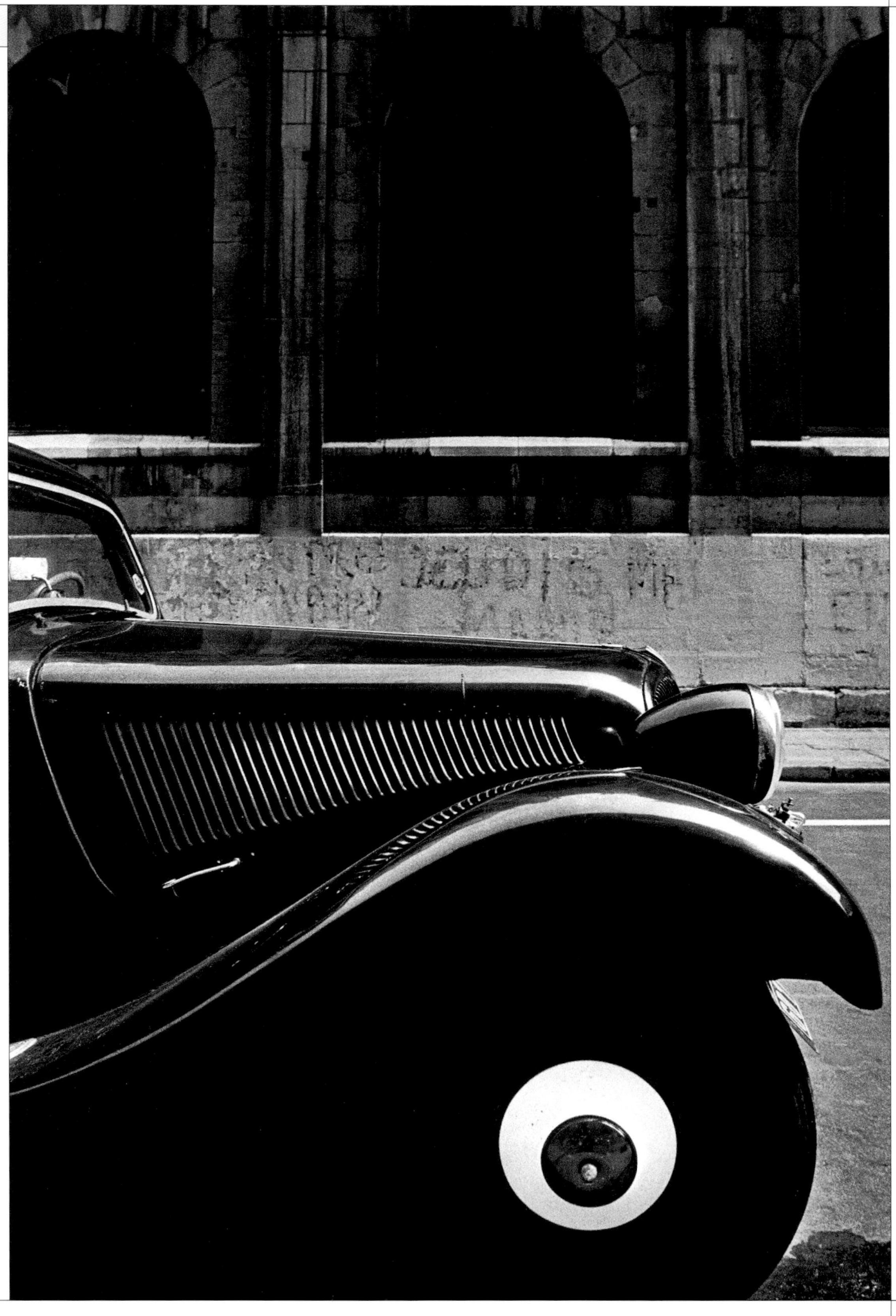

film choice

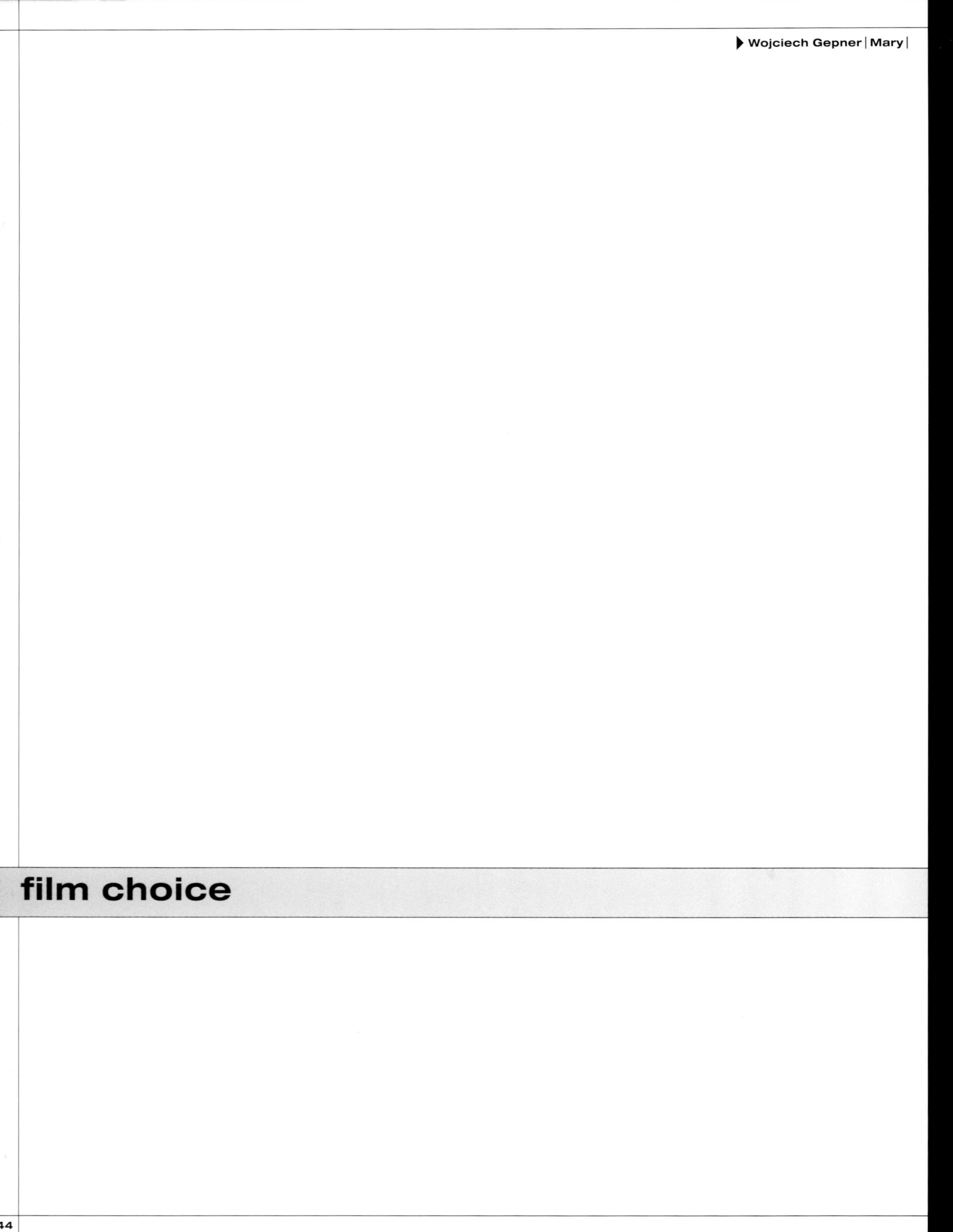

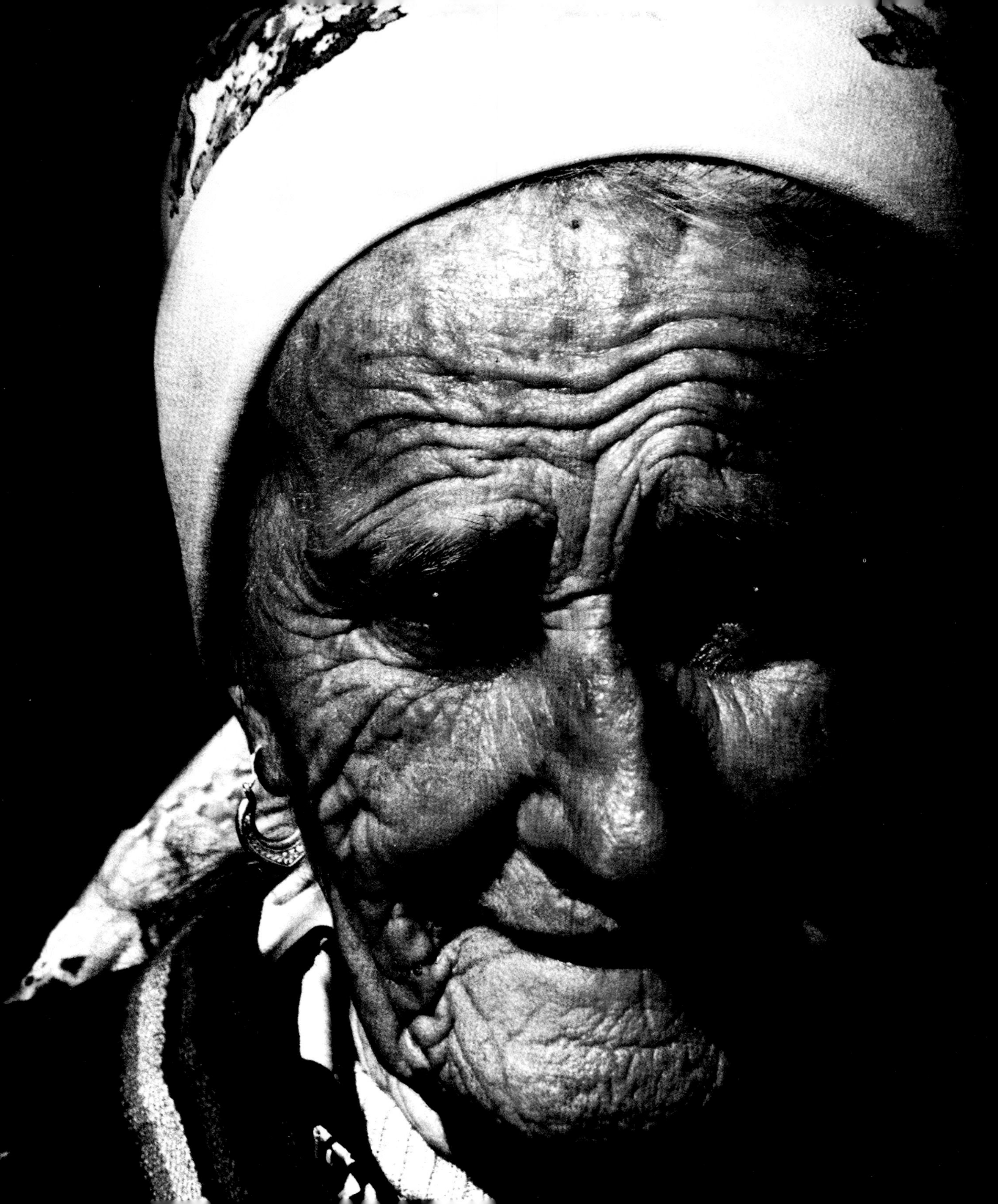

film choice slow film

Concept

I had been trying for over a year to get this picture and this was about my ninth attempt. It is only possible to get this view at a very low tide or from a boat, which means there is not much time during the year to gain the right perspective.

Severe storms hit this coast during the winter and so I wanted to show a stormy sky and movement in the sea, while still having a good light to retain the unique detail in the headland.

I always try to get a kind of haunting quality in my scenic images and I think I have achieved it here to a degree, but there is always room for improvement. The problem with spending such a long time in trying to get one particular picture is that you are never satisfied.

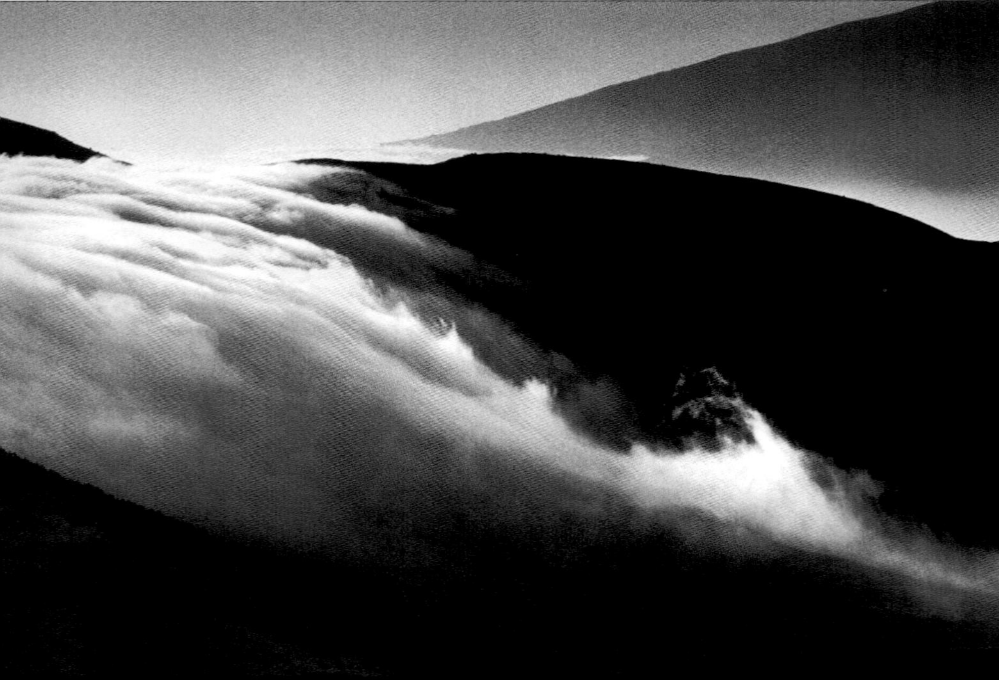

▼ Fact file 2 | Vince Bevan | Sierra Nevada | I was driving through the mountains in southern Spain and watching this huge blanket of mist slowly creep up from the coast. I realised I was going to be engulfed in it so I stopped the car and took a few frames until I could not see more than a few feet in front of me. I was using a slow film but the light was bright enough to allow a fast shutter speed to avoid camera shake.

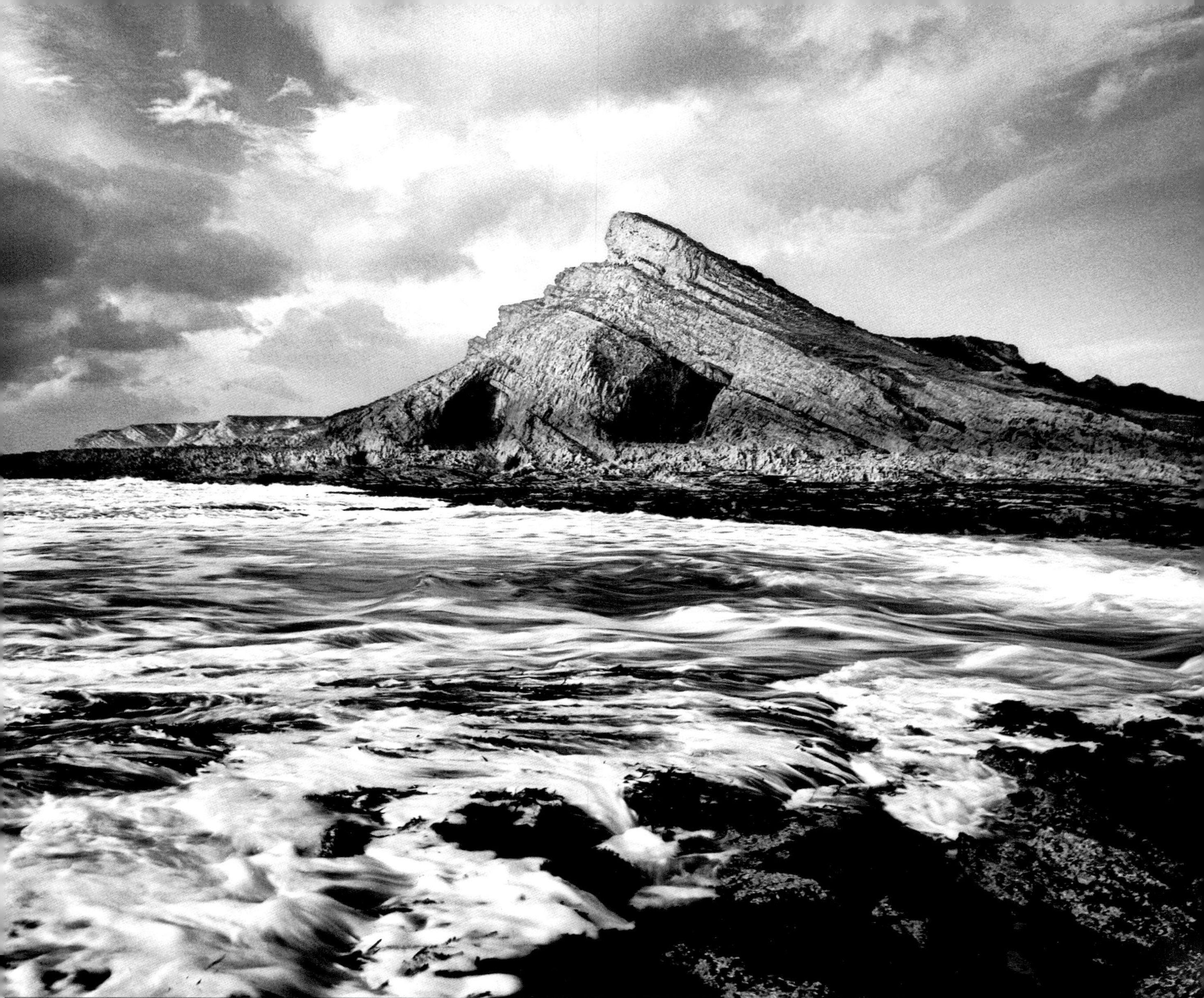

<table>
<tr><th>Composition</th><th>Technique</th><th>Camera tip</th></tr>
<tr><td>

Running the horizon through the middle of the picture does not always work but here it does. That is because the mountain, the focal point, is off-centre which helps bring the eye into the image. The graphic foreground also helps in this respect and darkening the sky stops the eye drifting out of the image.

</td><td>

I exposed for the shadows, taking a manual reading. I was conscious of selecting the correct shutter speed in order to blur the sea a little, but not excessively. Using an orange filter meant that the negative had plenty of detail, but I still found it necessary to burn it in to achieve the drama of the cloudscape. The bottom right and left of the print were also burnt in.

A solution of ferricyanide was applied to bleach out the highlights of selective areas of the headland in order to increase the contrast and emphasise the caves.

</td><td>

A bright sky can fool the camera's exposure meter to underexpose which will result in poor-quality prints. The quickest way to deal with this is to aim the lens down so that the meter reads more of the darker foreground and this will ensure plenty of shadow detail in the final negative.
If you are using an autoexposure mode use the camera's autoexposure lock to memorise the reading before recomposing the image.

</td></tr>
</table>

Fact file 1: Malham, Yorkshire Dales

Photographer: William Cheung

Camera: Canon EOS 3, lens: 20–35mm f/3.5–4.5, film: Ilford FP4 Plus, exposure: 1/50sec at f/5.6, developer: Kodak HC-110 1+31, 8.5 minutes

Technique

There was a strong cross wind so I opted against using a tripod. I thought it would cause more problems than it would solve and decided to hand-hold the camera. There was not much light around and the exposure meter indicated 1/50sec at f/5.6 so there was the risk of camera shake. I took a firm grip, gently held my breath and squeezed off a shot or two and hoped the picture would be sharp.

Concept

This limestone pavement is a little way outside the popular village of Malham and a short walk from the road. It was a very dull, windswept day although there was some tone in the sky and the scene had virtually no natural contrast. I decided to use a medium-speed film exposed normally and then during development I would extend processing by a couple of minutes to inject some contrast into the scene.

Composition

Aiming a wide-angle lens down accentuates the foreground and that is the effect I wanted here. The idea was for my dominant foreground to lead the viewer into the single tree. I tried some shots with just the lines of the pavement as foreground interest but after looking around, I saw the twisted remains of a tree which I thought would be more effective. I crouched down slightly to give more emphasis on the tree remains.

film choice medium speed

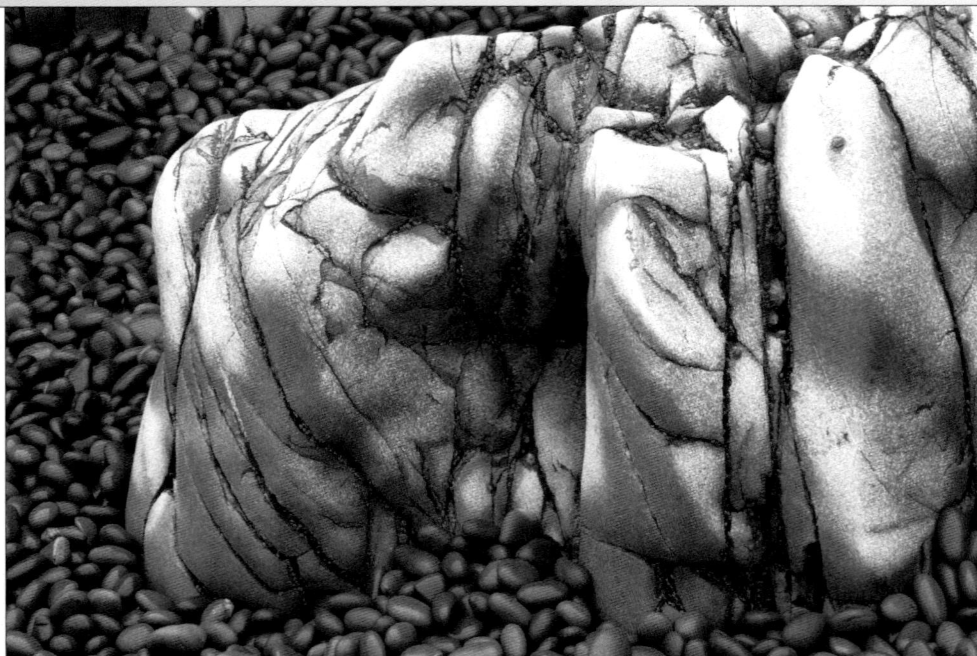

Fact file 2 | William Cheung | Bossington beach | It was a flat, grey day but the light falling onto this beautifully textured rock made it glisten. The light was so poor, however, that I should have been using a tripod but I had left it back in the car. I had to take the risk of hand-holding a 20–35mm zoom lens at 1/15sec to allow a lens aperture of f/5.6. As it happens, the picture is perfectly sharp and I love the mix of interesting textures.

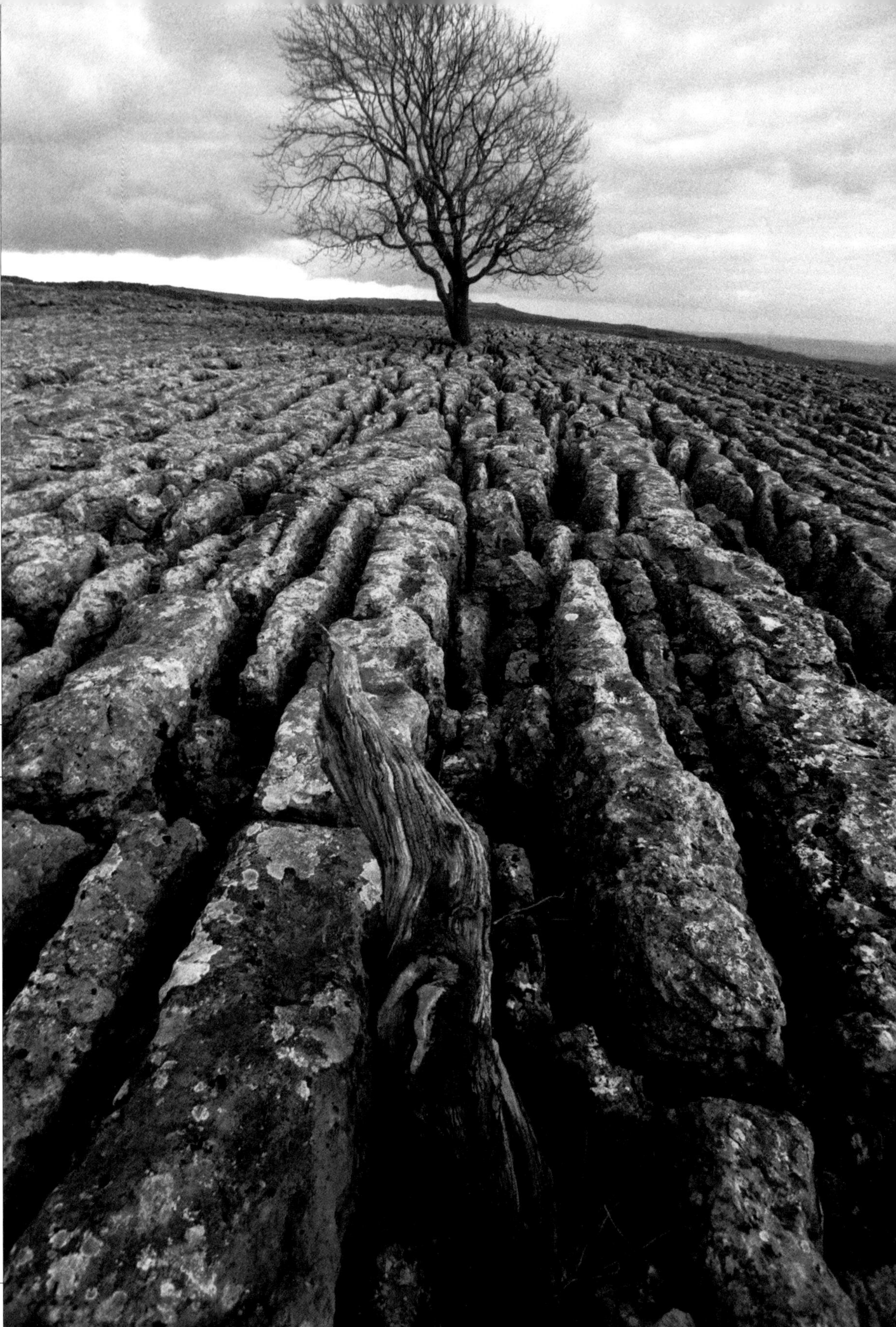

Camera tip

When the light is poor and you only have a medium-speed film available, try uprating or exposing the film at a higher speed than the manufacturer's recommended one. For example, if you have an ISO 100 medium speed you can set the camera to expose it at ISO 200 which effectively underexposes the film by one stop. To compensate you need to extend the film development. This technique is called push processing and in this example, the film needs a one stop push. If the film had been exposed at ISO 400, it would need a two stop push in development. Most black-and-white films respond favourably to this treatment and while grain and contrast do increase this is a small price to pay for sharp pictures. The film or developer will have instructions on how much to increase development by, but as a guide, increase the processing time by one-third for every one stop of underexposure. Many fast films can be pushed two stops before image quality starts suffering really badly.

Photographer: Ian McFarlane

Camera: Mamiya 6, lens: 75mm, film: Ilford HP5 Plus at ISO 400, exposure: 1/60sec at f/5.6, developer: Kodak T-max 1+4, paper: Ilford Multigrade FB, grade 2

film choice fast film

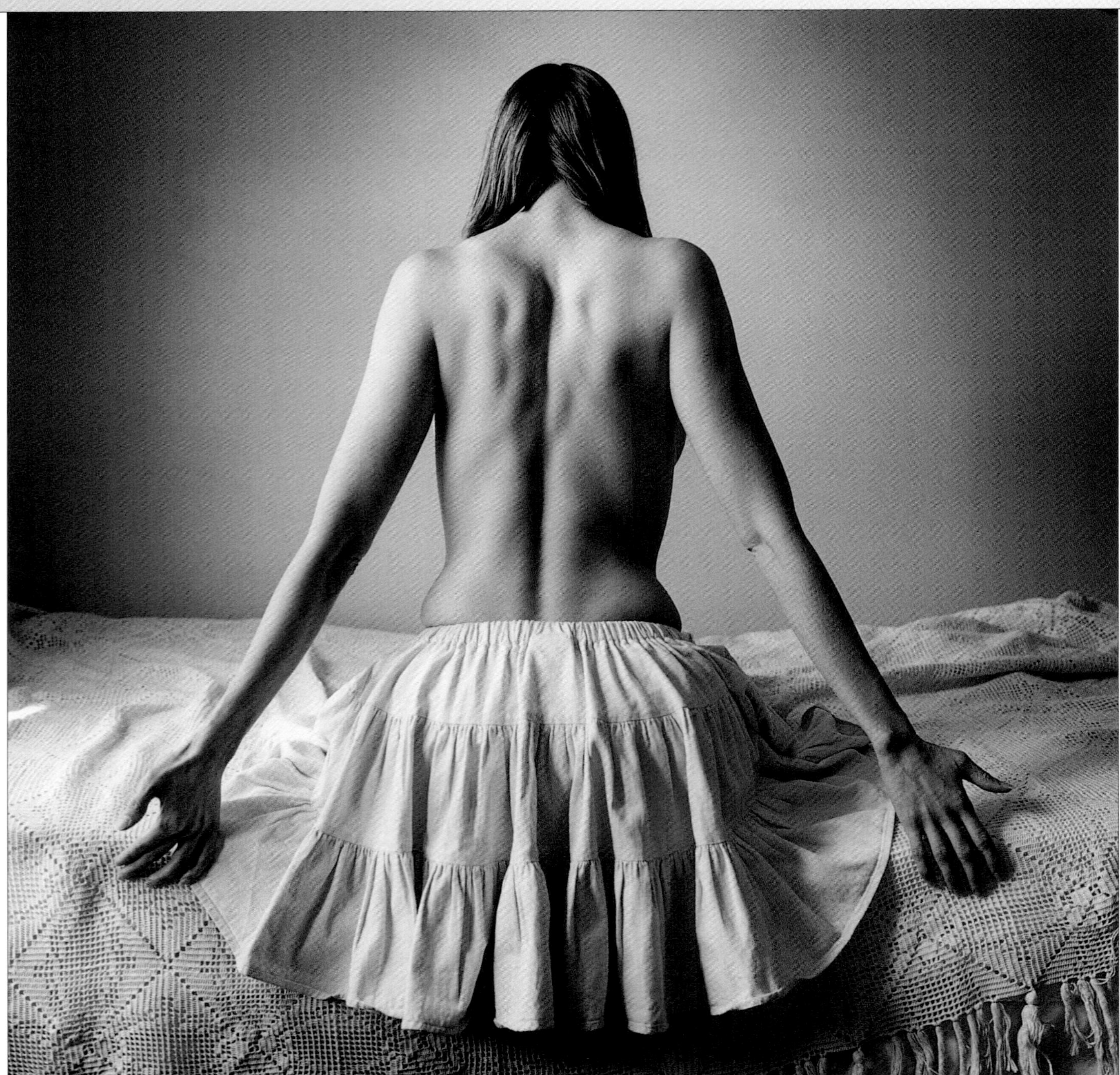

Concept

This is an image from a series centring around
the same white skirt with different models and in
different locations. It was taken at the model's
house, around the middle of the day and light
was coming in from one small window. She had
a very expressive back, being so thin and I liked
the balance of her body and the space around
her with the skirt.

Composition

I was using the 6x6cm square format so I
decided to place the model at the centre of the
frame, with her arms outstretched to create
symmetry. That halo of light around her holds the
viewer's attention on the side-lit back.

I really like the shapes and attitude generated by
the pose. I think it also works because you
cannot see the model's face. It has added extra
intrigue that holds the viewer.

Technique

I stepped in closer and took a manual meter
reading off the centre of her back. This ensured
that I had plenty of detail in that area. Despite
the low-lighting levels, the fast ISO 400 film
meant that I could expose at 1/60sec at f/5.6
and did not need to use a tripod.

I made the print myself and had to manipulate it
a little. The skirt and the top corners of the wall
were given extra exposure to darken them
down, while more exposure was given to the left
side of the blanket to reveal the highlight detail.

Camera tip

The film manufacturer's
quoted speed film is not
necessarily the best one
for you. With your first roll
of a film you have never
used before, expose it at
its normal speed but also
try a set of shots at
different exposures, i.e. in
one-third of a stop
intervals up to +/- two
stops. If you find that you
prefer results at, say, plus
two-thirds, in future rate
the film at that speed. For
example, in this case, an
ISO 100 film should be
rated at ISO 64 and an ISO
400 film at ISO 250. SLR
cameras have a DX auto
film speed setting feature
but this can be overridden
to allow this.

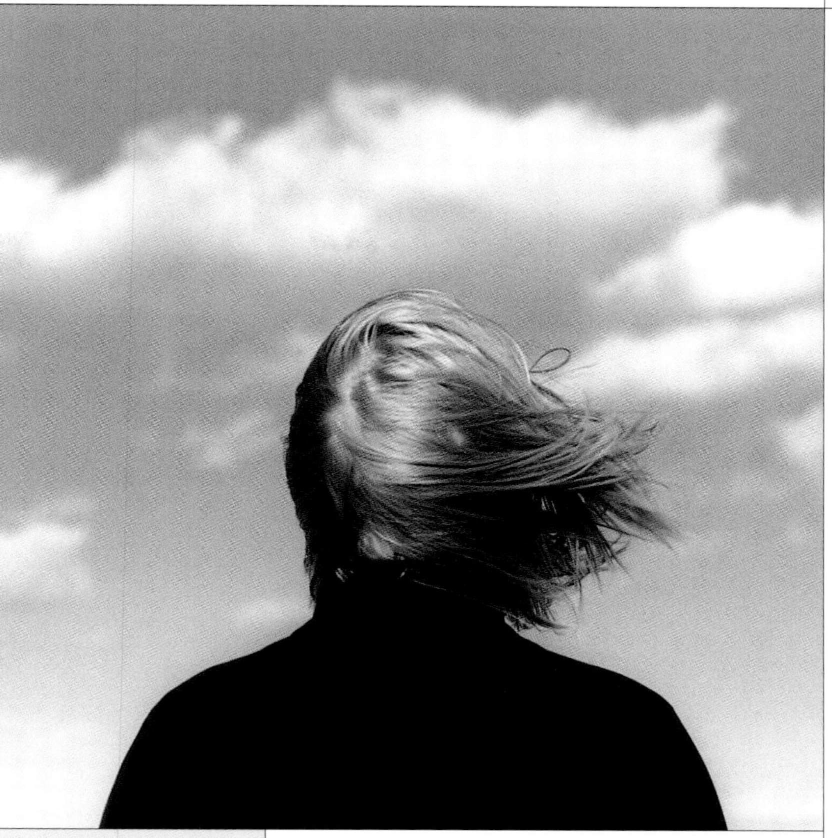

▲ Fact file 2 | Ian McFarlane |
Breeze | I am doing a series
of portraits from behind,
trying to convey how we all
have the ability to know
someone from the simple
shape of their head and
body. You do not always
have to see the facial
features. I used a light-
orange filter to bring out
the clouds and the fast film
meant that I could set
1/500sec to stop any
motion in the model's
windswept hair.

Fact file 1: Cowgirl

Photographer: Gorden Thye

Camera: Canon EOS 3, lens: 28–70mm standard zoom, film: Kodak T-Max 3200 rated at ISO 3200, developer: Kodak T-Max, paper: Ilford Multigrade IV FB, grade 3

film choice ultrafast film

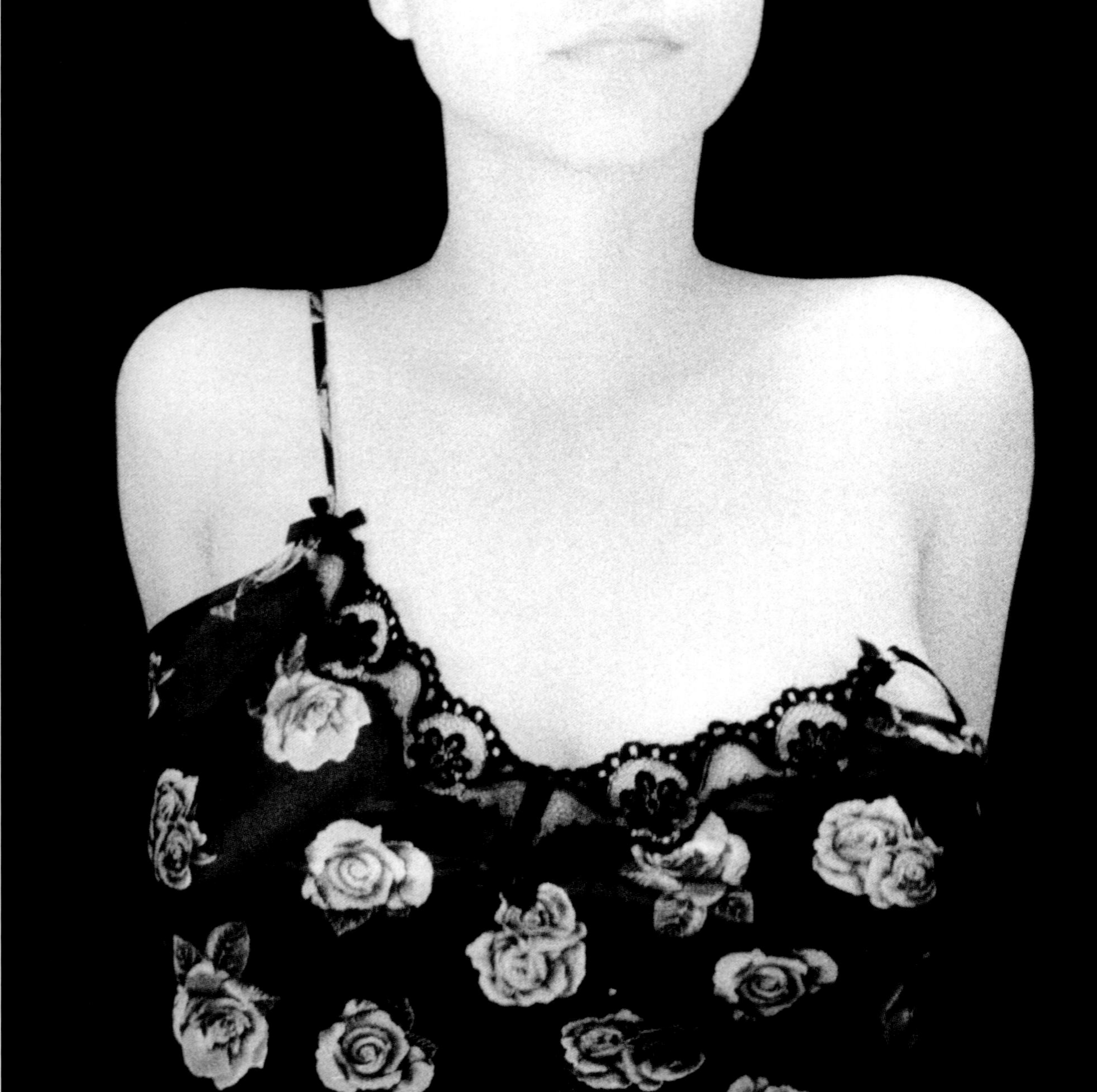

Concept

It was a test session for a model agency and the model got pictures to use in her portfolio. The agency was very satisfied with the pictures and the model used the image on her card. I made this picture in co-operation with Diana Fabbricatore, a very good make-up and hair artist.

Composition

Cropping in tight on the model's face helps to concentrate attention on her eyes even though she is not looking directly at the camera. Asking the model to look at something away from the camera can help when they are not very experienced and gives more natural-looking photographs. Getting in so close for a tight crop has also resulted in a nicely out-of-focus background.

Technique

It was afternoon on a rainy day so there was not too much light around. That is partly the reason why I loaded up with a very high-speed film so I could shoot hand-held without any risk of camera shake. The camera was set to aperture-priority automatic mode, so the technical side of this picture is very straightforward.

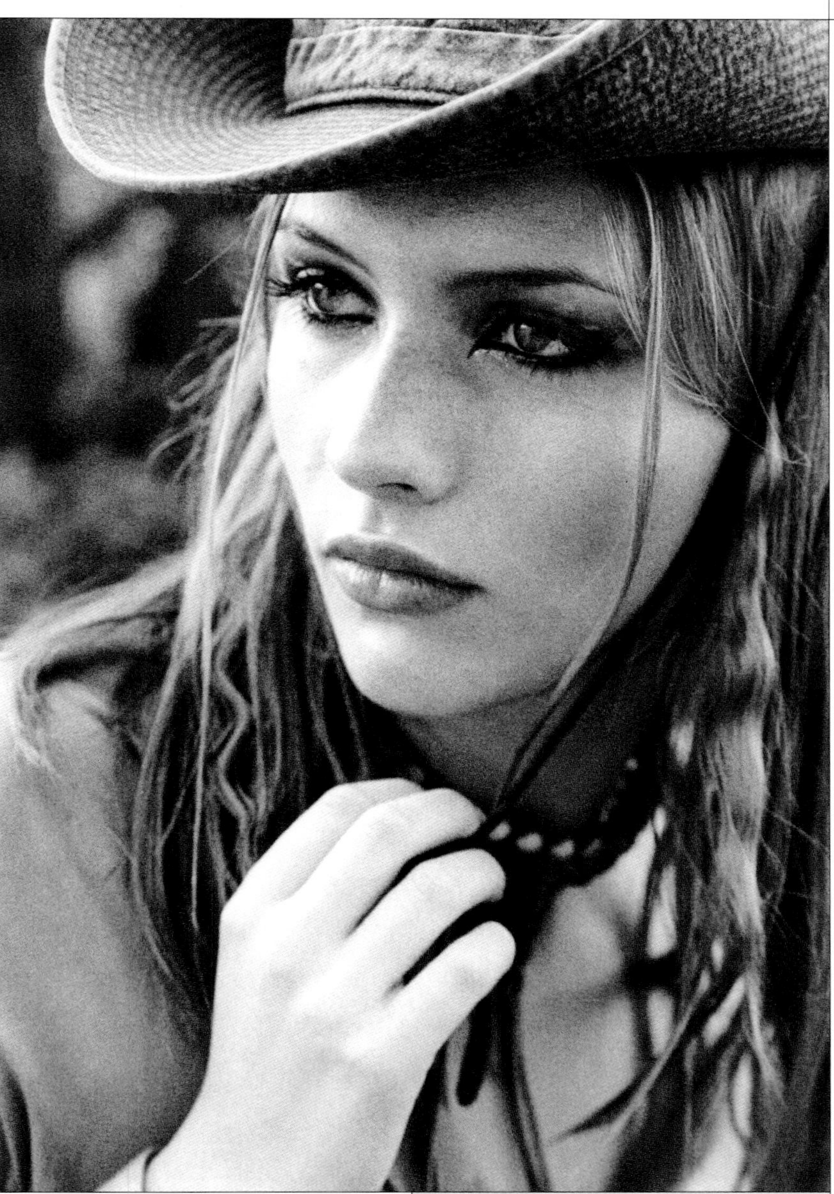

◀ **Fact file 2 | Jacek Pomykalski | A portrait with roses | I wanted a sensual portrait of a girl but without showing the whole face. The light source was a tungsten lamp which was placed above the model. I used Kodak T-Max 3200 film rated at ISO 3200 and this was developed in Ilford Microphen. A red filter was used on the lens to give the skin tones a pallid feel.**

Camera tip

Shooting in dull daylight can result in low contrast prints but you can increase contrast at the processing stage. Add a minute or two to the development time to increase contrast levels. If you do not process your own films ask the processor to extend development time slightly. This will marginally increase grain as well as contrast but levels should remain within acceptable limits. With a high-speed film you are going to get coarse grain anyway so there will be little difference in the results.

<table>
<tr><td>

Fact file 1: Spring

Photographer: Felix Tian

Camera: Contax RX, lens: 21mm f/2.8, film: Kodak High-Speed Infrared rated at ISO 200, exposure; f/16 aperture, filter: 25 red, developer: Kodak D76, paper: Ilford Multigrade, grade 2

</td><td>

Concept

This image was one from a series on spring I photographed using infrared film. I wanted to use this film to show more of spring's atmosphere, making the most of the white leaves against a very dark sky. I knew the characteristics of infrared film would suit the subject well, with the vegetation coming out light-toned and the blue sky recording as almost black. It was around midday and the sun was out so there was plenty of infrared radiation around.

</td></tr>
</table>

film choice shoot infrared

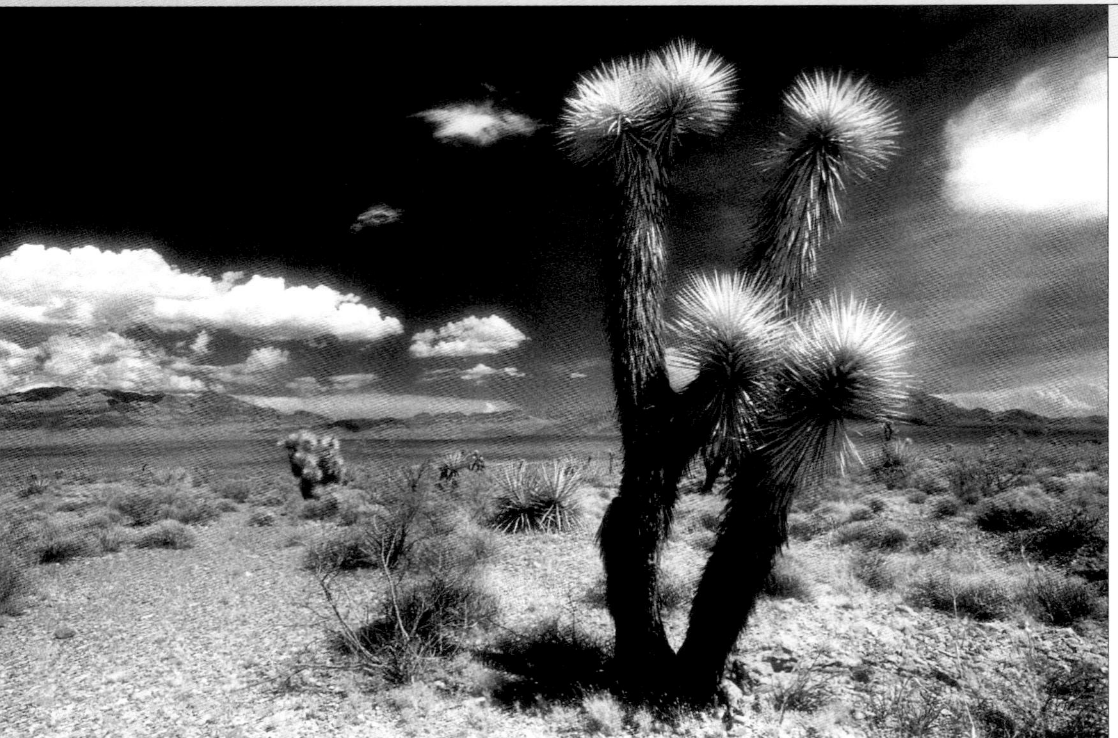

Camera tip

Buy a changing bag. Kodak's High-Speed Infrared film must be loaded and unloaded in total darkness otherwise it will be fogged. Consequently, a small changing bag is needed if you intend using this film on location. A changing bag is a special lightproof bag with armholes to allow access to the inside where the camera and film is contained. Most models are infrared-proof but this should be checked before purchasing.

Getting used to loading and unloading film by feel demands practice so do try this a few times with a dummy film before doing it for real. Double check that the film is correctly loaded before taking pictures.

▲ Fact file 2 | Felix Tian | Sierra | I decided to use black-and-white infrared film to make the Joshua trees look more vivid in the field and match the whiteness of the clouds, thus providing tonal balance in the picture. The strong afternoon sun gave a contrasty lighting which I knew would suit my intentions.

Composition

A wide-angle lens aimed upward produces the effect of converging vertical lines and this can give powerful compositions if used wisely. It is very effective with scenes featuring bold lines like the trunks of the trees in this picture. The film's extreme contrast has also contributed to this picture's composition.

The original is a full-frame 35mm negative but I cropped the image to give a square format which I felt suited the picture more.

Technique

Until you get used to the film, the filtration and how it reacts in different lighting conditions, infrared film can be awkward to expose correctly.

For this shot, I used aperture-priority automatic exposure mode with the spot meter selected. I took several readings from different parts of the frame and used the camera to average them out. The meter reading was taken with the red filter over the lens.

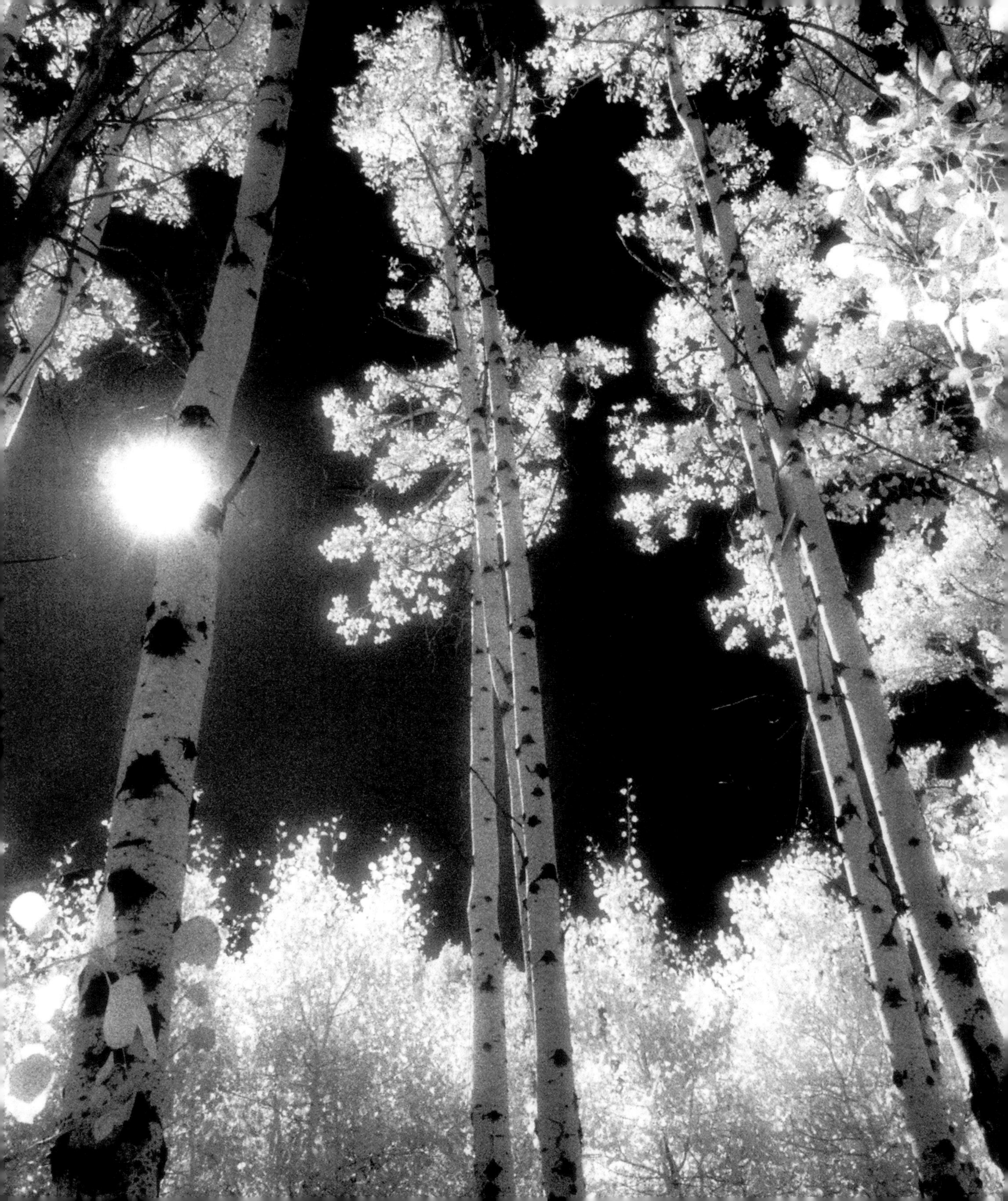

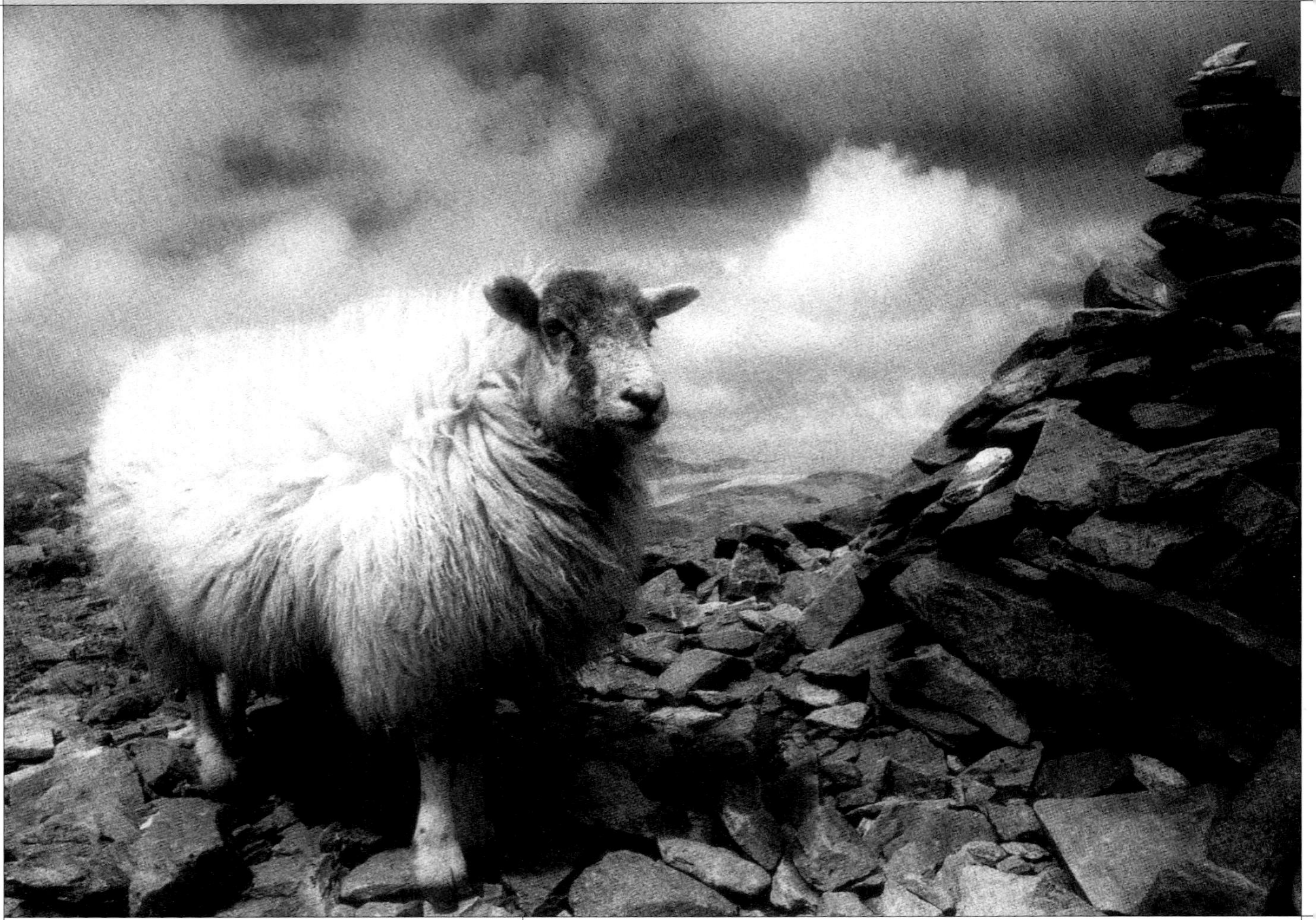

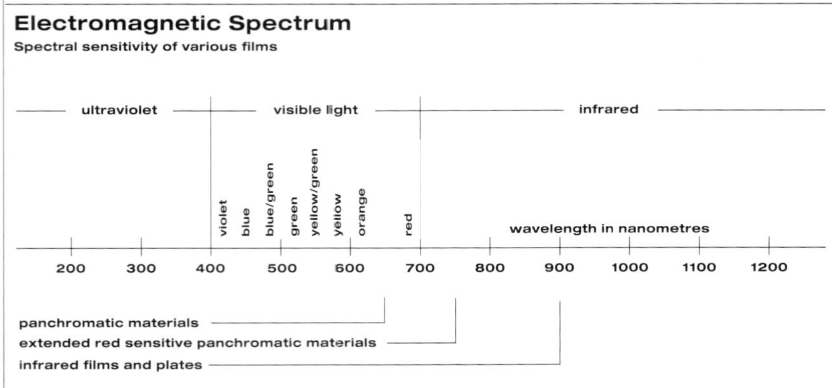

▲ Fact file 3 | William Cheung | Sheep | This was a lucky picture. Until I heard a noise I did not realise there was a sheep behind me. As soon as I spotted it, I brought my Leica M6, fitted with a 28mm wide-angle, red filter and loaded with infrared film, up to my eye and took the picture. It was the only shot I managed before the animal ran away. I like the sheep's coat, which seems to echo the cloud formation behind.

Electromagnetic Spectrum
Spectral sensitivity of various films

Infrared light has a different focal point from that of visible light. Thus, focusing the lens normally, especially with long focal length lenses or wide-lens apertures, results in out of focus pictures. Many lenses have an infrared focusing index marked on the barrel. With this, focus normally, note the distance then readjust the lens barrel so that the noted distance lies opposite the infrared focusing index. Failing this, the best thing is to shoot with wide-angle lenses at small apertures – f/8 and smaller – so that any focusing difference is accounted for by the amount of depth-of-focus at the film plane.

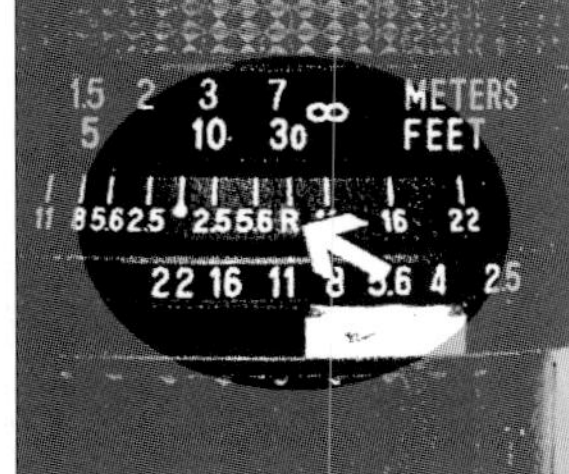

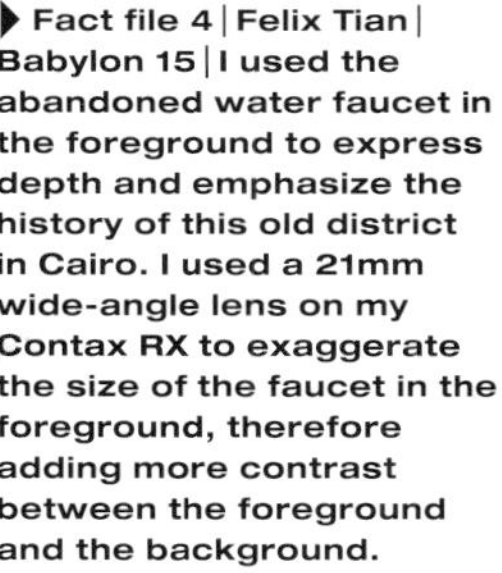

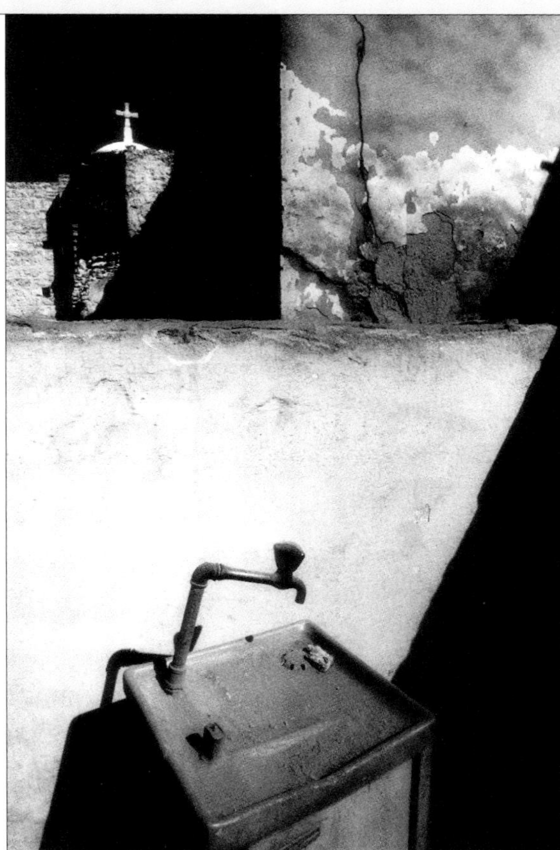

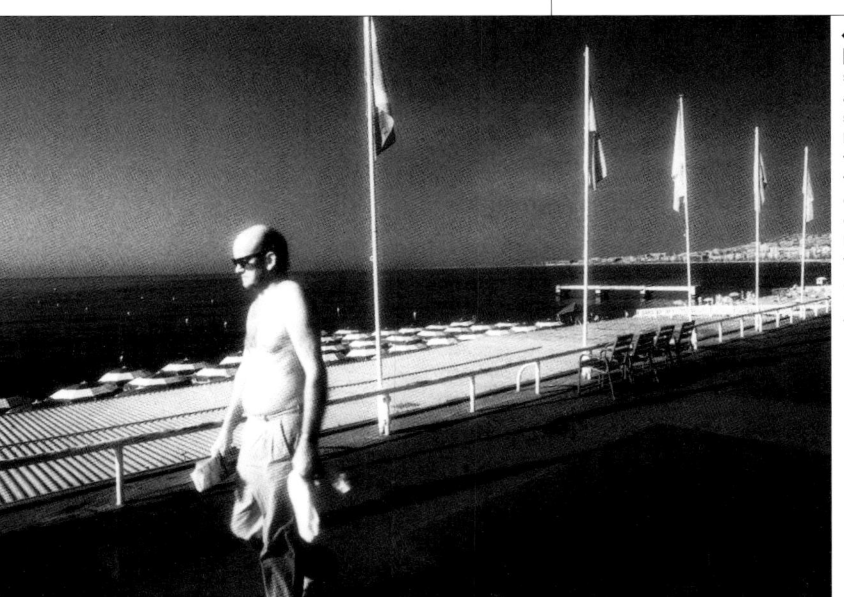

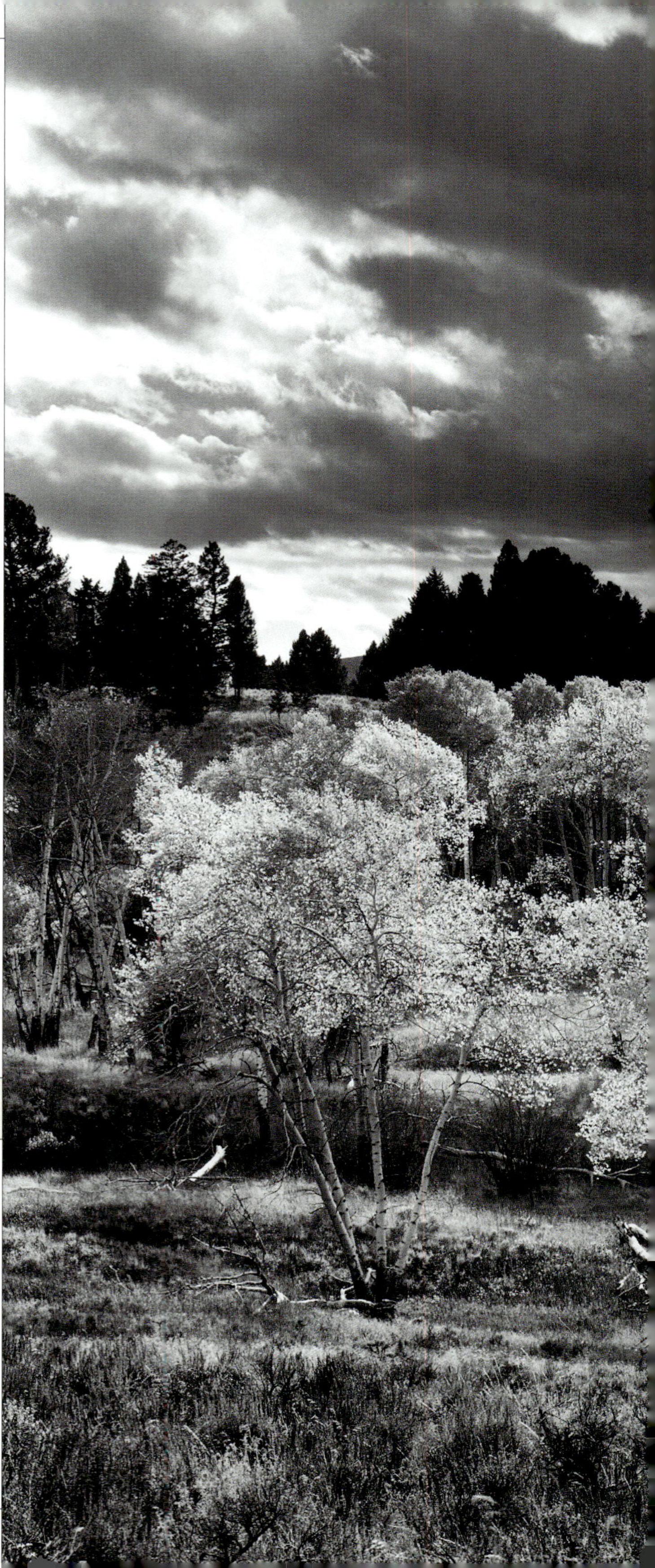

using filters

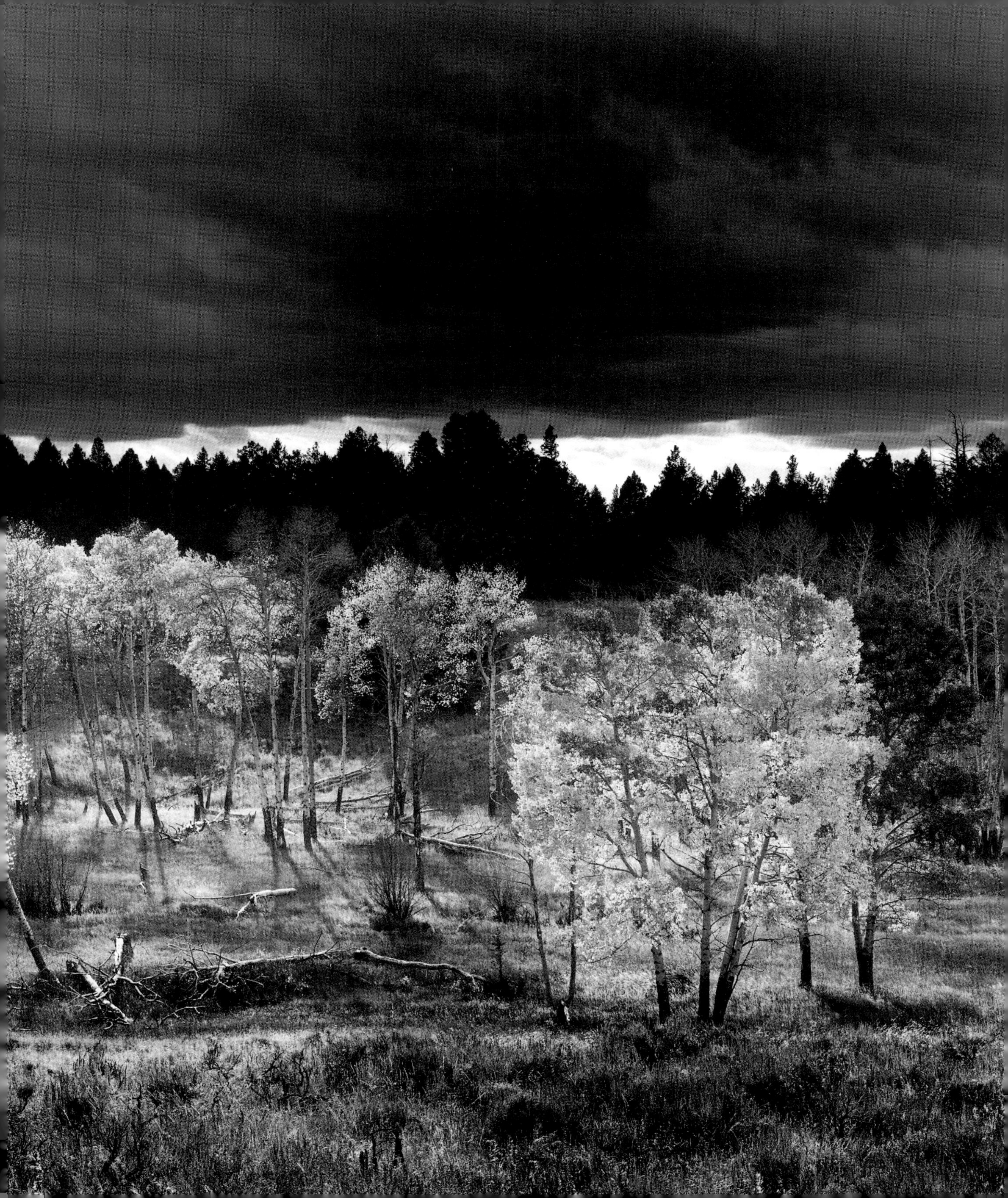

Fact file 1: Deserted farm

Photographer: Nökkvi Elíasson

Camera: Olympus OM-4, lens: 35–70mm, film: Kodak Tri-X, exposure: 1/125 at f/8, filter: red

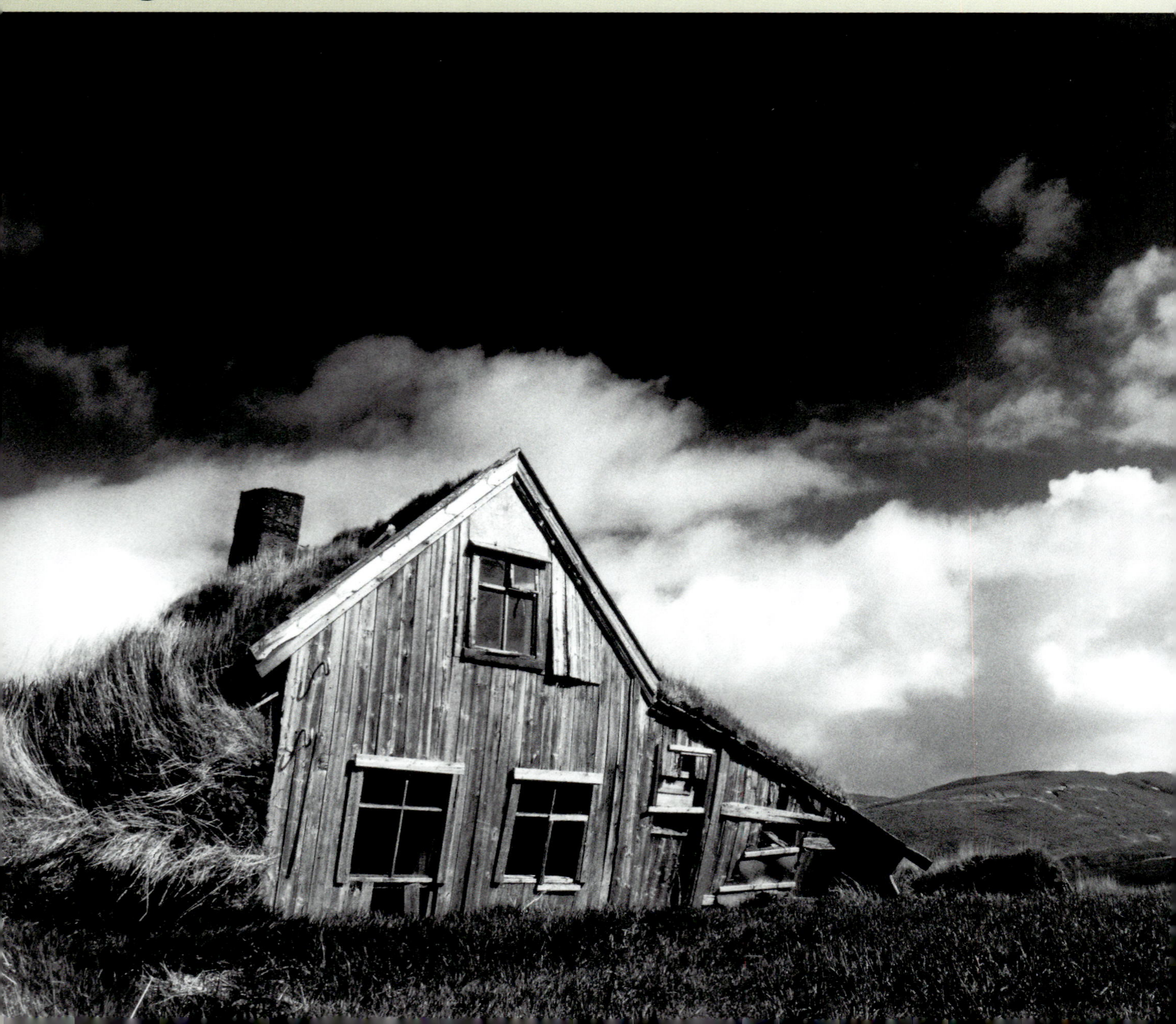

Camera tip

Darken a blue sky without affecting the tonal qualities of the foreground by using a red-graduate filter. An overall red filter can darken the foreground too much and this filter type avoids that problem. Meter for the scene before slipping the red graduate into position and use the camera's depth-of-field preview feature to check it is in the correct place.

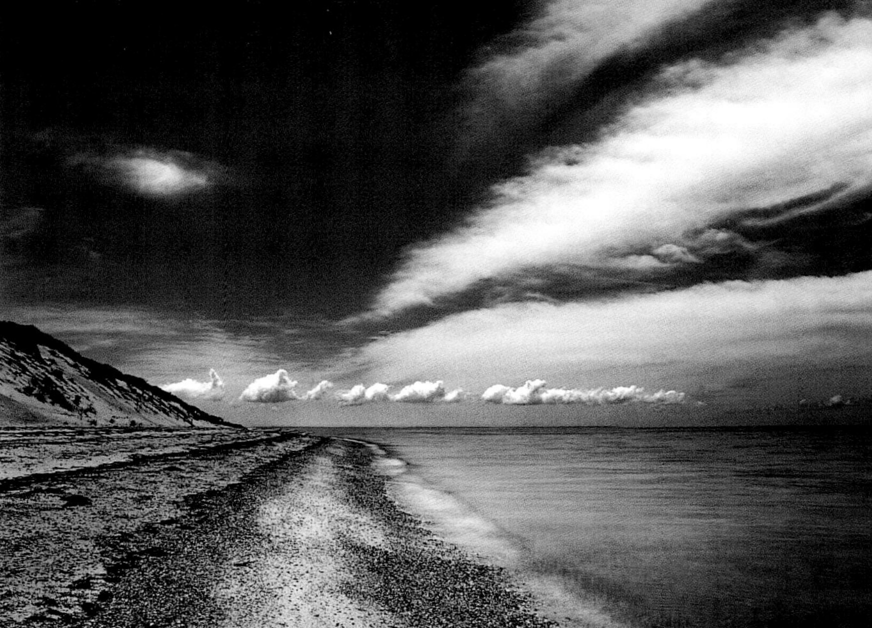

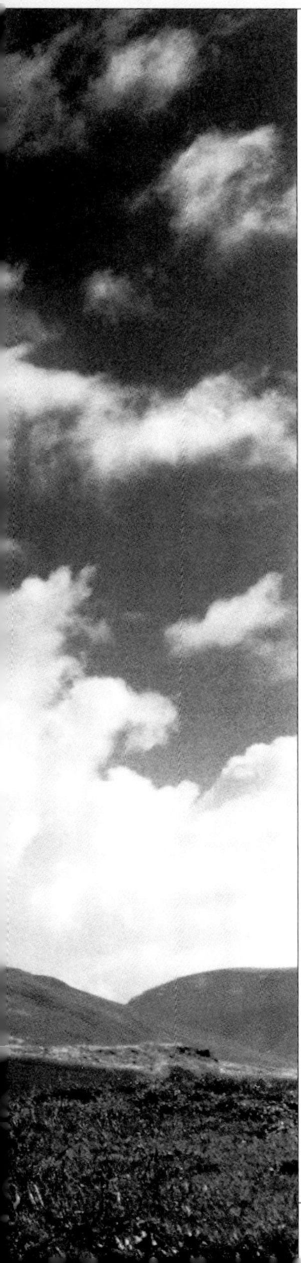

Concept

I am working on a personal project on deserted farmhouses in Iceland. This farmhouse was one of many that I photographed on this day. I wanted the sky to be dark and the clouds to be bold in the background.

Composition

The important thing was that I wanted the farmhouse to stand out strongly against the sky. I moved around for the best composition so that the building was placed against an area of white sky making it prominent in the image. Doing this also placed the farmhouse on one of the rule of thirds, which resulted in an attractive composition.

Technique

It was taken at noon, so the light was not very good, and the sky was almost clear. I knew without any filter the grass would come out light-toned and the sky too bland. Because I wanted the house to stand out I added a red filter. This has darkened the sky and grass but made the clouds and the house stand out.

After fitting the filter, I metered from the green grass in the foreground. This ensured plenty of detail in the shadows.

▲ Fact file 2 | Mario Abbatepaolo | There was little time to think comfortably when I was taking this because every element in the scene was changing quickly. I immediately metered, composed and shot a few frames knowing that I could do the rest in the darkroom. The darkroom work completed the pre-visualised photograph, but it took me many test prints to achieve that goal.

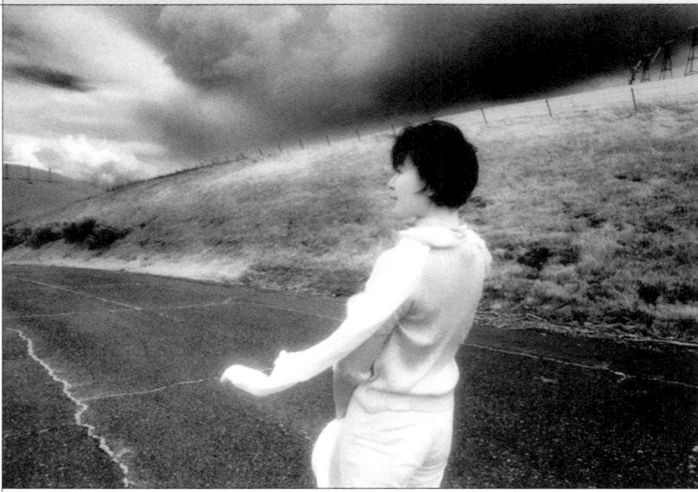

◀ Fact file 4 | Felix Tian | NuNu | The red filter is essential in black-and-white infrared photography. It cuts out the blue and green light wavelengths that the film is sensitive to while transmitting red and infrared wavelengths. A red filter has advantages over using an opaque infrared-transmitting filter only. Namely, you can compose and meter through a red filter so its use is much more convenient.

▼ Fact file 3 | William Cheung | Brighton | Exciting skies are enhanced further with a contrast filter. A red filter gives the most powerful effect and in this picture was used in conjunction with a grey graduate which allowed an exposure to give some foreground detail. In such instances, where more than one filter is used in bright light, flare is a risk so watch for this through the viewfinder.

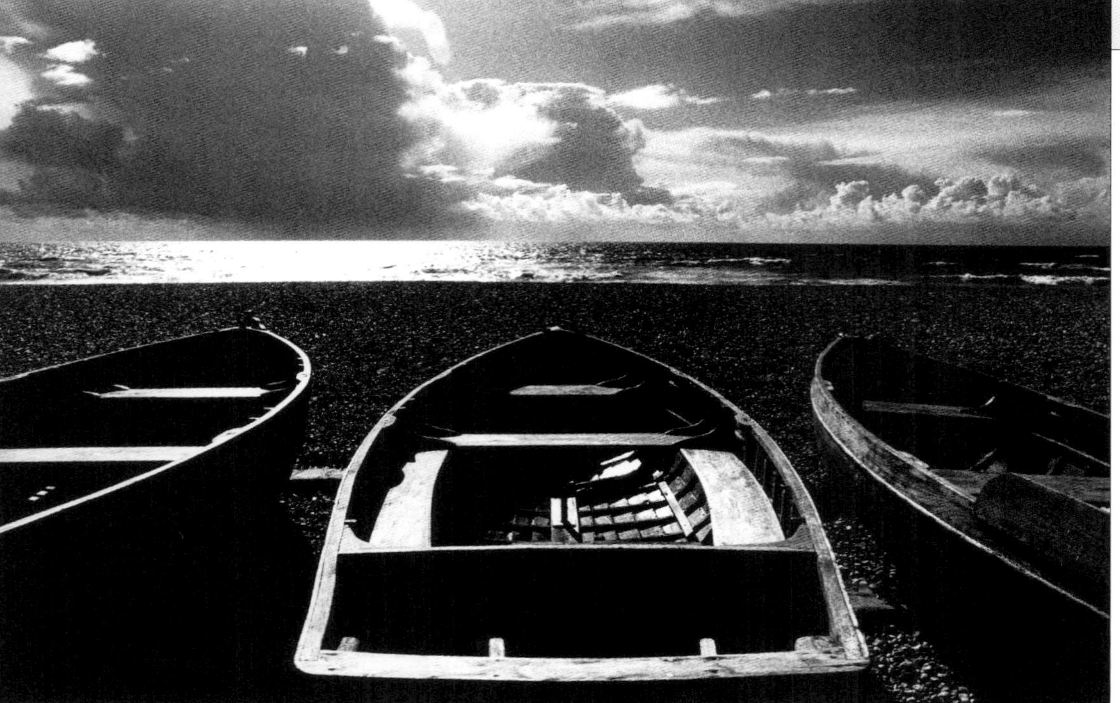

Camera tip

If using a red filter on its own is not graphic enough, try combining it with a polariser for extreme contrast effects. First, make sure you have a polariser filter suitable for your camera. Cameras that are autofocus or have spot/selective metering systems need a circular polariser; others will be fine with a linear polariser. Check the camera's instruction manual for more details.

A typical red filter has a filter of 8x so there is a loss of three stops of light. Polarisers have a filter factor of 4x so will absorb another two stops. Therefore, this pair of filters would absorb five stops of light which, even on a bright day, will mean a tripod is essential if you want sharp pictures.

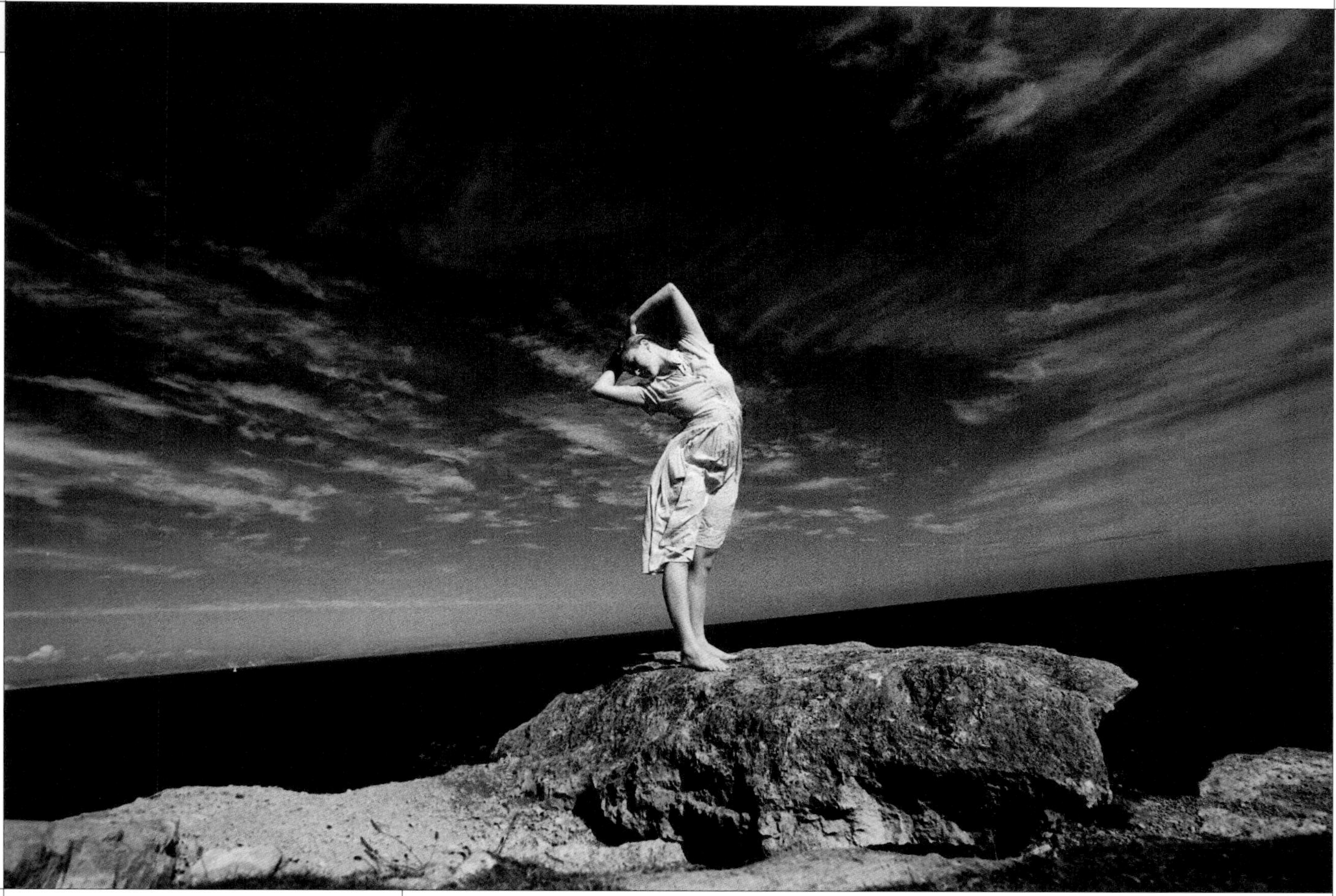

▲ Fact file 5 | Nic Tucker |
Red filters, such as the Wratten 25, can give incredibly dramatic results and, quite possibly, might not be to everyone's taste. I took this picture in the afternoon and the vivid blue sky has gone very dark indeed, helped by some work in the darkroom. The sea in the background has gone even darker but the net result is that the model is dominant in the frame and that is what I wanted to achieve.

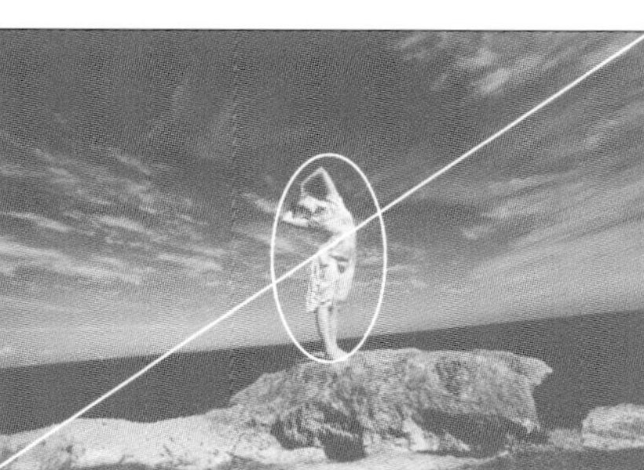

Fact file 1: Aspens, afternoon thunderstorm

Photographer: Bob Hudak

Camera: Wisner 5x4inch, lens: 210mm telephoto, film: Ilford FP4 Plus rated at ISO 64, exposure: 1/15 at f/22, filter: yellow

Concept

I came across this particular stand of trees one afternoon in Wyoming and it just so happened that a storm was starting to form some distance away. I set up the camera and looked at the scene from several different positions. The composition looked best from this spot and then it was just a matter of waiting to see what would happen.

For the next hour, I waited and watched the light. Finally, the light broke through the clouds and lit the aspens from behind. I had time for just one exposure before the light disappeared.

Composition

I took my time with the composition concentrating on the trees because they were my main interest. At the time of setting up the composition, I had no idea that the sky would end up looking like this nor that the trees would be so dramatically backlit.

▶ Fact file 2 | Lynn Radeka | Trailside | I decided to use a deep yellow filter to provide a good separation between the blue sky and the snow on the tree branches. I also hoped the filter would cut through the distant haze. I was happy with the final result, although perhaps next time I would use a slightly gentler filter to darken the sky a little less.

using filters yellow

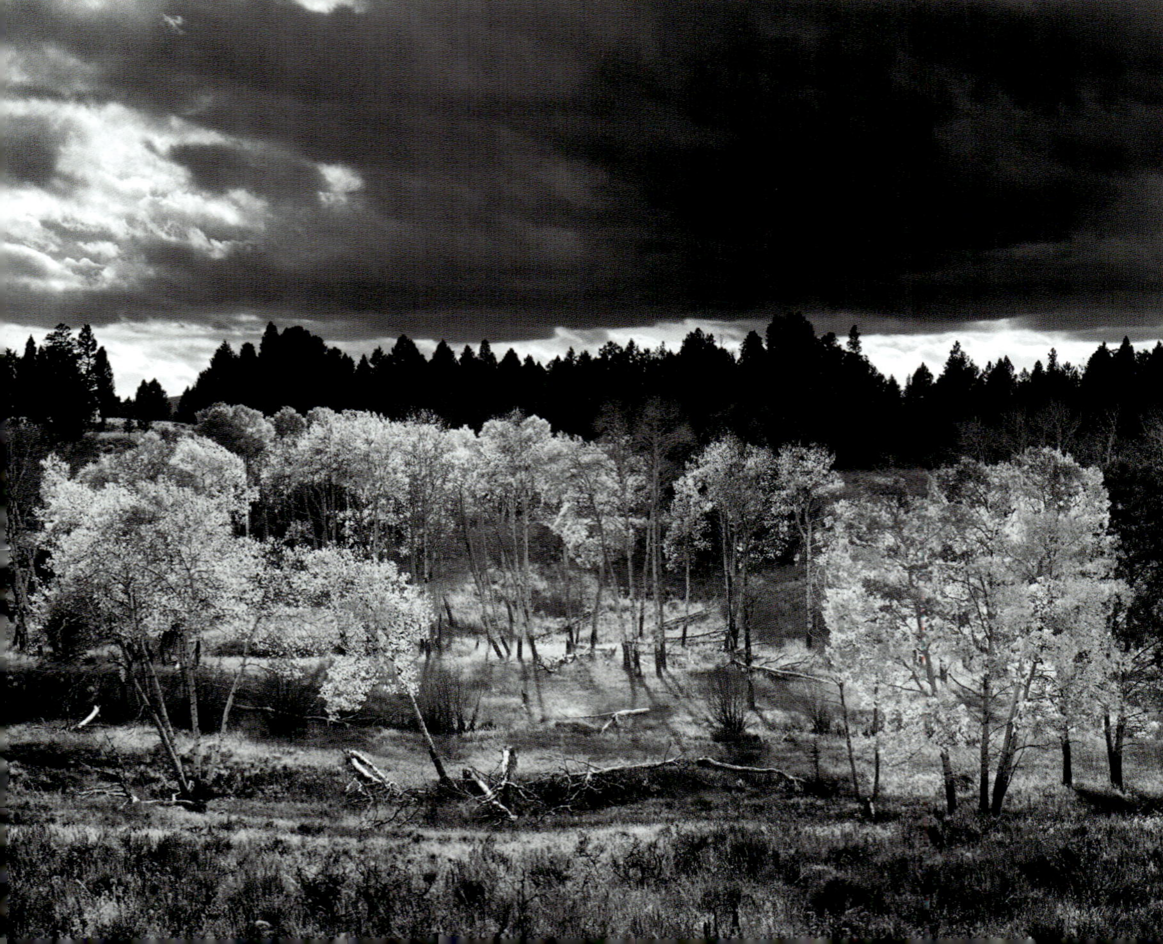

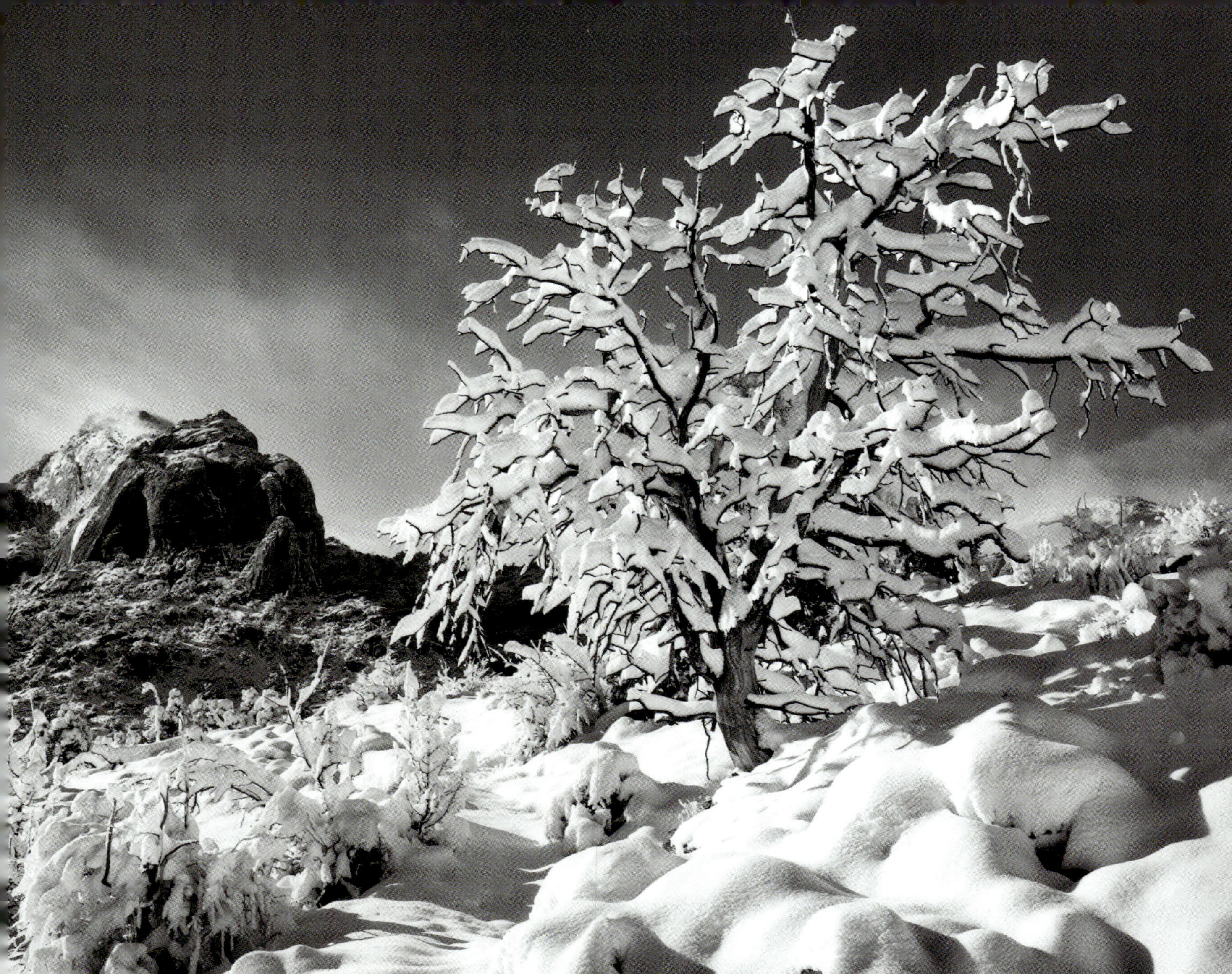

Technique

Apart from waiting for the light to be right, there was nothing difficult about this picture. The sky was dramatic but I knew using a medium-yellow filter would just enhance its impact even more.

Spot meter readings were taken of the darkest area of the trees and of the brightest area of the sky. The film was developed so that I kept the detail in the bright areas of the sky.

In the darkroom, I did some burning-in of the sky just to darken it slightly. The bottom area was also given extra exposure just to give some separation between the grass in the foreground and the closest aspens.

Camera tip

Placing any filter in the light path brings with it a risk to picture quality. Buy the highest quality glass filters possible, preferably multi-coated versions rather than single-coated. Multi-coating is designed to minimise flare and improve light transmission. Resin filters are not coated. Obviously, keeping them in pristine condition and free of dust are important considerations too.

Fact file 1: Fatima's hands

Photographer: Vince Bevan

Camera: Olympus OM2n, lens: 35mm, film: Kodak Tri-X, exposure: 1/250sec at f/11, filter: 4x orange, developer: Agfa Rodinal, paper: Ilford Multigrade FB Warmtone

using filters orange

▼ Fact file 2 | Nana Sousa Dias | Cabo Raso | This photograph is part of a study I am doing about the effect of slow shutter speeds on water. The orange filter brought out detail in the sky but because it absorbs two stops of light it let me set slow shutter speeds to maximise the amount of blur in the water. I did give extra exposure to the sky during printing to darken it down.

Concept

The picture was shot as part of a personal project on the town of Chefchaouen in Morocco, which lies in the Rif mountains in the northern part of the country. These hands appear in Islamic countries in different forms, and are said to warn off evil spirits. Fatima is the daughter of Muhammad, the prophet of Allah.

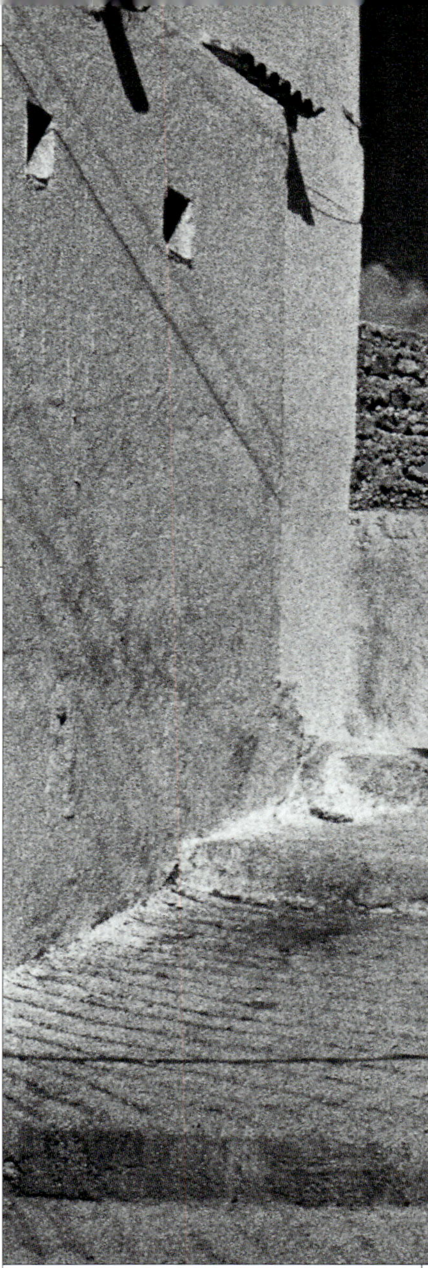

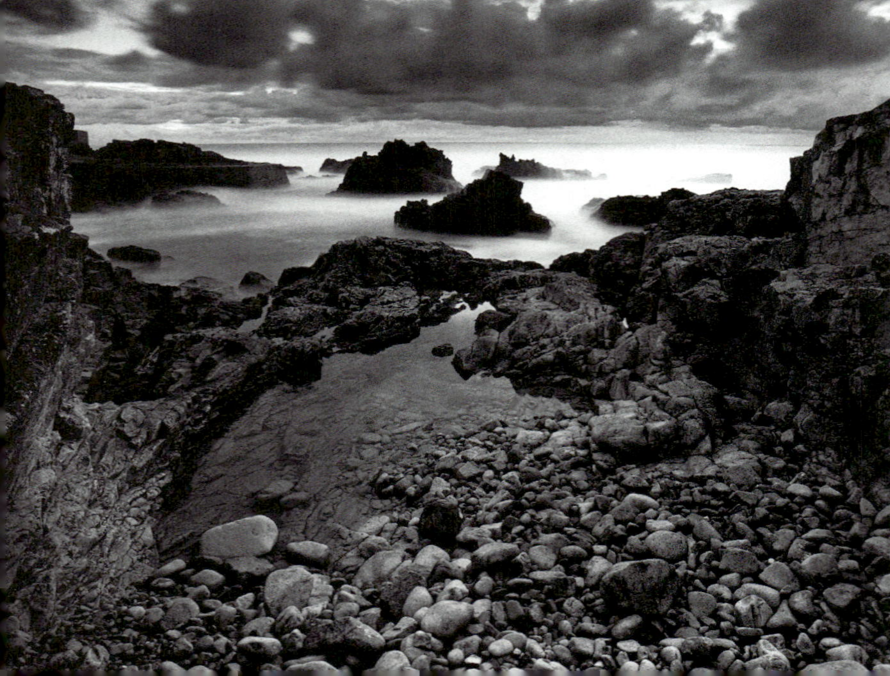

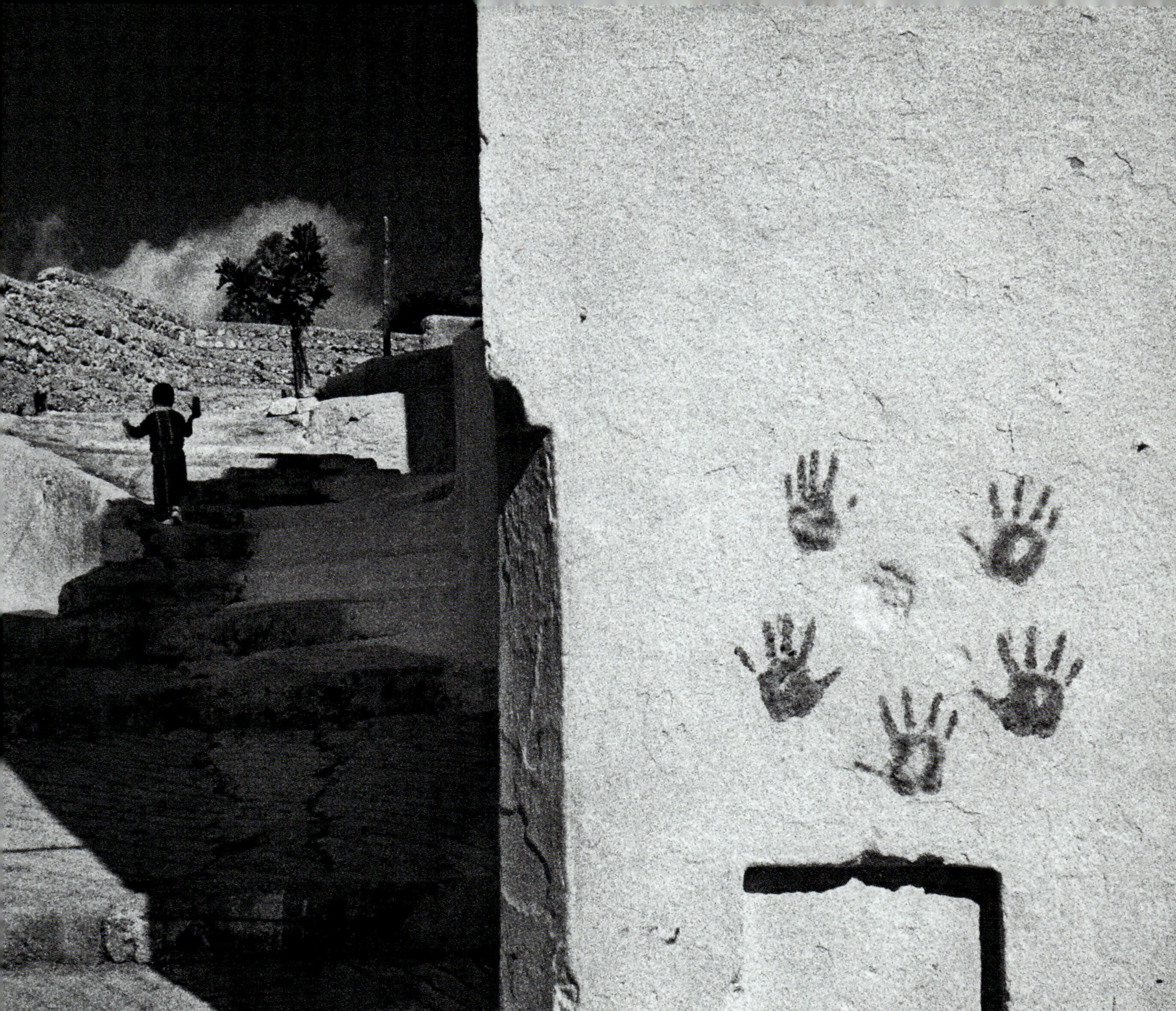

Composition

I had passed this alleyway and photographed it many times but I had never got it quite right. On this occasion a young boy wandered into the shot, singing and carrying a small bag, and proceeded to slowly meander his way up the steps through the shadows. At the top he held out his hands and the bag he was carrying. What also helped was the passing cloud, framing the tree at the top of the alley.

This was one of those times when everything clicked into place.

Technique

I metered manually, taking the reading from the shadows. The contrast was very high so I had to do some extra work during printing. I masked off the shadow area and exposed the rest of the print for part of the total exposure. Then the mask was removed and the shadows exposed to bring out the details. Some of the other shadows such as the boy were then slightly bleached with ferricyanide to bring out a little more detail.

Camera tip

An orange filter can come in very useful for black-and-white portraits if your subject has lots of freckles. The orange filter will make them much less obvious and look more flattering.

Photographer: Mario Abbatepaolo

Camera: Pentax 67 on a tripod, lens: 55mm wide angle, film: Agfa Agfapan 100 rated at ISO 100, filter: polariser, developer: Agfa Rodinal, paper: Ilford Multigrade IV fibre-based, grade 2.5

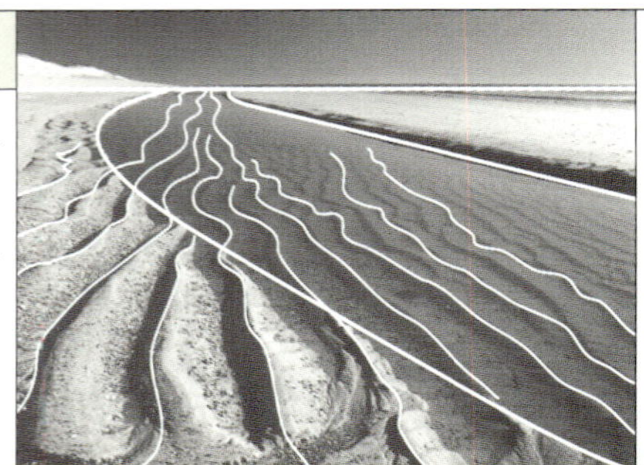

Concept

This is an image from a long-term project I am working on called 'Where the Sea Lands' (see page 76) featuring images that represent the relationship and the interactive dynamics between sea, earth and sky. The low angle and the direction of the lighting helped bring out the strength of the patterns and this has helped the composition.

Composition

The combination of a low camera viewpoint and aiming the wide-angle lens down has helped to make the foreground dominant. The lines of side-lit sand and the gentle shapes draw the viewer into the scene. The lines of sand visible under the shallow water are very important to the composition so the use of a polariser to cut out any reflections was important to the image's success.

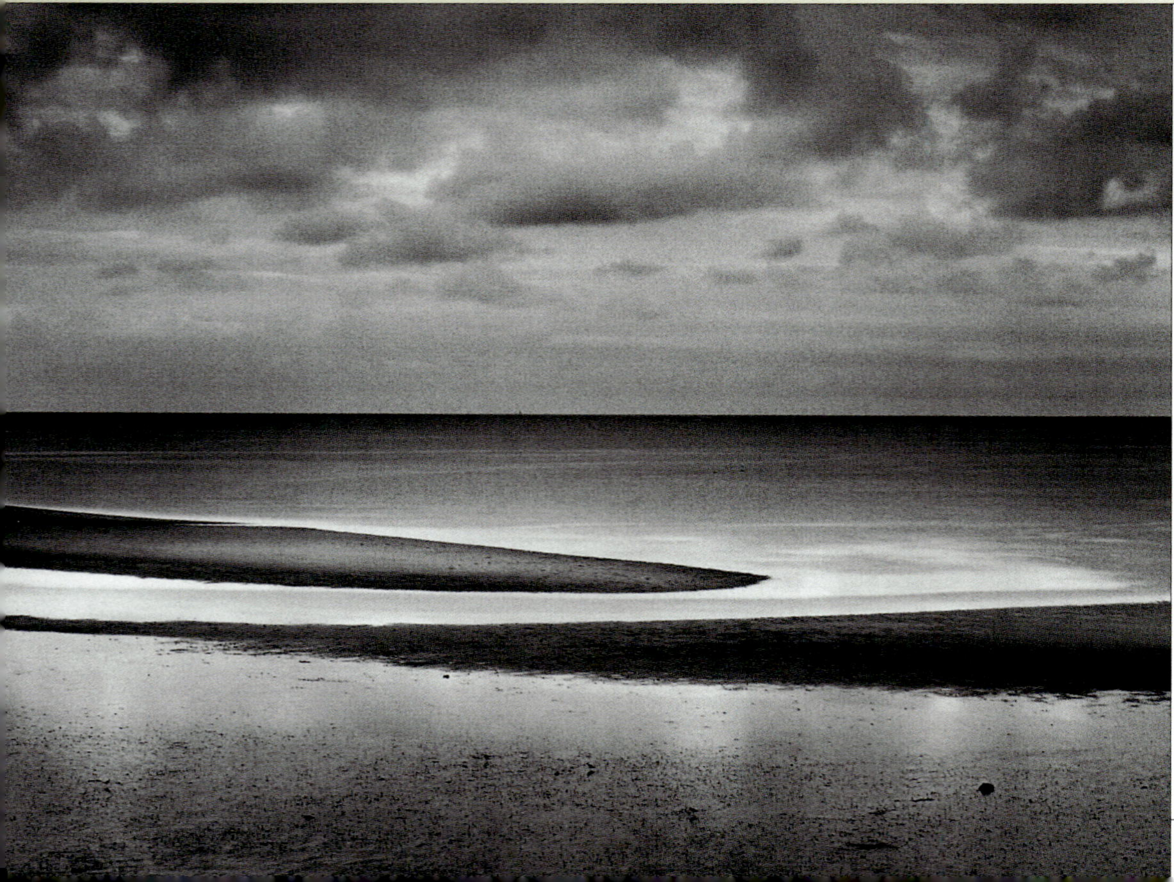

using filters the polariser

◀ Fact file 2 | Mario Abbatepaolo | Provincetown | I like to accentuate the grain in minimalist images like this one. I do this by under-exposing and over-developing the negative and this increases grain as well as contrast. At the time of shooting I knew that in the final print I would like the central part of the sky lighter and the edges darker to preserve the sense of space and dimension.

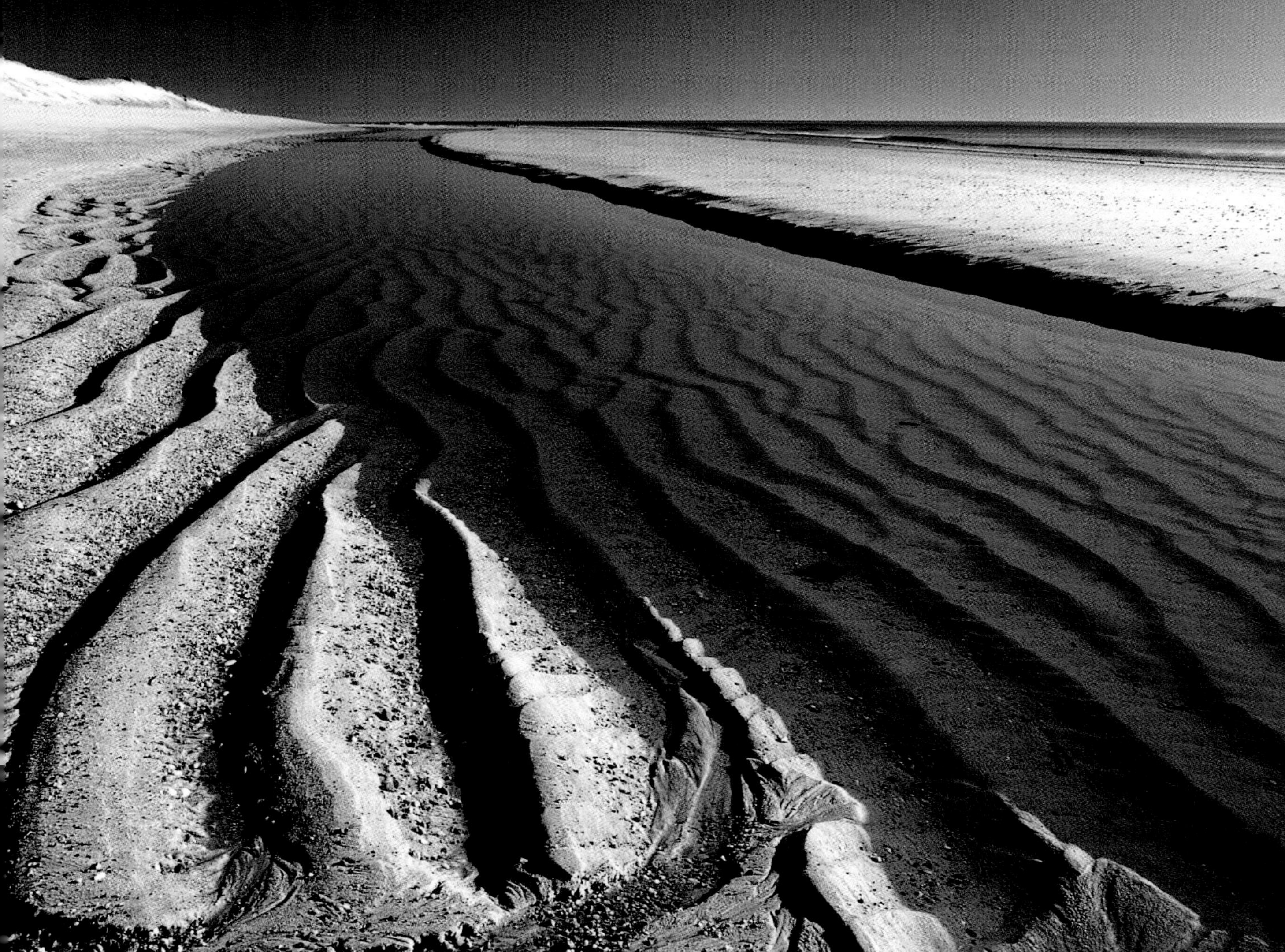

Technique

There is nothing technically complicated about the image. I try to previsualise the final print and this enables me to make immediate choices about the technique, processes and materials that I use. I used a hand-held spot meter to take an exposure reading and then added a polariser filter to enable me to bring out delicate details of the sand through the shallow water. The exposure was increased to take into account the filter. The polariser also helped to darken the early morning sky without affecting any tonal relationships.

Camera tip

While the polariser filter is best known for its usefulness in colour photography, it works for black-and-white photography too. It will eliminate reflections (at the right angle) off water, glass and painted surfaces and darken skies, giving an effect similar to that of a plain yellow filter. However, make sure you use the correct type of polariser to suit your SLR camera. For autofocus and spot metering SLR cameras you will need a circular polariser while a linear model is fine for manual focus models.

better composition

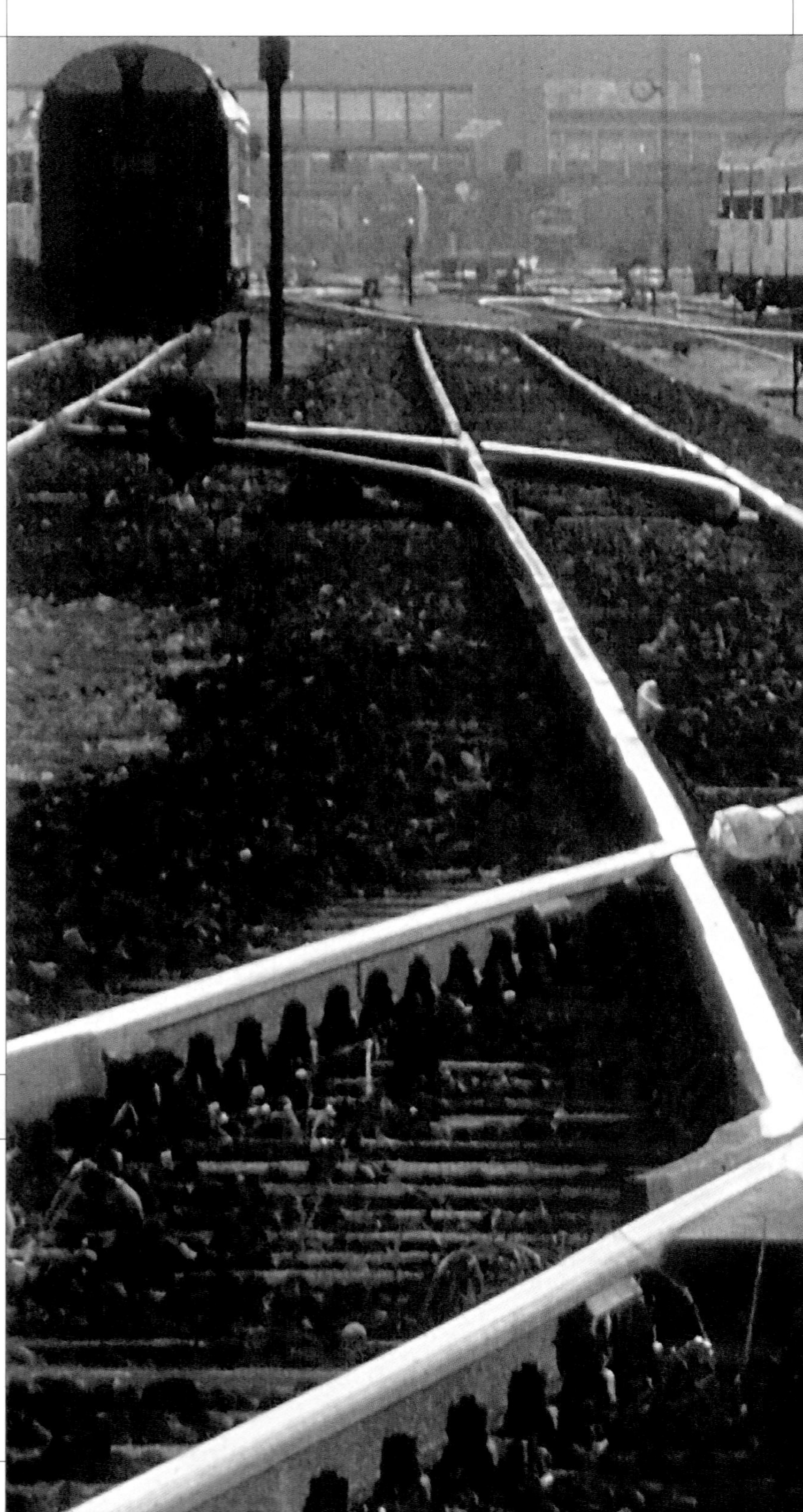

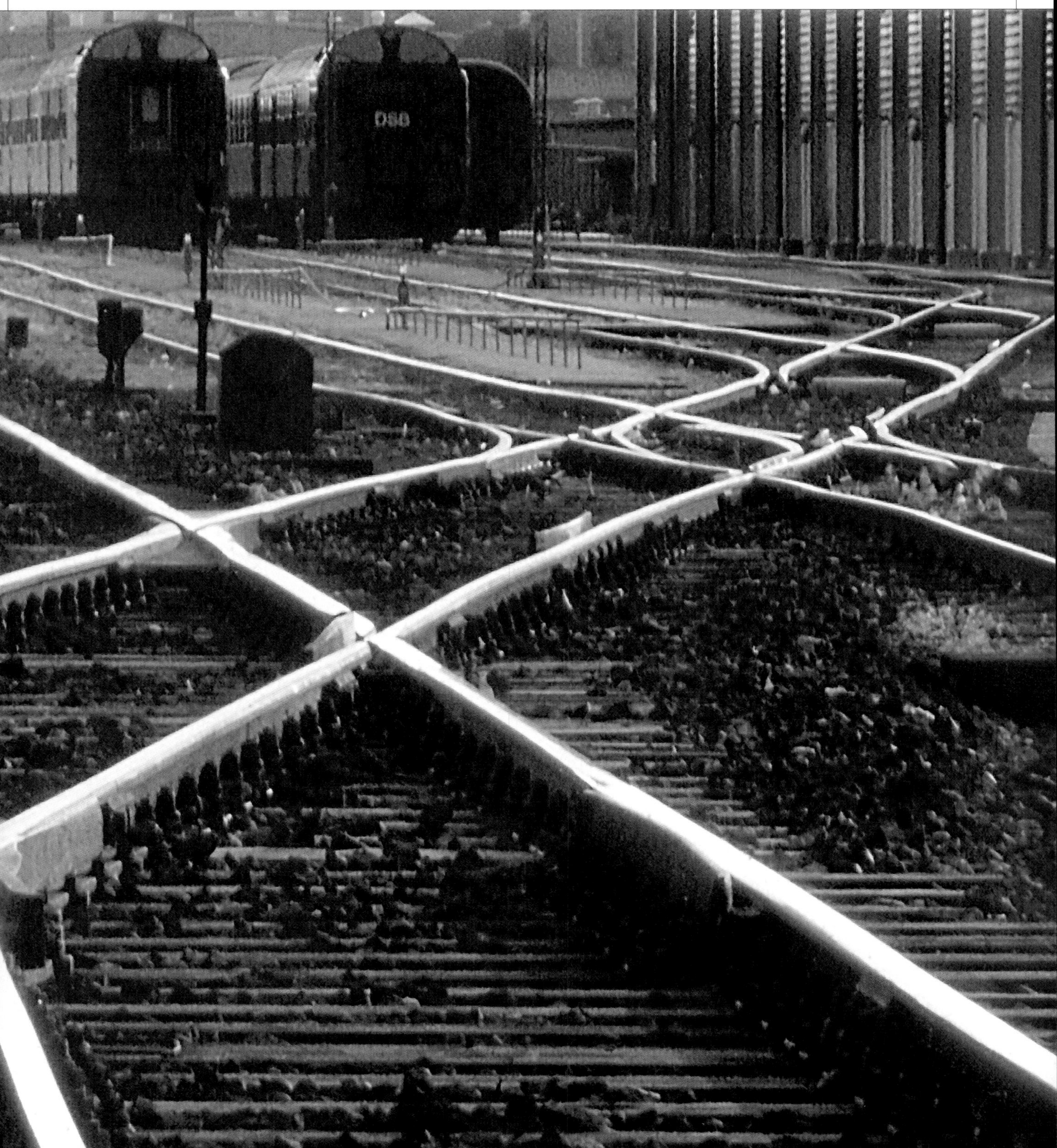

Fact file 1: Road in fog

Photographer: Dan Burkholder

Camera: Nikon F4 on a tripod, lens: 28–85mm, film: Kodak T-Max 400, developer: Kodak T-Max

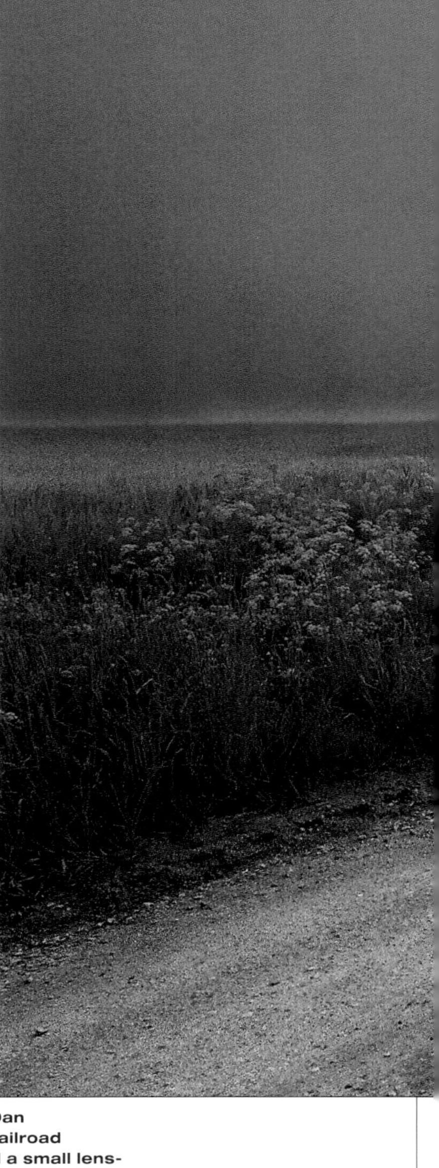

Camera tip

Bracket exposures if you want to ensure that you get a perfectly exposed picture in awkward lighting. How you bracket depends on which exposure mode is used and how you prefer to work. This is how to bracket in an automatic exposure mode. Meter as normal and take your first picture. Next set –1 on the exposure compensation dial and take another shot. Finally, set +1 and take your third shot. This is a three-shot bracket at +/– 1 stop. One of the three should be correct.

Of course, you can shoot more frames and the amount you bracket can be altered. Generally speaking, a bracket in smaller degrees, i.e. 1/2 or 1/3 stops, is best for slide films. A few SLR cameras have automatic bracketing features.

Concept

The rising sun was starting to burn through the early morning fog. At the time, I remember wishing that the sun was rising directly over the road. Now, I am happy with the feeling of the image. I just wanted a handsome photograph that captured the gentle drama of the early morning conditions.

Technique

The key thing was for good depth-of-field to record the entire scene sharply, so aperture selection was important. I had the camera on the tripod to give me freedom in this respect. Mist can cause underexposure so it was important to aim the meter down so that it was not affected by the sun.

better composition dynamic diagonals

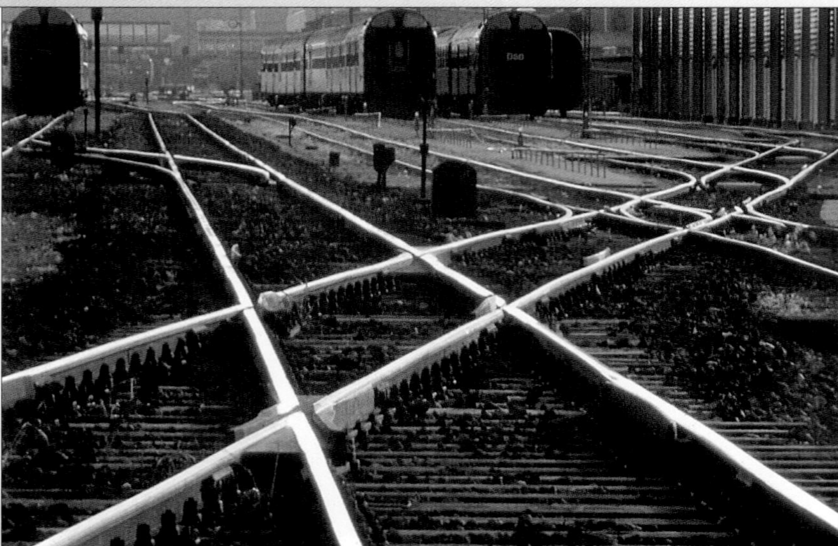

◀ Fact file 2 | Dan Burkholder | Railroad station | I used a small lens-aperture to provide extensive depth-of-field so all the rails were sharp. I positioned the camera to cross at a compositionally pleasing angle and the sky light reflected off the rails did the rest. It was early evening and the soft light was just right for the mood of the picture I wanted.

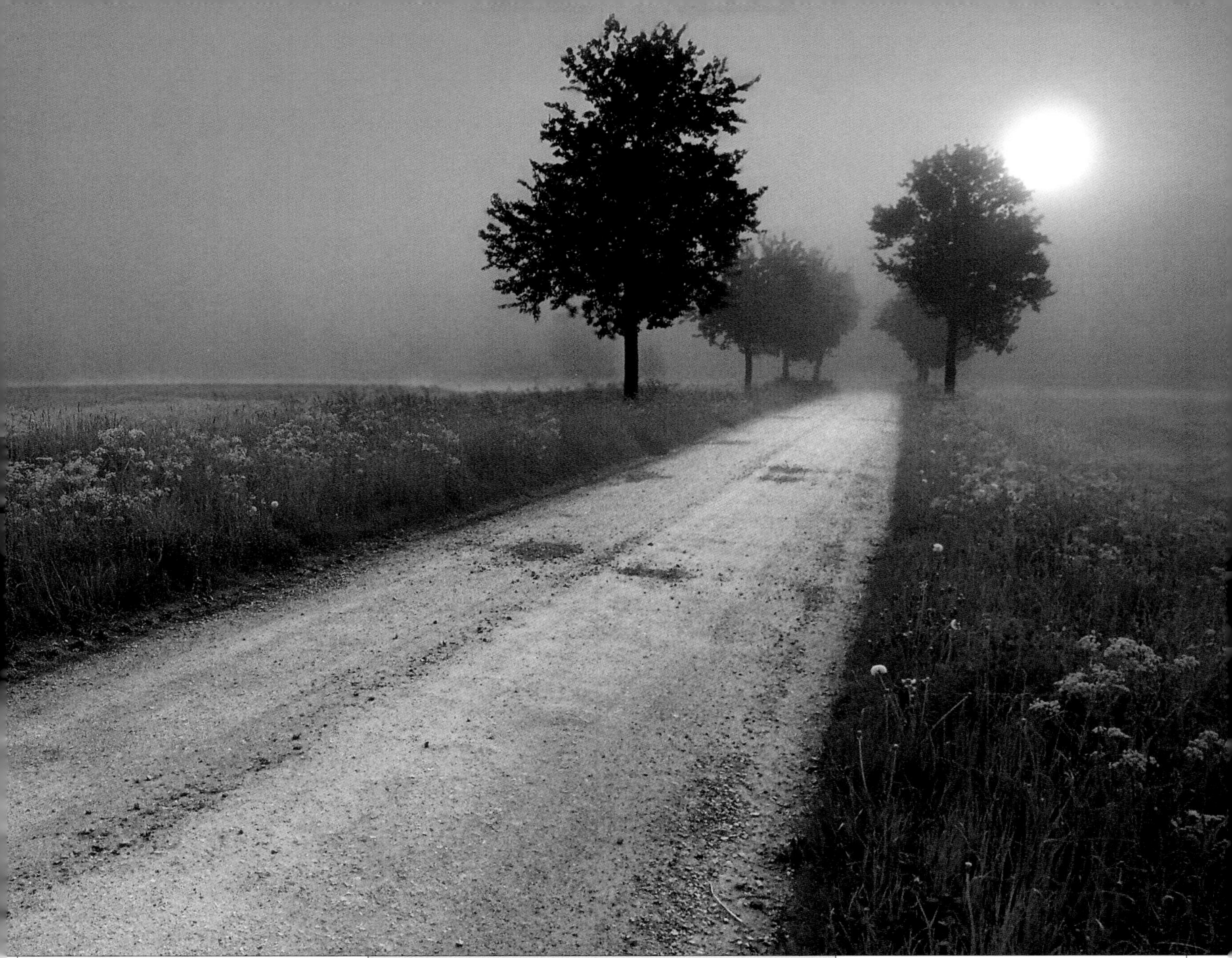

Composition

The diagonal of the road is the strongest and most immediate compositional element. It takes the viewer to the background where the atmospheric perspective of the fog and sunlight complete the image.

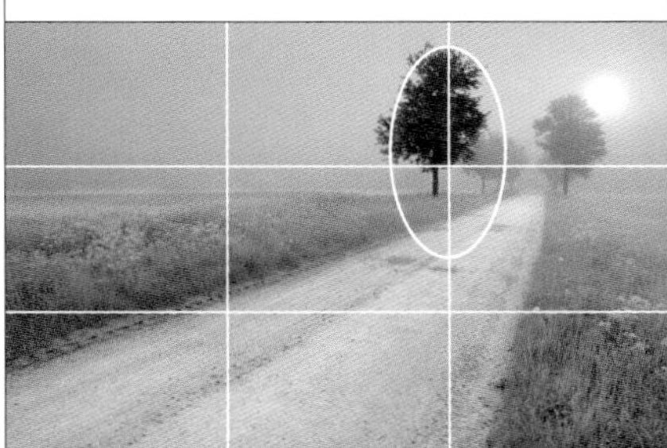

<table>
<tr><td colspan="2">Fact file 1: Polder landscape</td></tr>
<tr><td colspan="2">Photographer: John Braeckmans</td></tr>
<tr><td colspan="2">Camera: Nikon F100 on a tripod, lens: Nikkor 24mm f/2.8, film: Kodak T-Max 100 rated at ISO 100, exposure: 1/250sec at f/11, developer: Kodak X-tol</td></tr>
</table>

better composition use lines

Concept

It was a cloudy day but I was relying on the strong lines to create an eye-catching composition. I believe any picture with bold lines will always catch someone's attention. A wide-angle lens was used and this made the most of the lines, which seem to pull the viewer into the scene.

Technique

Because the scene was evenly lit, taking the exposure reading was straightforward. I used the camera's multiple segment lightmeter and aimed down slightly to ensure there was plenty of shadow detail in the negative.

I had the camera on a tripod so I closed the wide-angle lens to its smallest aperture to guarantee complete sharpness, from the closest part of the scene all the way to the far distance.

Composition

The bold lines really do pull the viewer into the picture but of course you need to hold their interest. I did this with those farmhouses on the horizon that act as a simple but effective focal point.

With such a bold foreground it always pays to explore the possible variations and the effect they have on the final result. I could have had the lines coming in at different angles but I went for a straight on viewpoint. Camera height also has an effect too and I could have opted for a lower viewpoint which would have made the lines even stronger but at the expense of the distant detail.

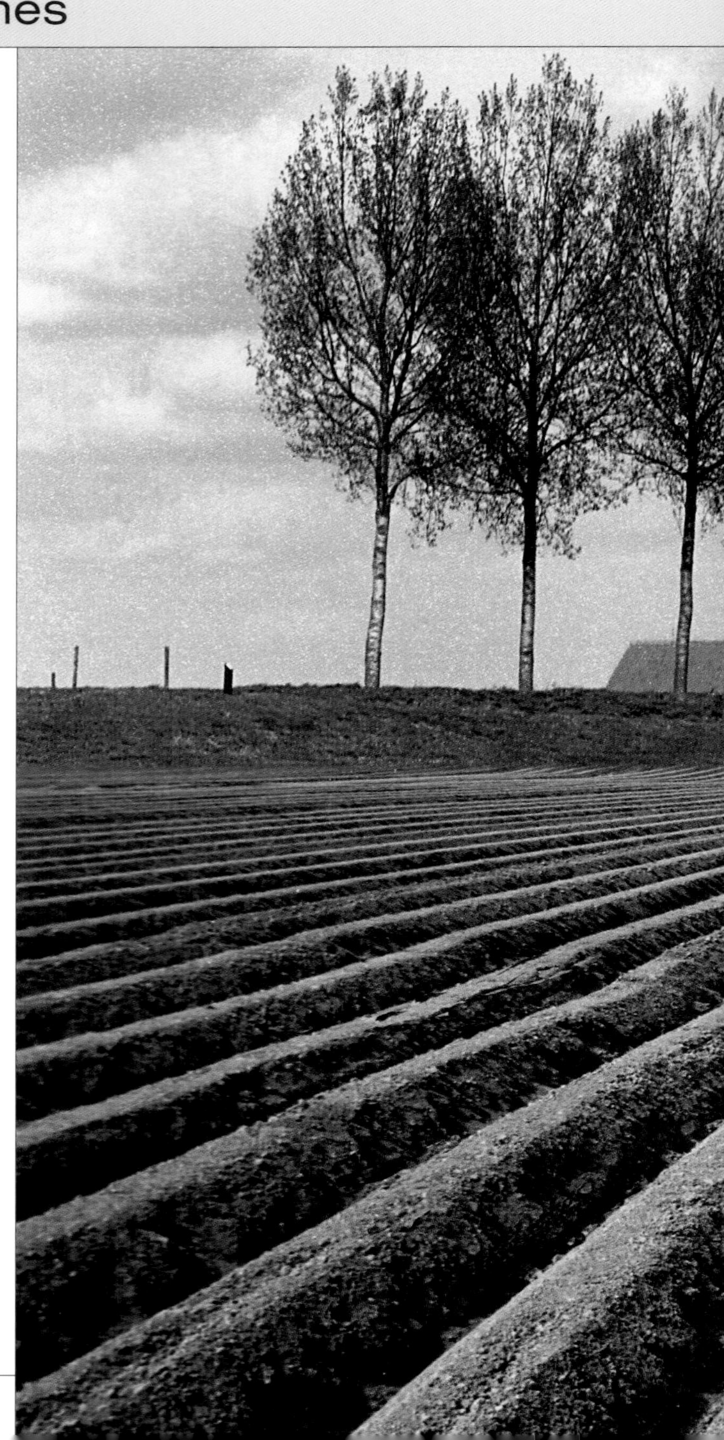

Camera tip

Most cameras have a depth-of-field preview feature. Operating it closes the lens' aperture to the set value so that the viewfinder image darkens and lets you see how much of the scene is in focus and how the background and foreground interact. Allow a few seconds for your eye to get used to the darker image before making a judgement especially when the lens is at a small aperture.

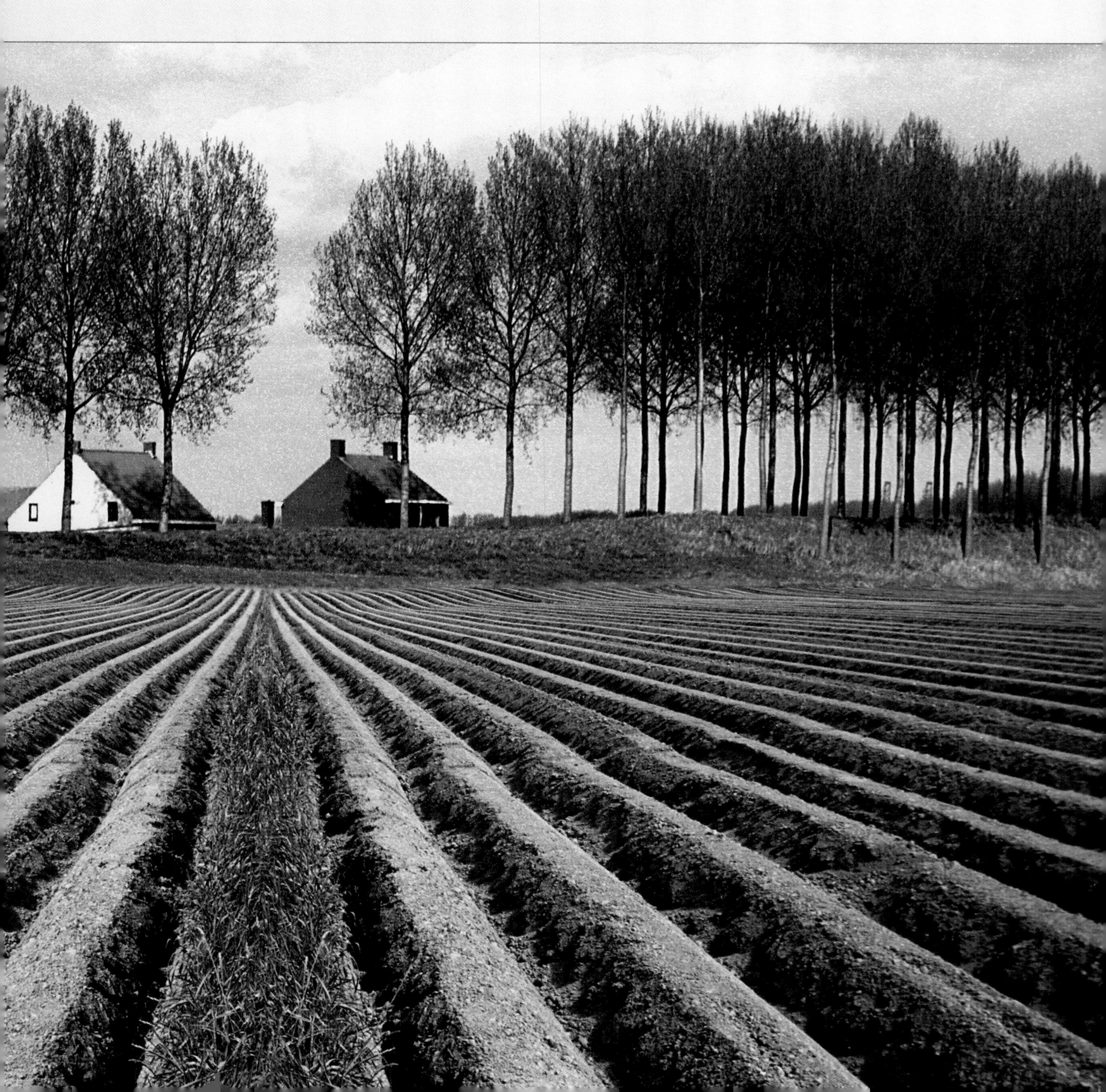

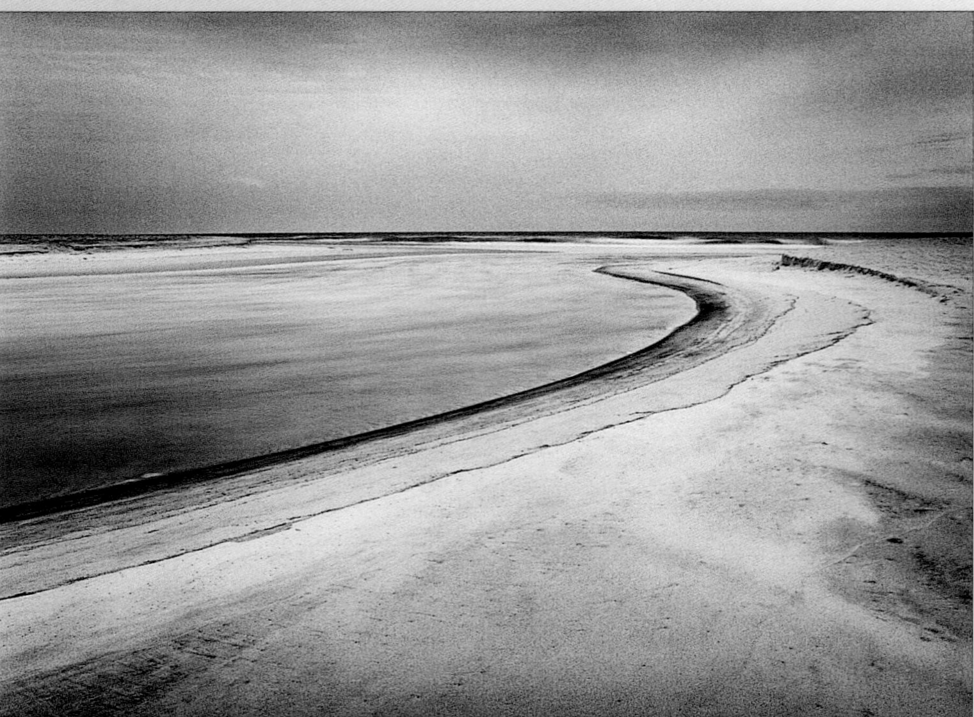

◀ Fact file 2 | Mario Abbatepaolo | Flying Point Beach | I wanted this picture to show the quietness and silence of the place. It is part of a project I am working on called 'Where the Sea Lands' (see pages 68–69). The images present the relationship and the interactive dynamics between the earth, sea and sky. The sweeping curve is wonderful and it leads the viewer straight to the only other bold line in the composition; the horizon.

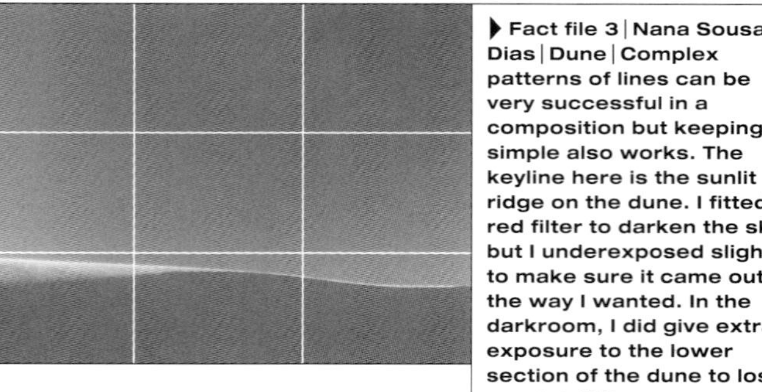

▶ Fact file 3 | Nana Sousa Dias | Dune | Complex patterns of lines can be very successful in a composition but keeping it simple also works. The keyline here is the sunlit ridge on the dune. I fitted a red filter to darken the sky but I underexposed slightly to make sure it came out the way I wanted. In the darkroom, I did give extra exposure to the lower section of the dune to lose any detail there.

Experiment with fast film for obvious grain effects. The latest ISO 1600 and 3200 films have relatively fine grain considering their speed but the grain is still very obvious and suits images with bold lines. With the right subjects, the grain effect gives prints a lovely texture. Grain works well for moody landscapes and whenever you want a harsh, gritty photo-journalistic feel to your images. Slight overdevelopment will enhance the grain even further.

▶ Fact file 4 │ Aguinaldo Calheiros Vera-Cruz │ Ambiences │ It was mid-morning on a foggy day and it was completely quiet. The sides of the path gave two bold lines in a very dull scene and these lead the viewer to the focal point; the figure right at the centre of the composition. The trees just visible through the mist add an extra dimension. I am rarely satisfied but I do like this picture very much.

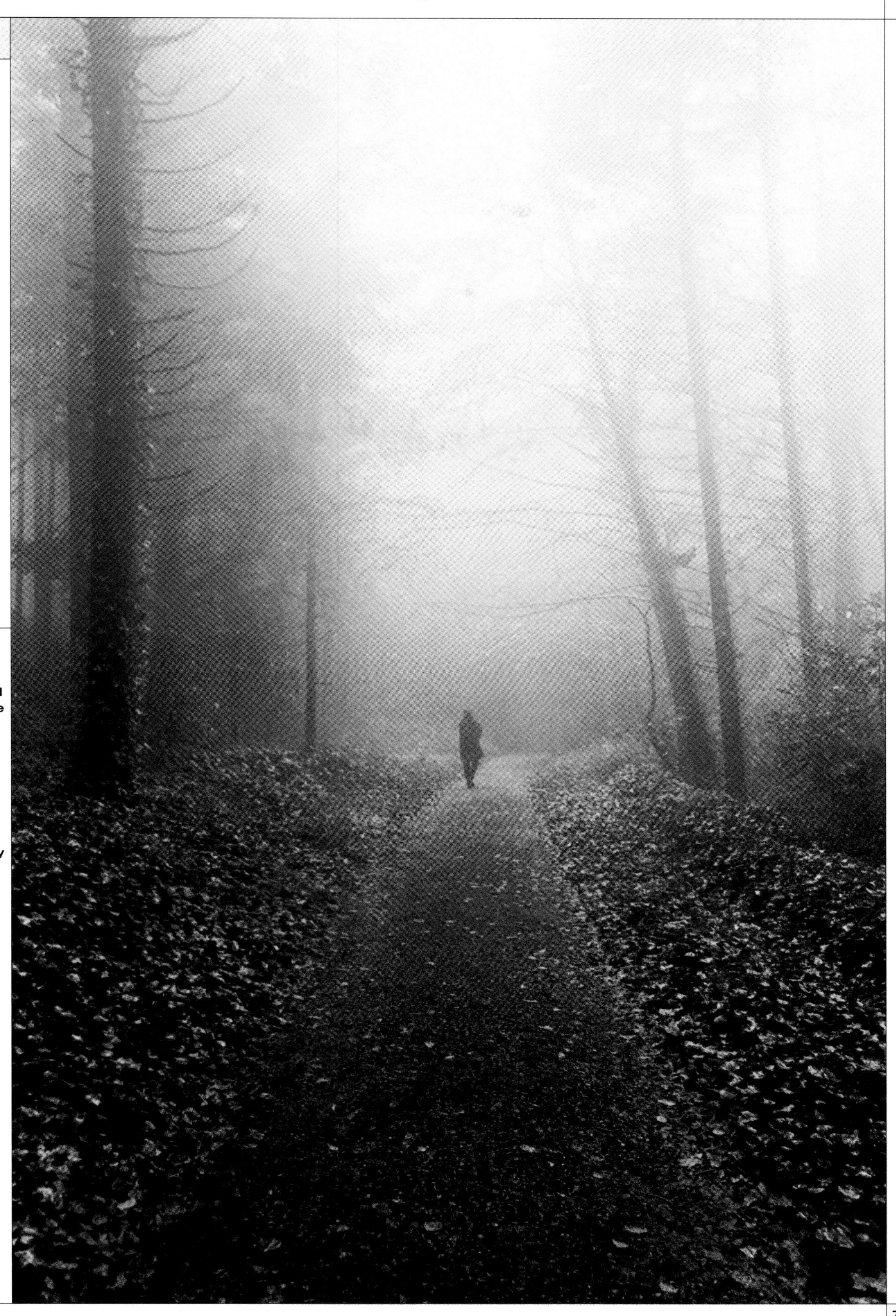

Fact file 1: Grandma 1

Photographer: Zosia Zija

Camera: Hasselblad 2000, lens: 80mm f/2.8, film: Ilford Delta 100, developer: Kodak D76, software: Adobe Photoshop

▼ Fact file 2 | Zosia Zija | Grandma 2 | It was late in the day and the natural light was very soft but it fell nicely on the old lady revealing character in her face. I wanted to show the woman with a good background and I used the dog and the cattle to help this. The picture has a fairy tale feel to it and I enhanced that mood by using the computer to add sepia to make the picture stand out more.

Concept

It was a late summer's day and the light was very flat because of heavy clouds. But this diffused light looked good and suited the fairy tale interpretation I wanted for this shoot. The old lady, cattle and the confused dog were key elements as I wanted to show a different world, the world of an older woman.

Camera tip

Autofocus cameras are wonderful but they are not infallible. If the subject is low contrast, off-centre or there is a lot happening within the scene, learn to use the camera's focus lock feature. Aim the focusing target (usually a letter-box shaped window at the centre of the viewfinder image) at a sharp edge within the frame and then partially depress the shutter release to make the camera focus. Now you can recompose the shot but keep the shutter release depressed to lock focus. When you have the composition you want press the shutter release all the way to take the picture.

better composition get in close

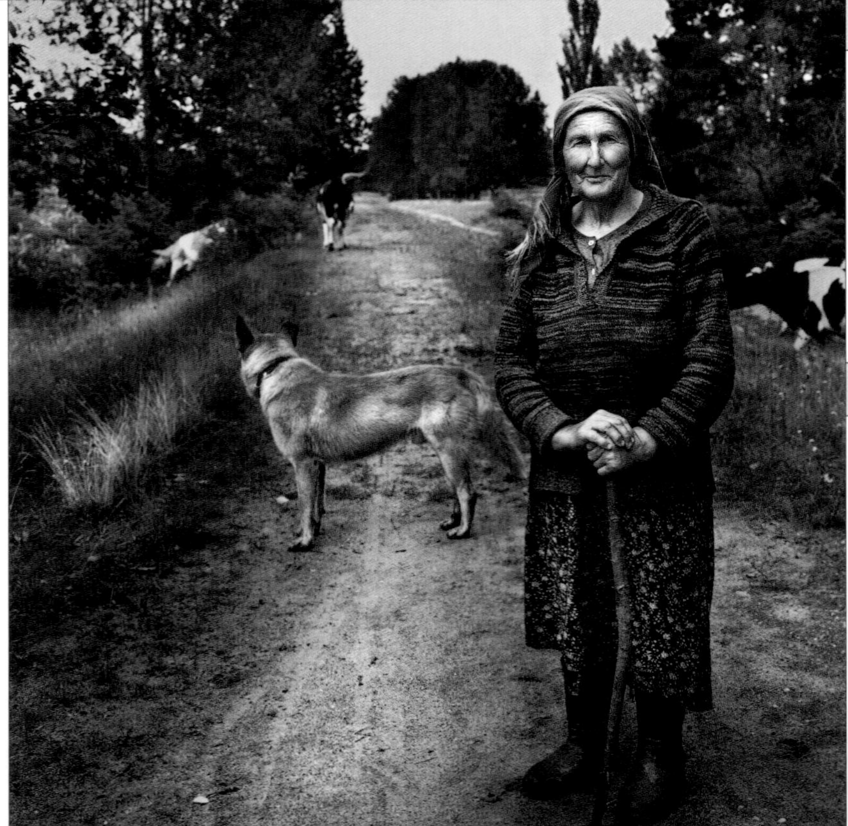

Composition

Both pictures here show how different the compositions can be but also how they can be equally effective. For this picture, I moved in closer to fill the frame with the old lady but still used one side of the square frame for the background. I asked my subject to move slightly to one side so that I could see the dog and even though it is out of focus, having it lurking in the background finishes off the composition nicely.

Technique

The contrast of the scene was low and I took an incident light reading using a separate meter. Exposure was straightforward because the lighting was so dull. The only difficulty I had was that I was not using a tripod and keeping the camera steady was not easy.

I developed the film and scanned in the negatives. Then I adjusted the picture on the computer. I altered the contrast, dodged and burned in and then added a touch of sepia before making the print. I prefer to print digitally compared with traditional printing because I feel the effects are better and I can get the maximum from the negatives.

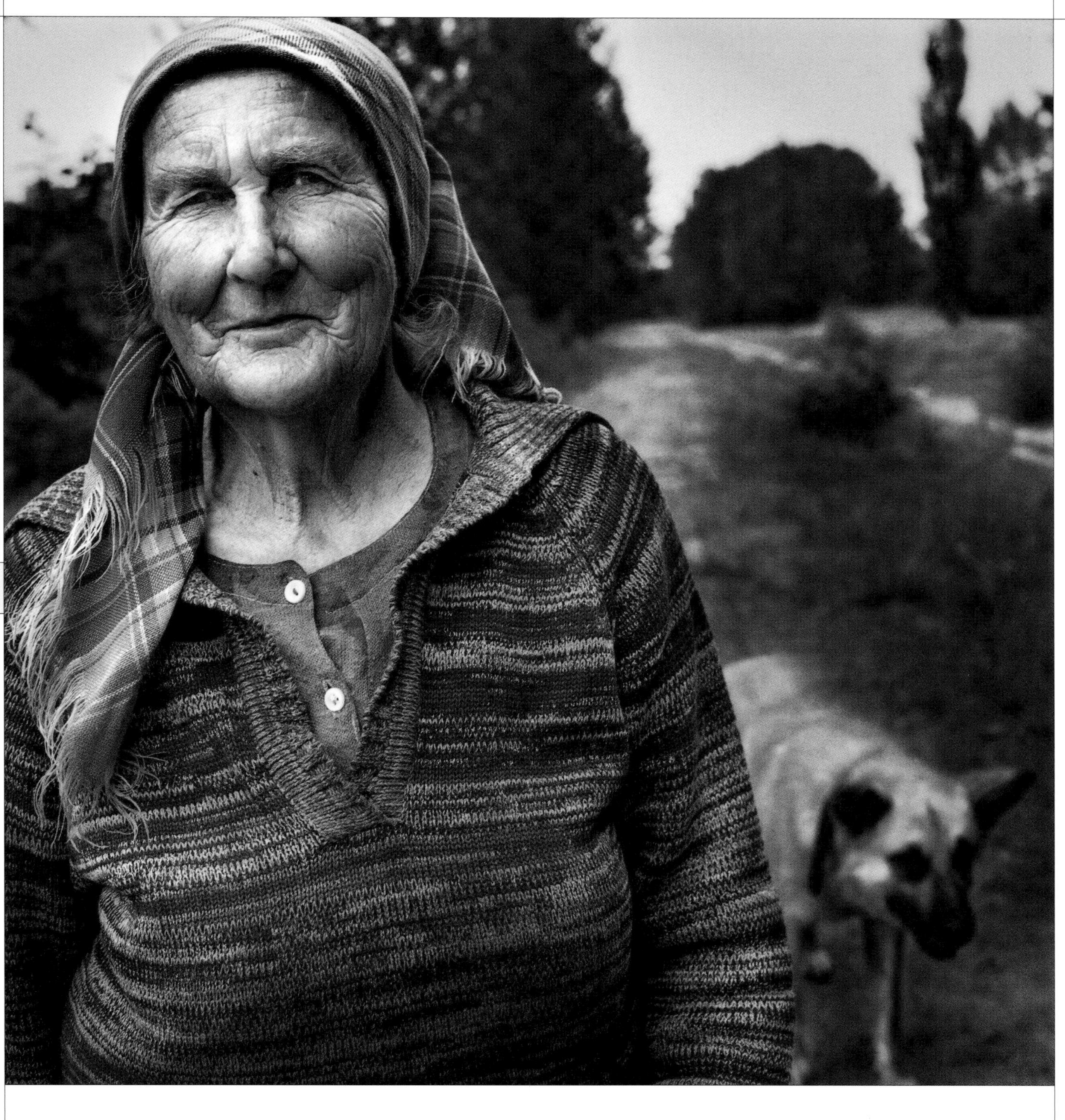

<table>
<tr><td colspan="2">

Fact file 1: Kathrin's eye

Photographer: Gorden Thye

Camera: Canon AE-1, lens: 85mm, film: Ilford HP5 Plus, rated at ISO 400, developer: Ilford Ilotec, paper: Ilford Multigrade IV

</td><td>

Composition

Quite possibly the most radical aspect of this picture's composition is where I placed the model's eye, right into the corner of the frame. But I feel that is well balanced by the incredible hair and the neutral background. The whole effect is very potent, probably because the viewer has to work a little to enjoy the picture.

</td></tr>
<tr><td></td><td>

Concept

I did this picture for a model test. She had asked me to take pictures of her for her 'book'. I worked with the make-up artist, Anke Thot, who liked to experiment and that is why the hair is so adventurous. I moved around the model trying different compositions until I found this perspective and the radical crop.

</td><td>

Technique

The light was a mixture of daylight and two spotlights. It was reasonably bright so I did not need a tripod. Using a tripod would have slowed the session down and there would have been less spontaneity. I set the camera to its automatic shutter-priority mode and relied on it to give the correct exposure, which it did.

</td></tr>
</table>

better composition cropping

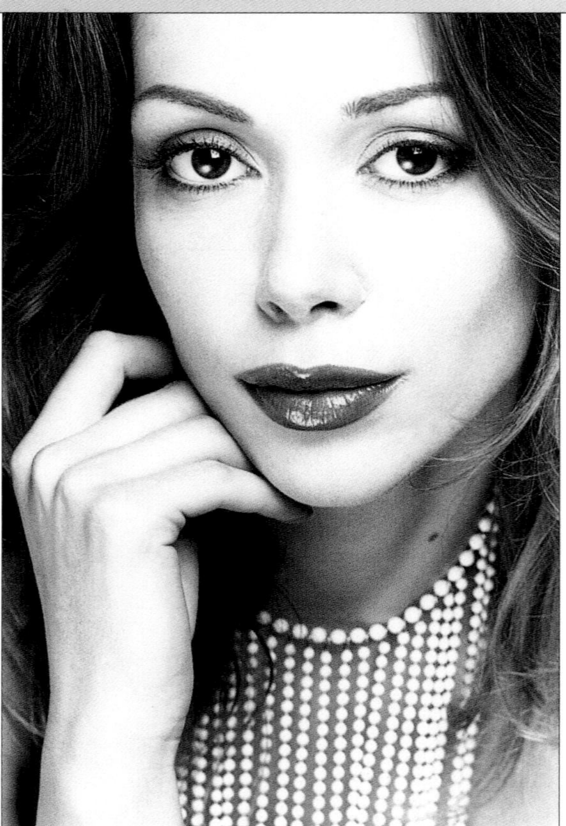

◀▶ **Fact file 2 and 3 | Marco Girolami | Sonila | Cropping** has a profound impact on the final photograph. In this case, I did a traditional, more 'friendly' picture first and that looks fine. But by swinging the lens slightly away so that I only got half of the model's face, I managed a much more intriguing and less conventional image.

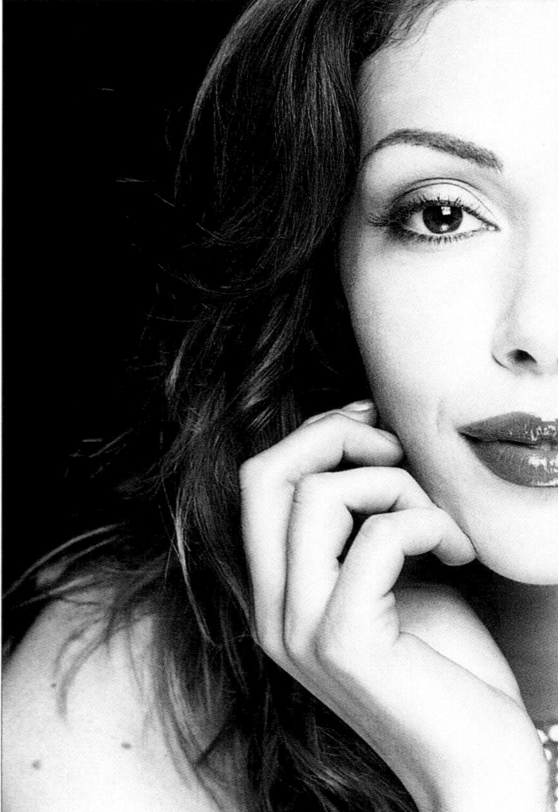

Camera tip

Cropping in camera is ideal. It means you get the right composition without sacrificing any of the film format. However, it is rare that compositions are absolutely perfect at the taking stage and often this aspect of the photograph has to be considered later. For this, make a pair of L-shaped masks from black card. Obviously, with slides, the masks can be much smaller.

With the two masks held at opposite corners of the print you can move them around and see how the composition is affected and improved. Then trim the unwanted areas of the print or mask off parts of the slide with silver foil.

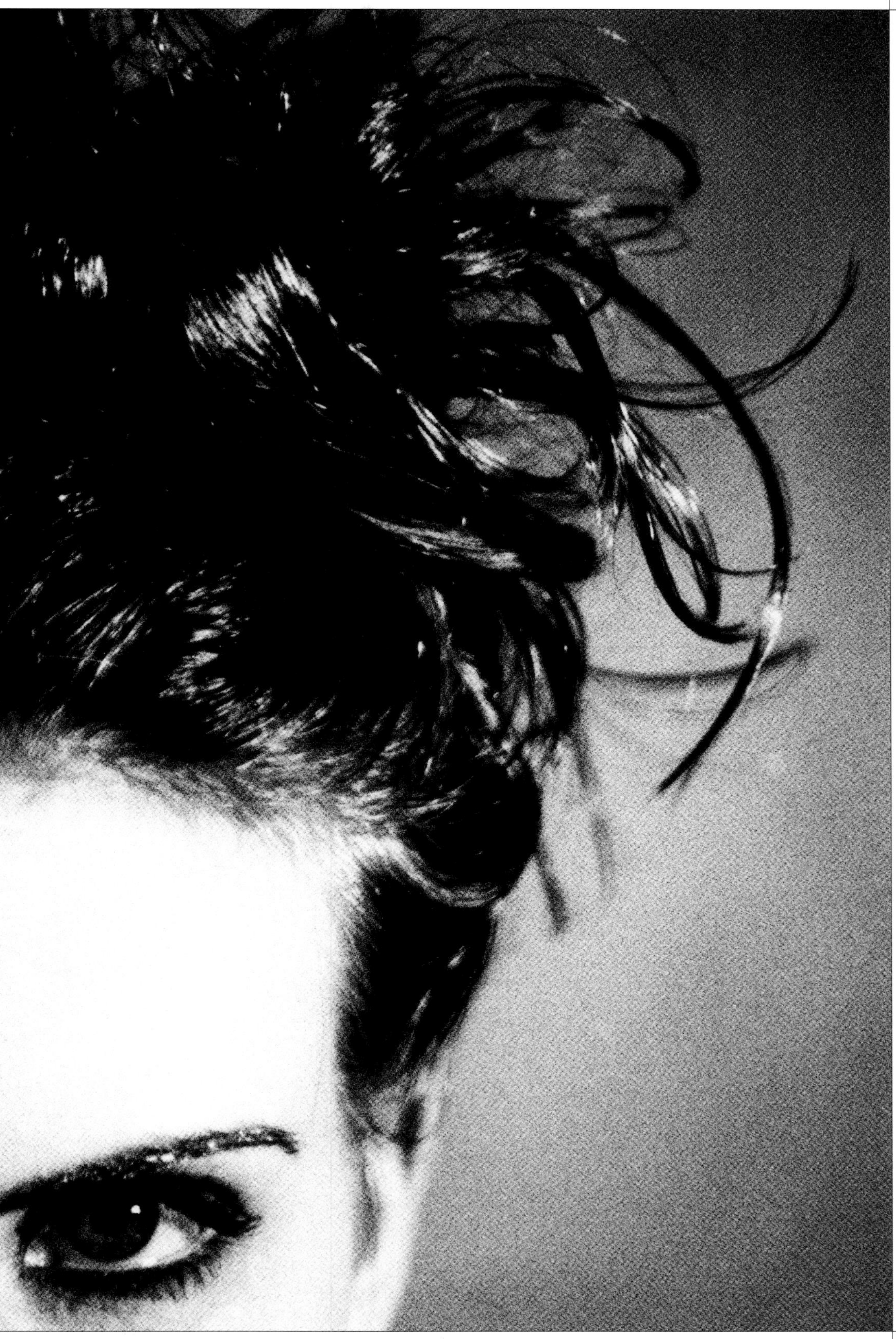

<table>
<tr><td>

Fact file 1: Fences

Photographer: Aguinaldo Calheiros Vera-Cruz

Camera: Canon F1N, lens: 20mm, film: Kodak High-Speed Infrared, exposure: 1/125sec at f/16, filter: red

</td><td>

Concept

It was a bright, sunny day and there were attractive clouds in the sky. When I saw this scene I just thought of the forms within the image and knew it would suit shooting with a very wide-angle lens like the 20mm that I used. I am a frequent user of infrared film because of the exciting effects that are possible.

</td></tr>
</table>

better composition perspective

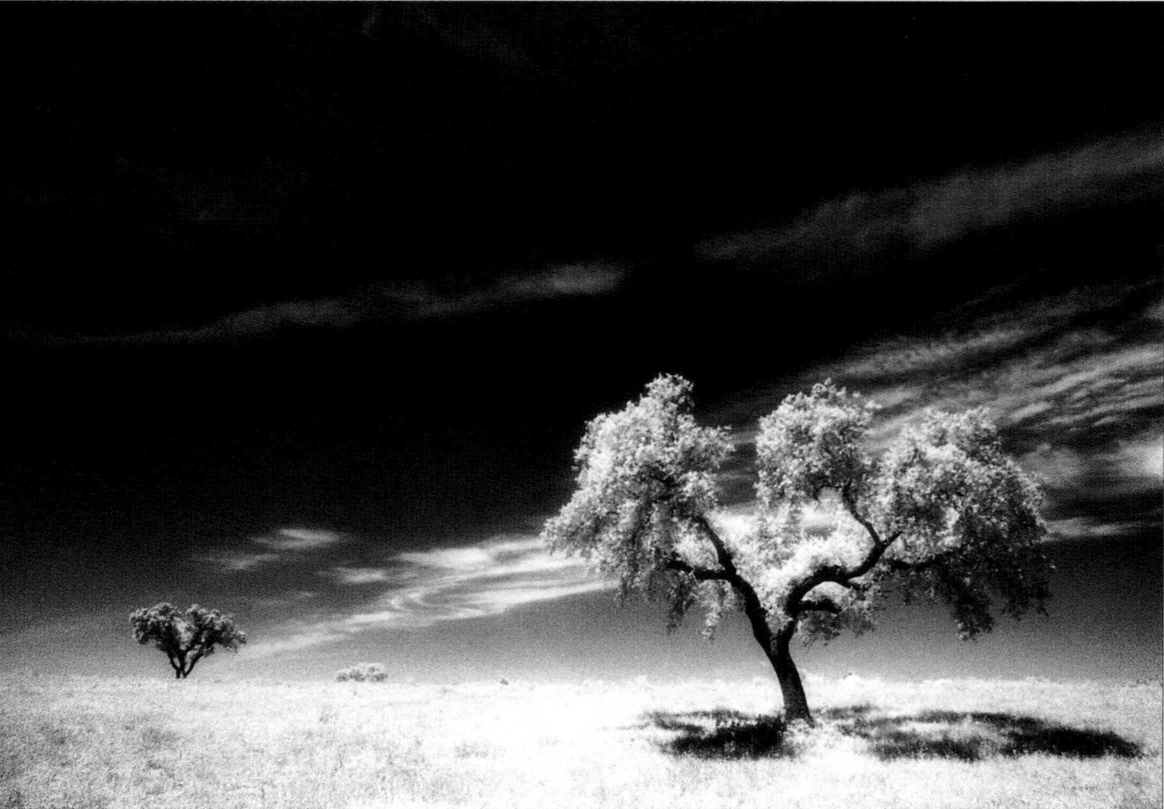

◀ Fact file 2 | Aguinaldo Calheiros Vera-Cruz | Zenith | This was taken around noon so the sun was high in the sky. With the 20mm wide-angle lens fitted I moved in near to the closest tree to make the most of the shadow and positioned the distant tree on the opposite side of the frame.

Composition

I am never truly satisfied but I do like this picture. The fence makes nice patterns in the sand and the whole composition just pulls me into the scene. The scene was an obvious candidate for a vertical composition because that made the most of the powerful lines created by the fence and shadows. I closed the lens down to f/16 so that everything in the scene is very sharp.

Technique

Infrared film responds very differently depending on how much infrared radiation is around. Clouds absorb infrared so the effect is less pronounced. On bright, sunny days, however, there is a great deal of infrared around and it is in these conditions that you get the most dramatic effects. Blue skies go almost black as does water while healthy foliage comes out very light-toned indeed. A red filter is the most convenient to use because it still transmits visible light so composing an image is simple. It is also possible to use special near-opaque filters that transmit infrared wavelengths only but you will have to compose and focus the scene before fitting the filter in position.

Camera tip

Aperture choice has a profound effect on the final picture so merits careful consideration, whether shooting a landscape, portrait or still-life. The aperture directly affects the amount of depth-of-field, or the zone of front to back sharpness, in a picture. The smaller the aperture the greater the depth-of-field and the wider the aperture the more shallow the depth-of-field. Lens focal length and the camera to subject distance are other influencing factors. Moving in close to a subject reduces the amount of depth-of-field so be careful if you want sharpness from the near foreground to the distant horizon.

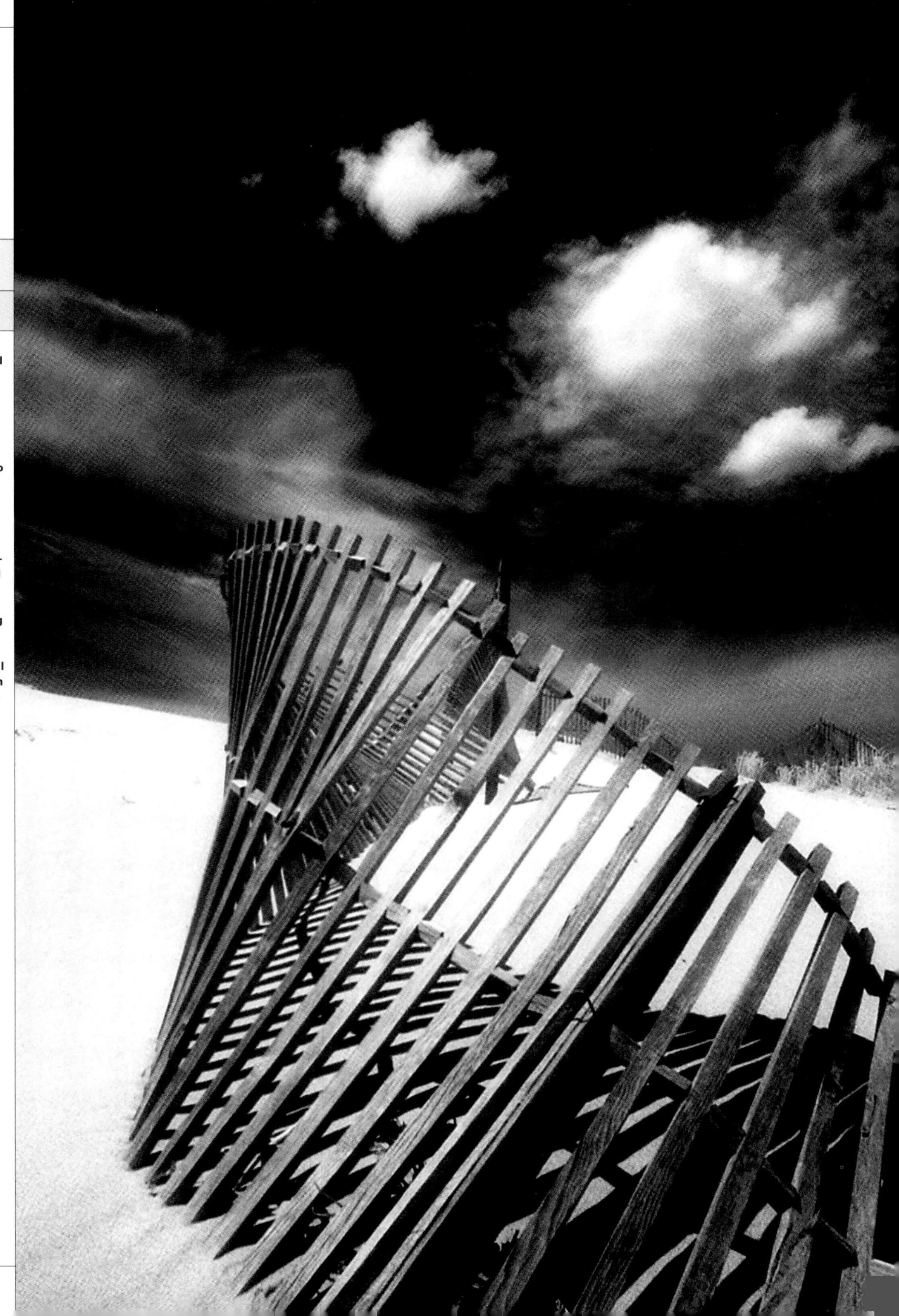

Photographer: Bob Hudak

Camera: Pentax 6x7cm on a tripod, lens: 135mm macro, film: Ilford Pan F Plus ISO 50, exposure: aperture of f/32, paper: Oriental Seagull, grade 3, toner: selenium 1+64 for three minutes

▼ **Fact file 2 | Bob Hudak | Dried leaf |**
Sometimes the most interesting pictures are right in front of you and my aim here was to present an object in a way that we are not normally accustomed to seeing it. It was the shape and textures of the leaf against the black background that caught my eye.

Composition

Getting in close with the camera looking for patterns is a great technique if you want to create abstract images out of everyday scenes. Close scrutiny of the viewfinder is important to make the most of patterns because you need to ensure the composition works as a whole. In pattern shots, there is not always an obvious focal point to catch the viewer's eye so the rhythm of the composition has to be strong enough to retain interest.

better composition look for patterns

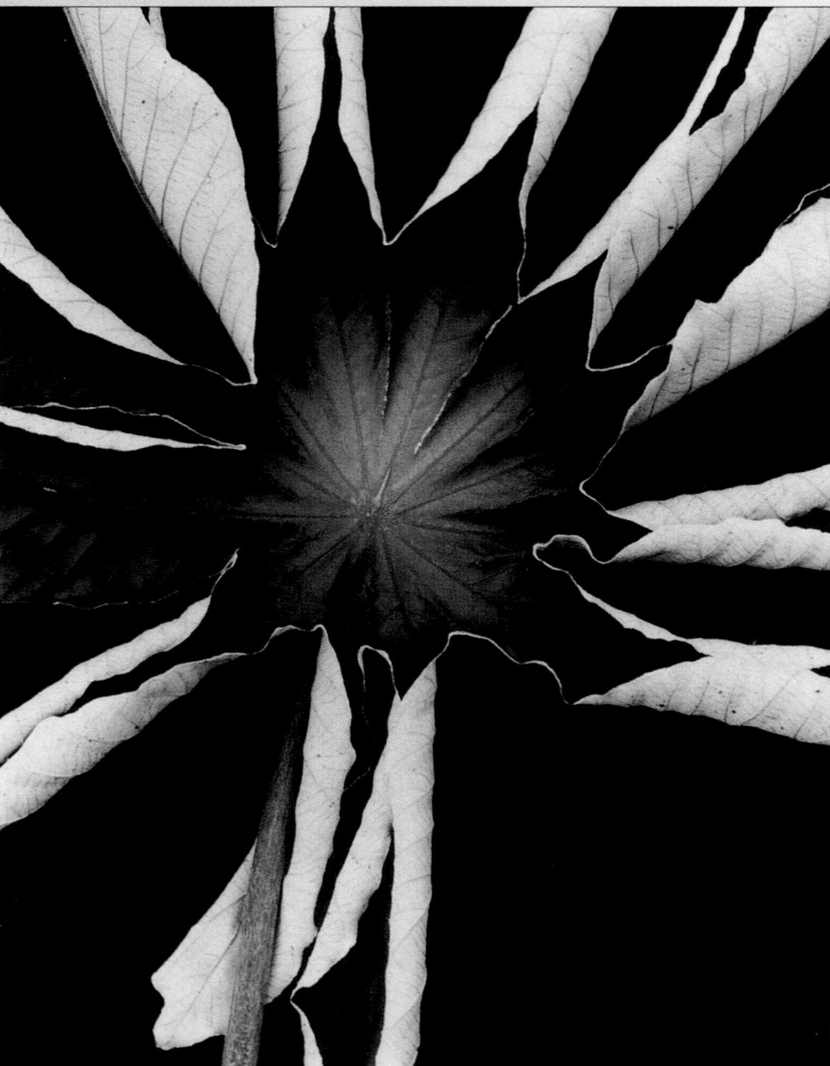

Concept

What initially caught my attention were the tones and shapes of the leaves. By exploring around the scene, I tried to find a rhythm to the arrangement of the forms as well as tones, and have them work together. The light was constantly changing which made taking the picture a little more difficult. I wanted to keep contrast down so I waited until the sun ducked behind some cloud before taking the picture.

Technique

The camera was set up on a tripod to allow me complete freedom with aperture choice. I set f/32 for maximum depth-of-field within the scene. Metering was done manually using the camera's exposure meter. With 35mm and roll film you cannot develop each frame individually so I usually bracket the exposure half-a-stop either side of the meter reading and then develop the film normally.

The print was made on grade 3 paper and I gave some extra exposure in the top right of the print to deepen the tone in that area. The leaf at the bottom right was also burned in for the same reason.

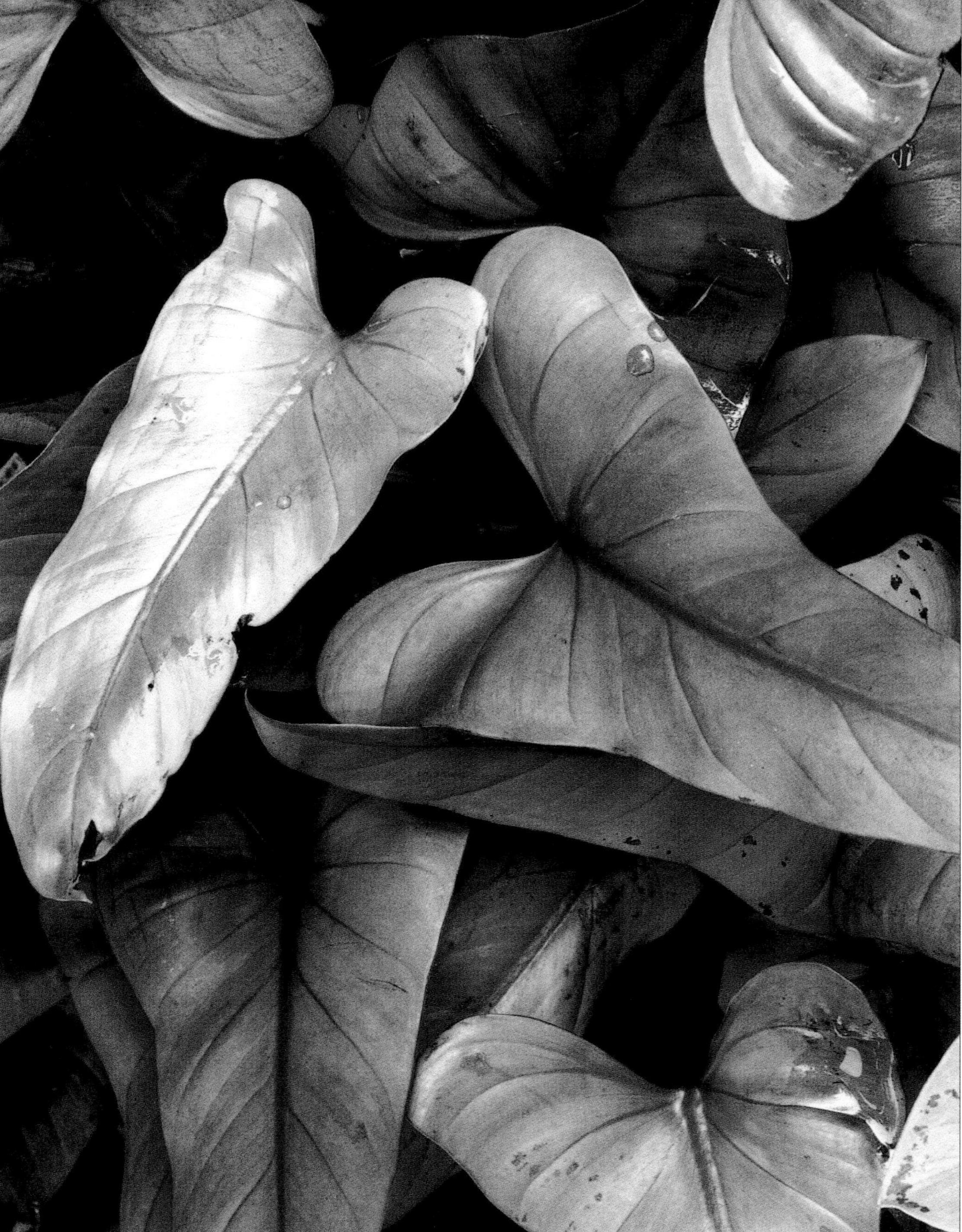

Camera tip

With the camera mounted on a tripod, fire the shutter using a remote release. If you do not have one use the camera's self-timer. Both methods mean that you are not touching the camera as the actual exposure is made so there is no risk of shake. Some cameras let you shorten the usual ten second delay to two seconds so there is much less of a wait.

shooting light

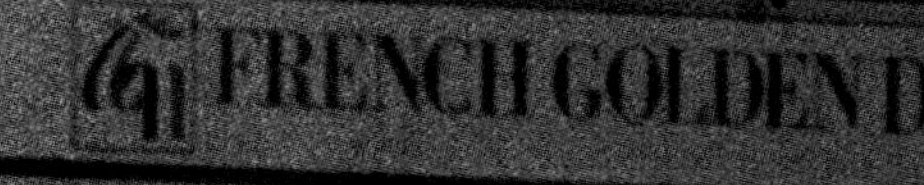

FRENCH GOLDEN D

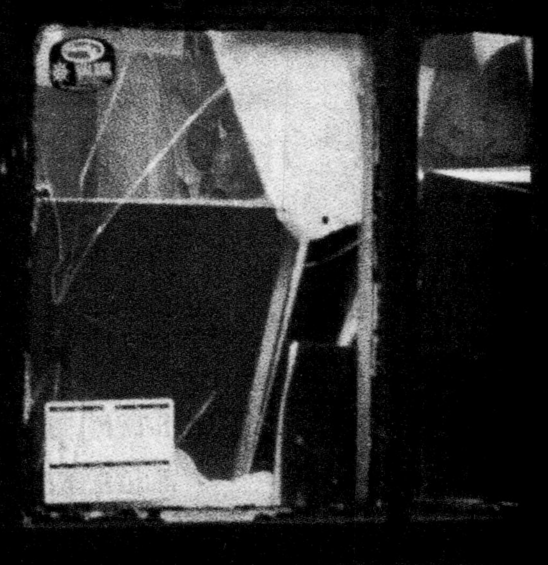

FINEST SELECTE
FRESH
COCONUTS

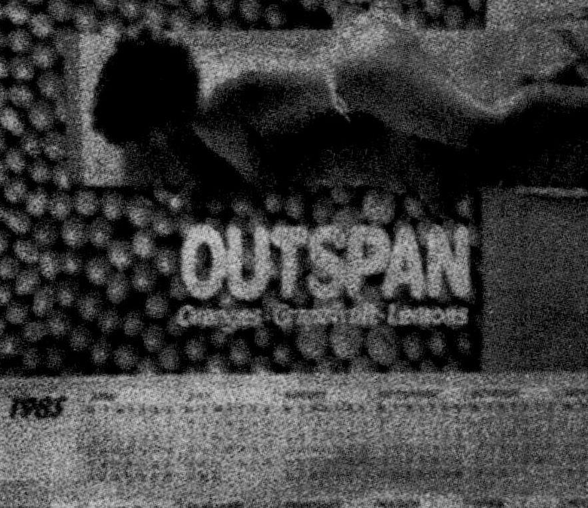

Fresh Citrus
OUTSPAN
1985
1986

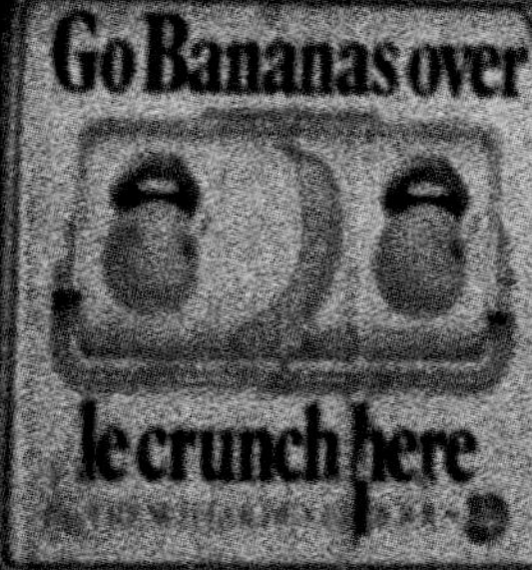

Go Bananas over
le crunch here

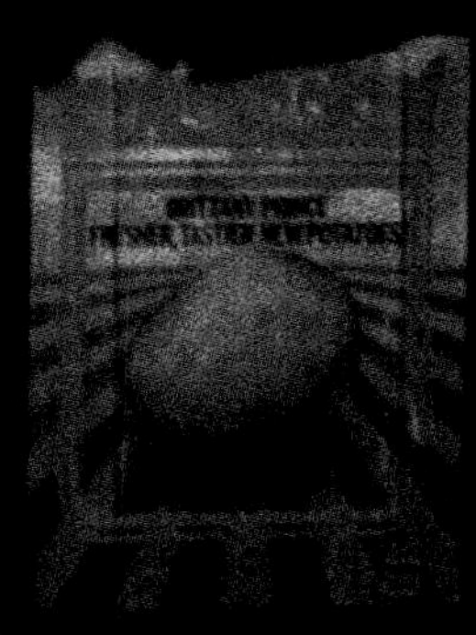

Go Bananas over

Fact file 1: The walk	**Concept**
Photographer: Zosia Zija **Camera:** Hasselblad 2000, lens: 80mm f/2.8, film: Ilford Delta 100, developer: Kodak D-76, software: Adobe Photoshop	Like many of my pictures, this was taken on the spur of the moment. I was fascinated by the beautiful vivid light of an early evening in summer and I just wanted to capture that wonderful feeling. I use a documentary style for my pictures and this shot looks like a still frame from a movie.

shooting light in sunlight

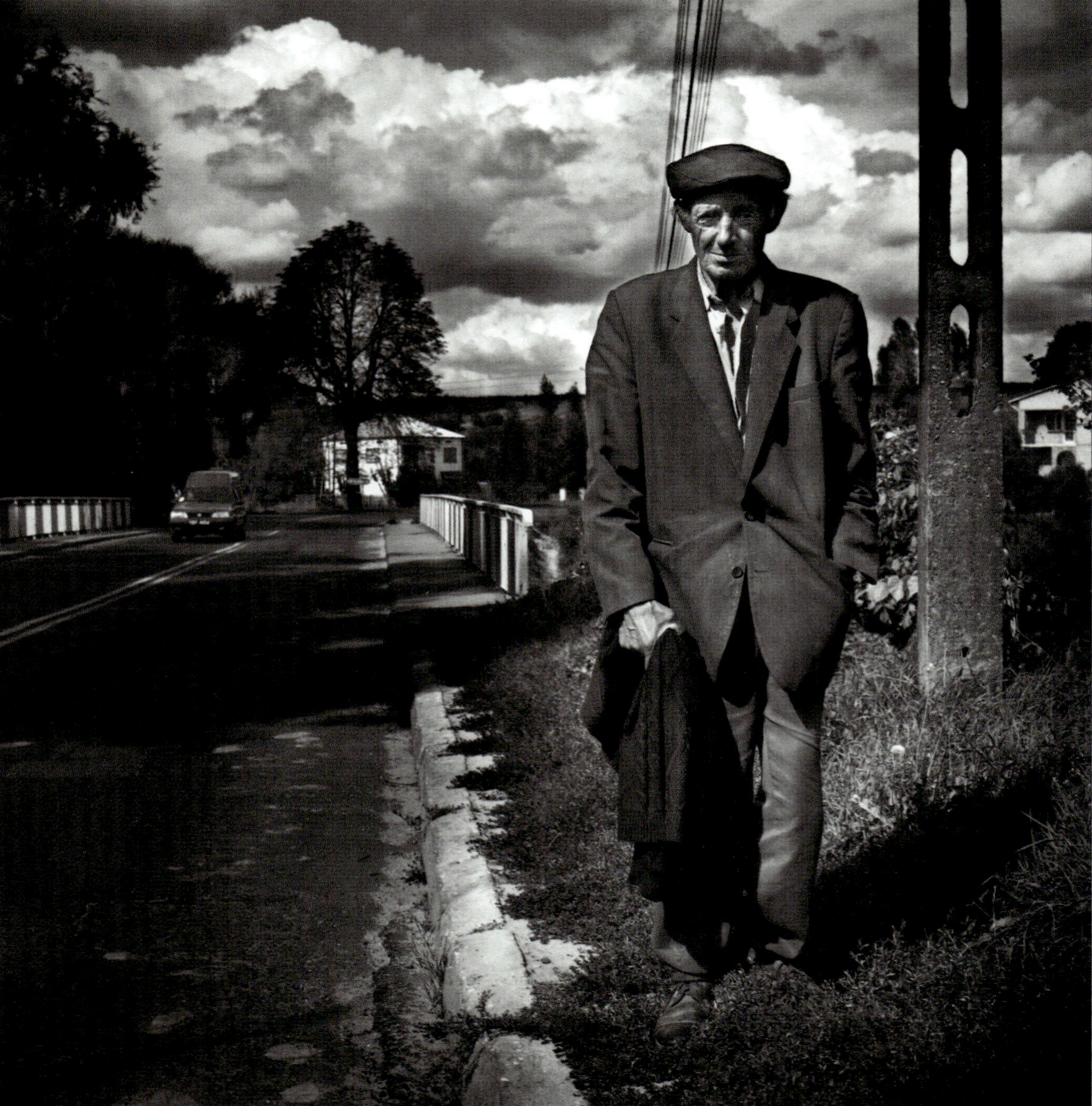

◀ Fact file 2 | Zosia Zija | The old man | Late afternoon in the summer produces a harsh light but good pictures are still possible. I was trying to show that modern day life in the countryside is mixed up with a certain kind of backwardness, so I composed this man with a passing car in the background. By doing this, I showed that this picture was not taken 20 years ago despite the appearance of the man.

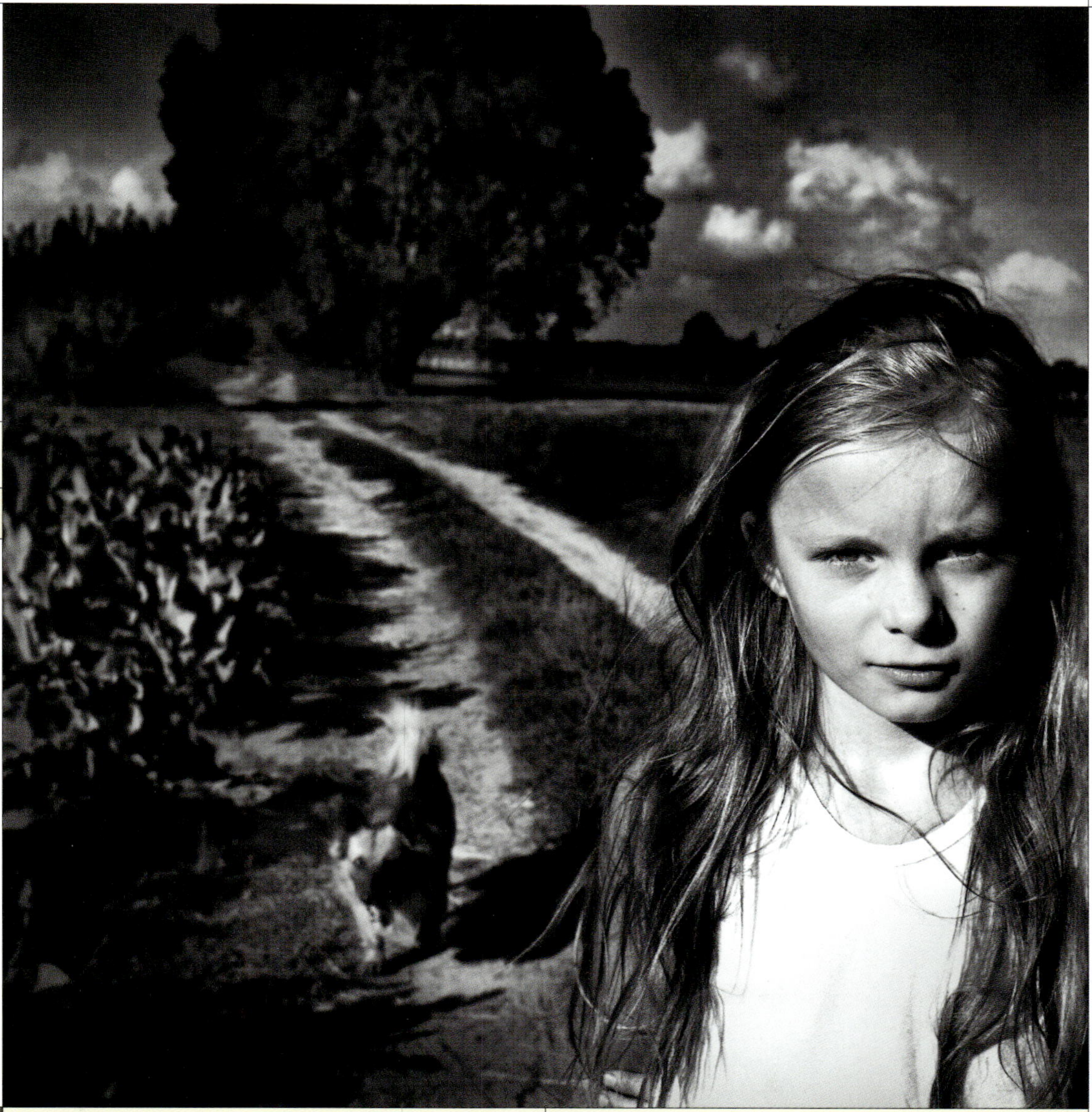

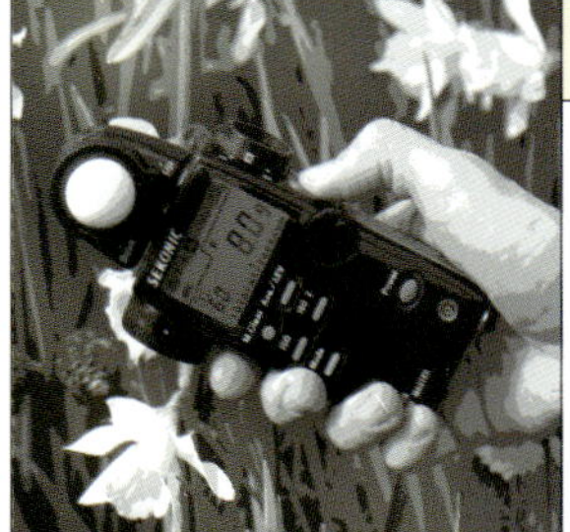

Composition

The pathway and surrounding trees created a nice composition but when I saw the dog I thought it was a great addition to the picture. Just as I was going to take the picture a girl suddenly jumped into the frame. I quickly re-focused and took the picture. The bright light, which was falling directly onto the girl, gives the feeling of anticipation and suspense.

Technique

I took an incident light reading using my hand-held meter. My only concern was that I did not have a tripod so I had to make sure of holding the camera steady during the exposure.

I scanned the developed negative and applied contrast, burning-in and dodging using Adobe Photoshop. I prefer using digital techniques over traditional printing methods because I feel the effects are better.

Fact file 1: Window nude

Photographer: Jamie Drouin

Camera: Leica M6, lens: 50mm, film: Kodak Tri-X, exposure: 1/30sec at f/2, developer: Agfa Rodinal

Concept

My wife and I had just arrived in Paris after several days of travelling through northern Europe. This image was taken the next morning as we slowly collected our energy to go out exploring. The sun was veiled by a thick layer of morning mist giving the room and my wife's profile, a bright luminescent quality.

shooting light backlight

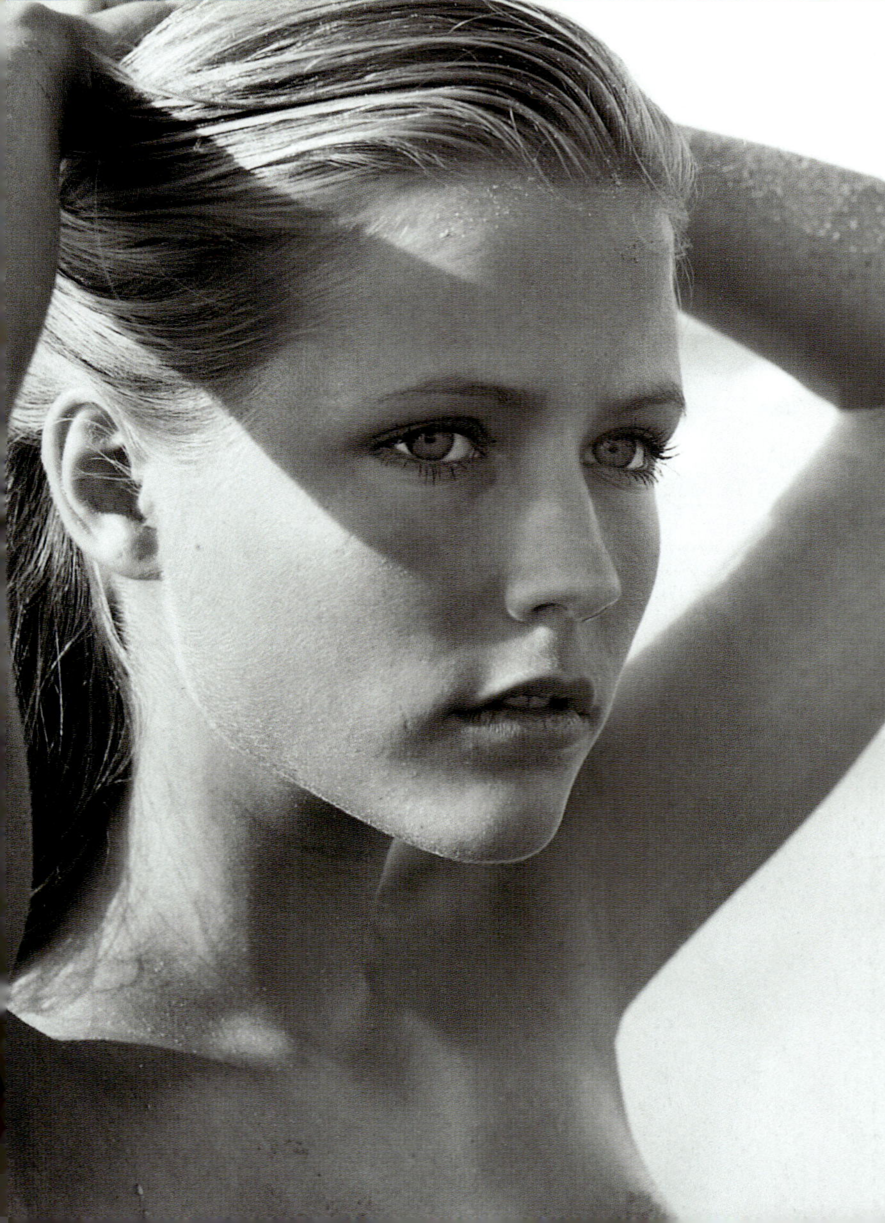

Composition

As with most of my work, these are moments recognised out of the corner of my eye. They both explain a real situation and communicate a state of being, where people, objects and places hold new meanings. I saw the parallel between the liquid nature of the figure and the sheets set against the rigid lines of the window frame. The figure remains in flux, continuing to change shape and meaning for the viewer, while the window frame is static and reaffirms the physical nature of space.

Technique

This was an extremely high-contrast situation. The biggest technical issue was retaining interesting textural detail in the highlights while avoiding an excessively 'chalky' look to the tones. I used my camera's spot meter and took a reading off an area of backlit skin and opened the aperture up by two stops.

During printing, I gave extra exposure to the window frame and the bed foreground to focus attention on the edge of the figure. This also gave the foreground a more textured effect.

◀ **Fact file 2 | Rene de Haan | Myrthe 66 | It was late afternoon and the sunlight was coming in from an angle from behind the girl. I used the girl's arms to keep direct sun off her face so that the composition appeared less flat. I used the camera's lightmeter and moved in close to her face to take a reading then recomposed.**

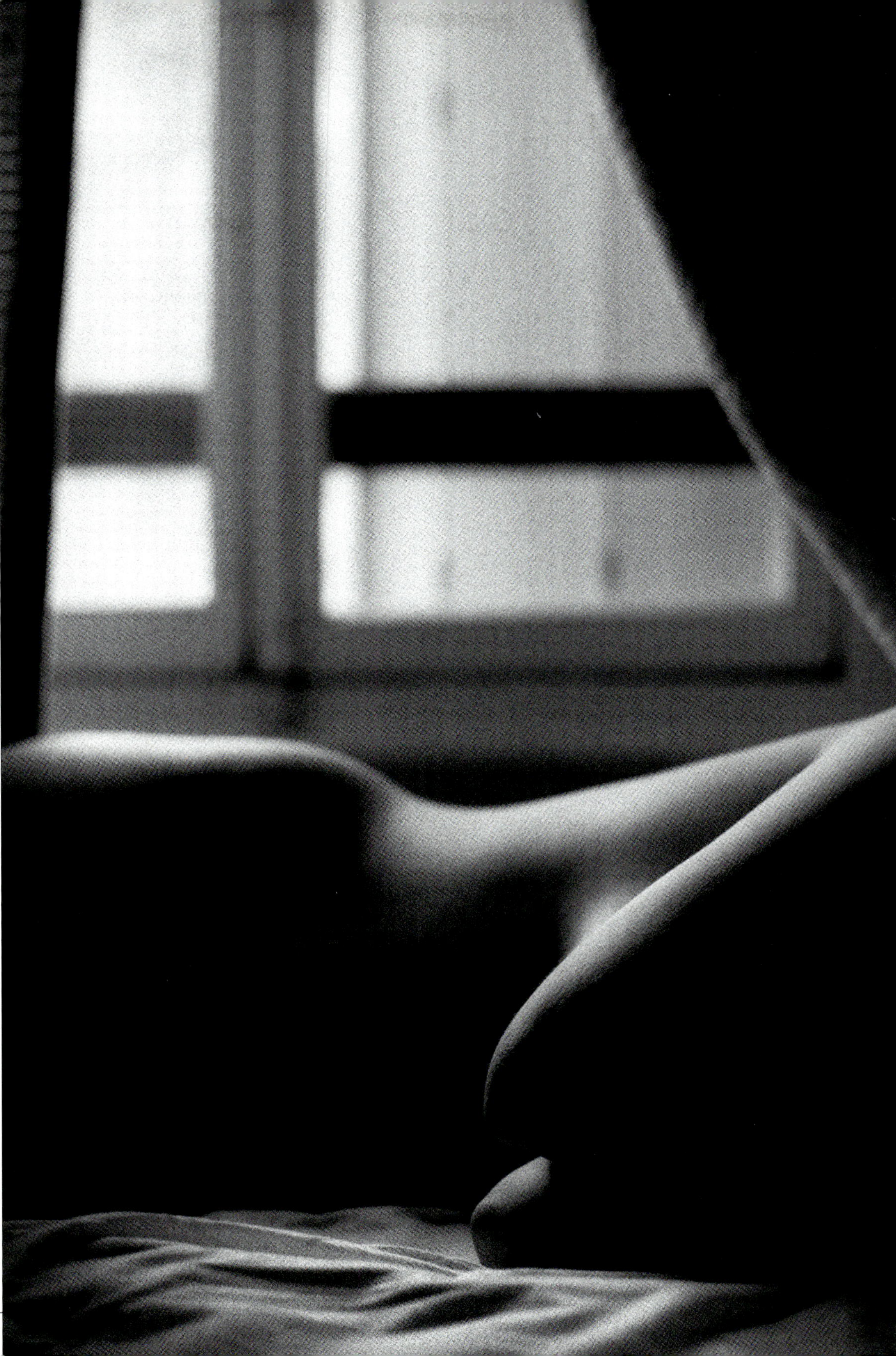

Camera tip

Intense backlighting often
fools the camera's meter
into underexposing the
foreground but, unless you
want a silhouette, it is easy
to avoid this by using the
autoexposure lock (AE-L).
Aim the camera down
slightly to fill the viewfinder
with some foreground and
operate the exposure lock.
This might be a separate
control or it could be
incorporated with the
shutter release. Look at
your camera's instruction
manual. Operating the AE-L
memorises the reading so
you can now recompose
the image knowing that the
foreground will be correct.

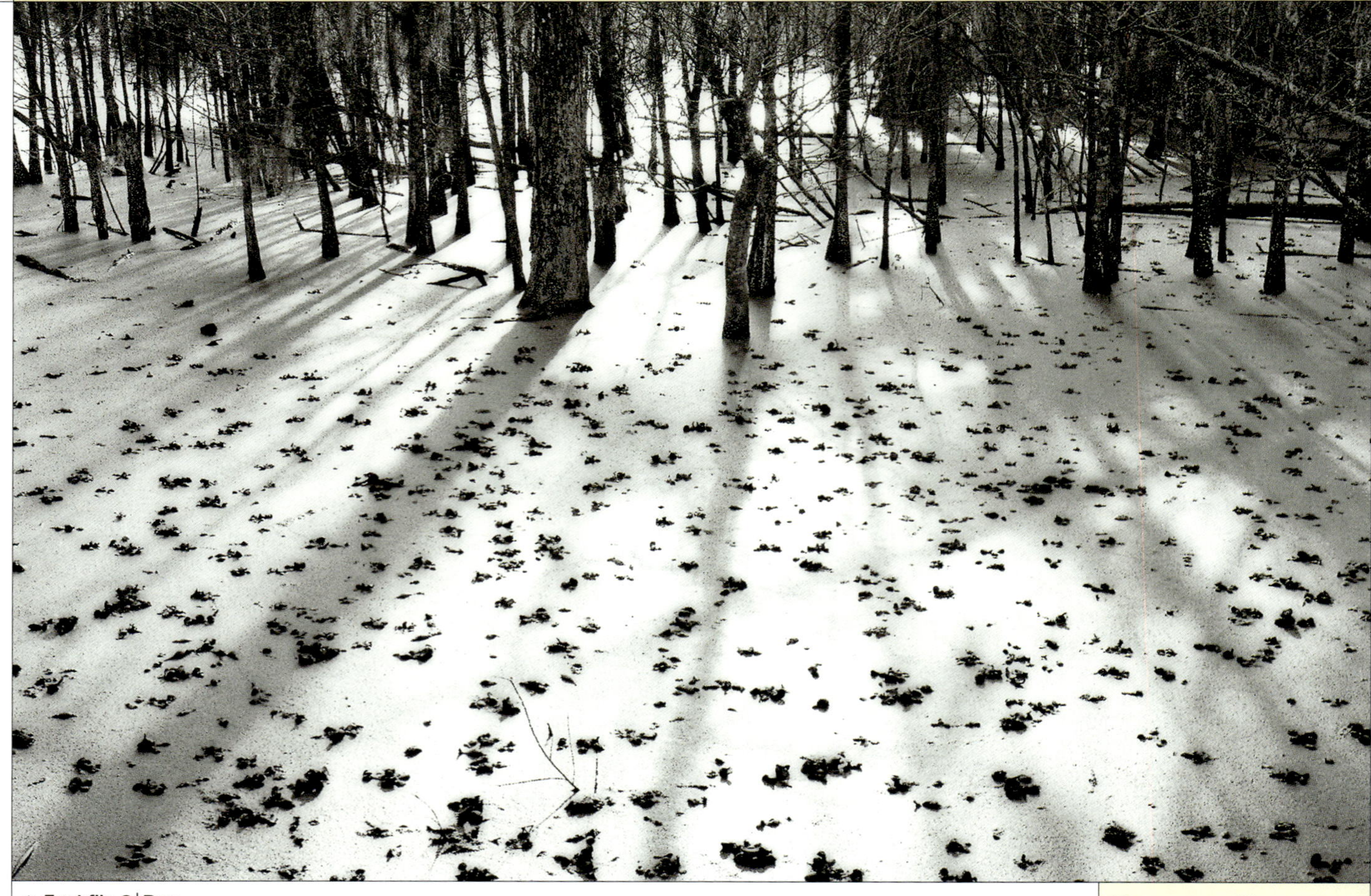

▲ Fact file 3 | Dan Burkholder | Leaves on swamp | Shooting backlit pictures is my favourite technique. This was taken late afternoon and the lighting was making great patterns on the swamp. I fitted a wide-angle lens to make the most of the shadows of the backlit trees and set a small aperture to ensure enough depth-of-field. To avoid any risk of underexposure of the leaves I dialled in +1 stop exposure compensation in automatic exposure mode.

Camera tip

Using a hood minimises the risk of lens flare when shooting into the light but unless you have a bellows lens hood, a typical hood is not effective throughout the range of a zoom lens. If flare is visible in the viewfinder, use a hand or a sheet of stiff card to shield the front of the lens from the sun. The most comfortable way of working is having the camera on a tripod and then looking through the viewfinder for the improved result as the hand or card is moved into position. Obviously, the hand or card should be out of frame and it is worth making doubly sure by using the depth-of-field preview facility.

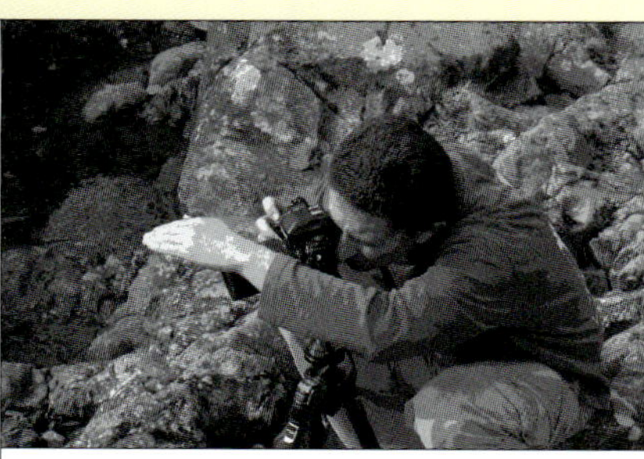

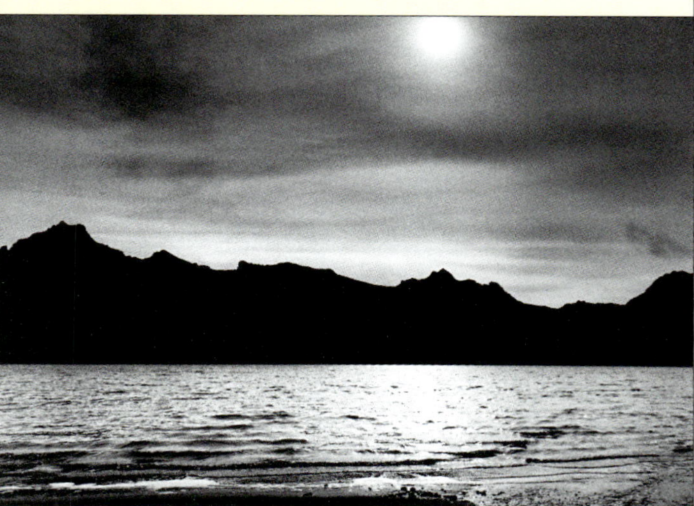

▶ Fact file 5 | William Cheung | Iceland | The sun was diffused by low cloud but it was still strong enough to fool the meter into underexposing the interesting detail in the stream. To ensure some foreground showed up in the final image the camera was angled down for a manual meter reading before returning to the original composition. Exposing using these camera settings would have overexposed the sky greatly so I fitted a 0.9 grey graduate to keep detail in the sky.

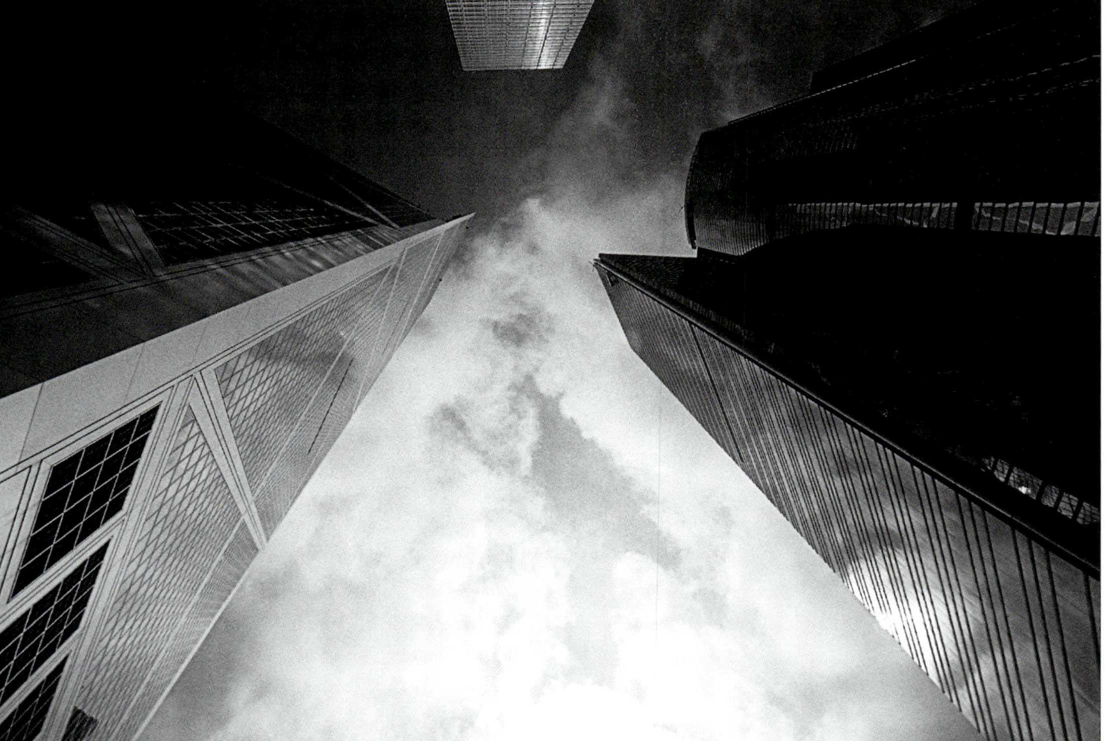

◀ Fact file 4 | William Cheung | Hong Kong | It was the clouds that encouraged me to take this picture. Looking straight up at these skyscrapers with a wide-angle lens gave a dynamic composition with powerful shapes and lines, but the sun was rather too intense until a few clouds arrived to diffuse the light. A red filter was used to bring out the blue sky and I did several shots at intervals because the quickly changing cloud formations significantly changed the composition.

Fact file 1: Madeleine

Photographer: Éric Soulé

Camera: Leica M6, lens: 50mm f/2, film: Kodak T-Max 400 rated at ISO 200, exposure: 1/60sec at f/2, developer: Kodak D76, paper: Ilford Multigrade IV FB

Concept

I took this portrait for a project on an old peoples' home. It was morning and I placed my subject in front of a curtained window. I had little time so I had to work quickly which is why I hand-held the camera.

shooting light low light

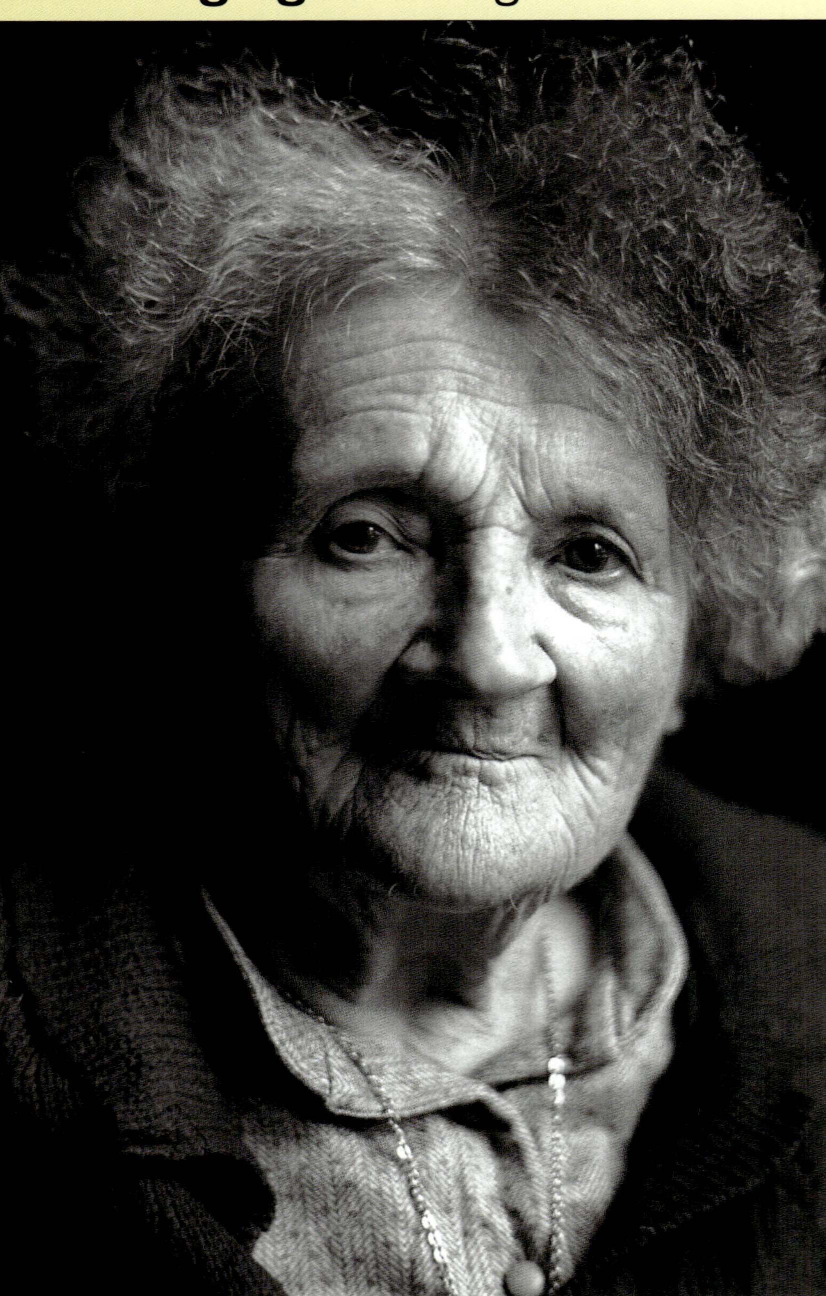

Composition

The upright 35mm format suits portraits very well as it allows you to make the most of the image area. I placed the face above the centre line so that Madeleine's eyes are resting on the top-third which I feel gives portraits more impact. Inexperienced photographers put the subject's face right in the middle of the frame but that style of composition does not suit me.

Technique

I wanted to take pictures quickly and without too much fuss so I did not use a tripod. The good thing about the Leica M camera is that there is no reflex mirror and it is possible to get very sharp pictures in low light conditions with minimal risk of camera shake. The exposure was straightforward and I took a meter reading from the side of her face that was in shadow.

◀ **Fact file 2 | Éric Soulé | Jeanne | The room behind the old lady, Jeanne, went dark naturally because it was receiving little light. The dark background has allowed her to stand out very well. The diffused, low-contrast light has delicately revealed the subject's character without the need for harsh, extreme tones.**

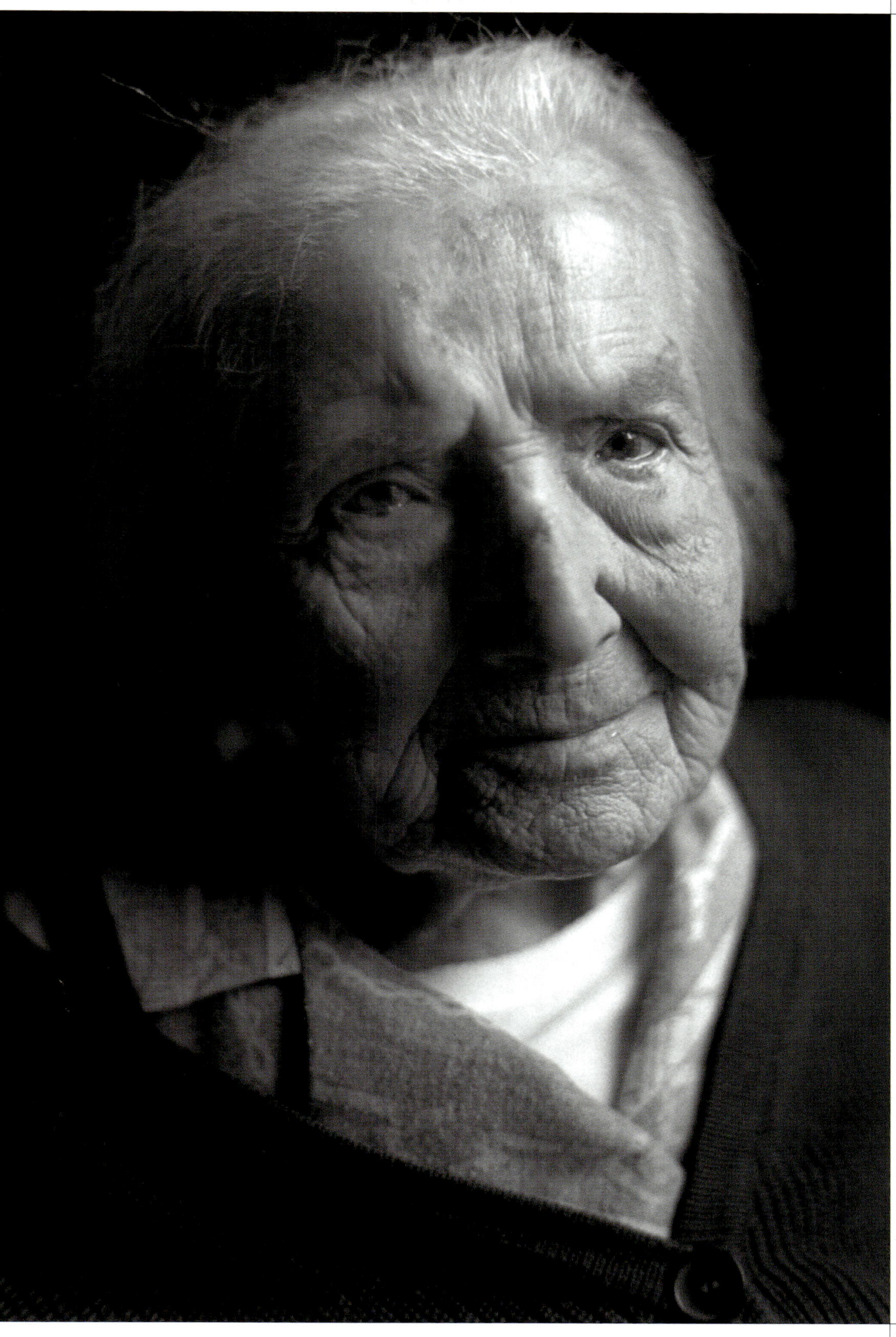

Camera tip

Squeeze the shutter
release slowly and
smoothly when taking the
picture. Inexperienced
photographers often stab
the shutter release and are
then surprised that their
pictures are ruined by
camera shake. This is a
fundamental technique to
practise. At shutter speeds
of 1/30sec or slower try
this: support the camera
firmly in both hands, tuck
your elbows into your body
and then squeeze the
shutter release while very
gently holding your breath.
If you find yourself tensing
up and shaking, relax and
start from the beginning.

Photographer: Vince Bevan

Camera: Olympus OM1n, lens: 100mm, film: Kodak Tri-X 400 rated at ISO 1600, exposure: 1/30sec at f/5.6, developer: Agfa Rodinal, paper: Ilford Multigrade FB

Shooting in low light can lead to camera shake if there is no tripod available. However, there are other ways of gaining some much-needed support. Leaning back against a solid wall or resting on a streetlight or signpost can make the difference between acceptable pictures and failures. As always, squeeze the shutter release smoothly and gradually rather than stabbing at it.

shooting light very low light

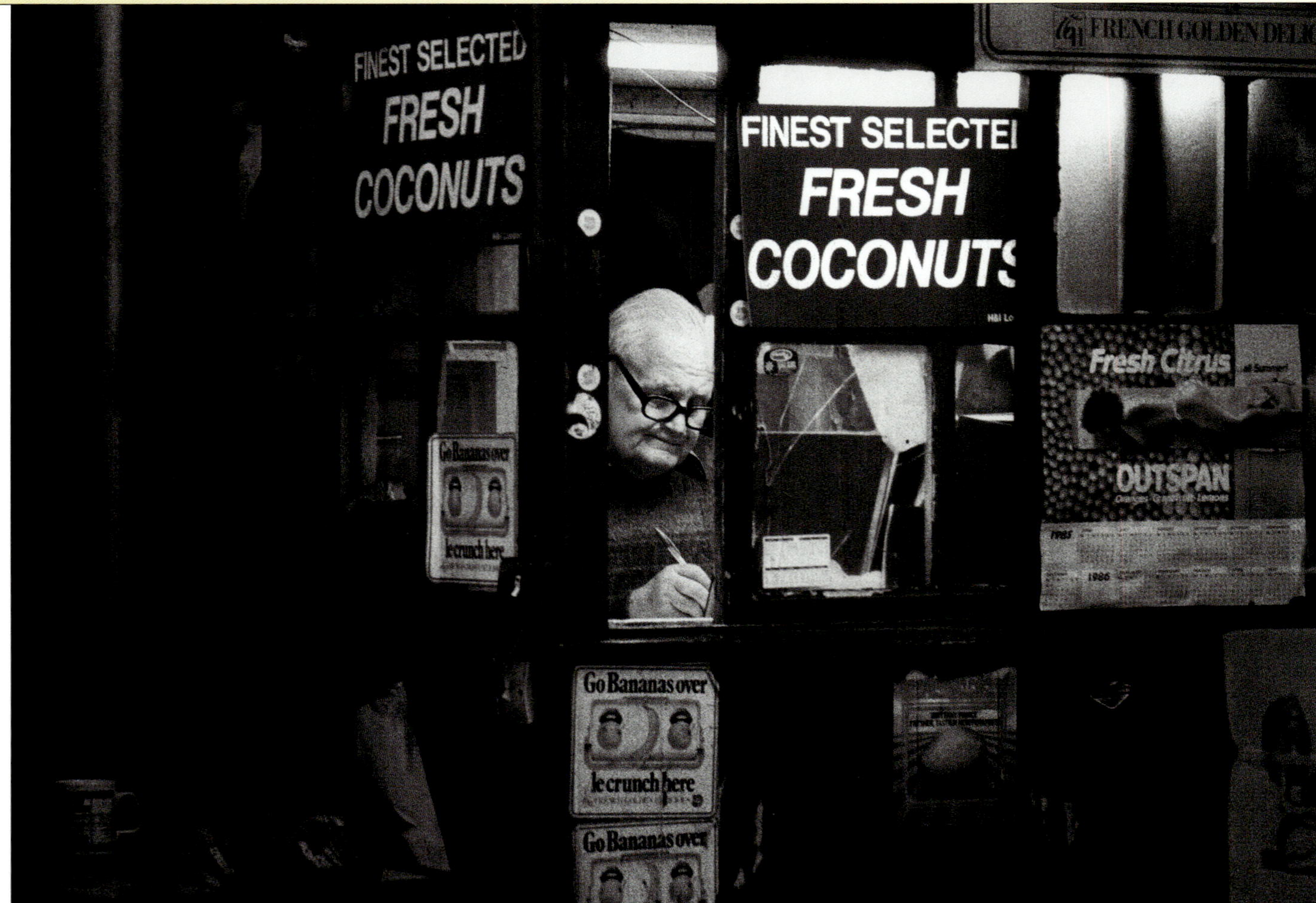

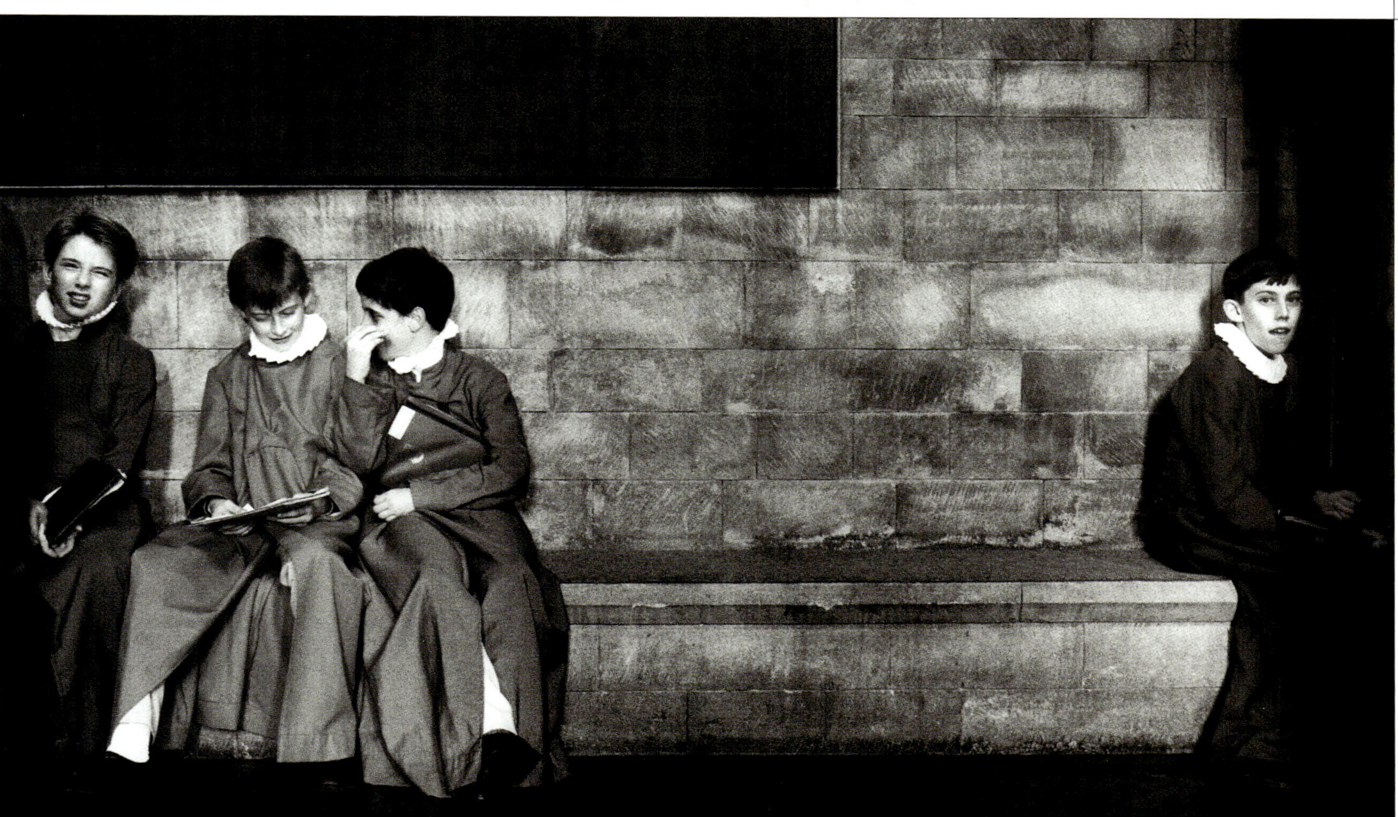

Concept

This image was taken using available light at 4am for a photo essay I was doing on an area of South London. This includes Borough Market, which is one of London's oldest vegetable markets still in use. I wanted to give the feeling of the timeless atmosphere of the place through a series of portraits and candids of the characters that worked there.

Composition

What I think makes this image work is the busyness of the posters surrounding the stillness of the man's expression, working in his own pool of light seemingly oblivious to the hustle and bustle of the market around him. Placing the main subject right at the centre of the frame rarely works but it does here because of the man-made frame.

Technique

I exposed for the shadows, using the camera meter. It was at a slow shutter speed so I was careful to keep the camera steady. When printing the image I had to give extra exposure to slightly darken the striplight, forehead and poster.

Kodak Tri-X is a marvellous film that responds well to push-processing. So instead of rating it at its usual ISO 400 I exposed it at ISO 1600 and then gave extra development in the darkroom to compensate for the deliberate underexposure.

▲ Fact file 2 | Vince Bevan | Southwark Cathedral | I had already shot some gritty pictures of a local market and its characters so I photographed the choirboys as a contrast. But I wanted something different from the usual pictures of them singing, so I hovered around before their practice trying to grab a candid shot. The composition suddenly appeared in front of me. While two boys acknowledged that I was taking their picture, the other two were caught unaware. The image was there and gone in an instant.

Concept

It was late morning and the light was giving a lovely interplay between the wall and the steps. This picture is part of an on-going project called 'Umbra', which is Latin for shadow. I wanted to show the graphic interplay of light and shadow while keeping the composition simple and striking.

Composition

I prefer clean compositions so I cropped in tightly on the scene. The sweep of steps curving upward towards the top left of the picture draws the viewer in and during printing I gave extra exposure to darken that area. That was one strong diagonal and I contrasted that with the straight, angular lines of the steps themselves going in a different direction.

shooting light light and shade

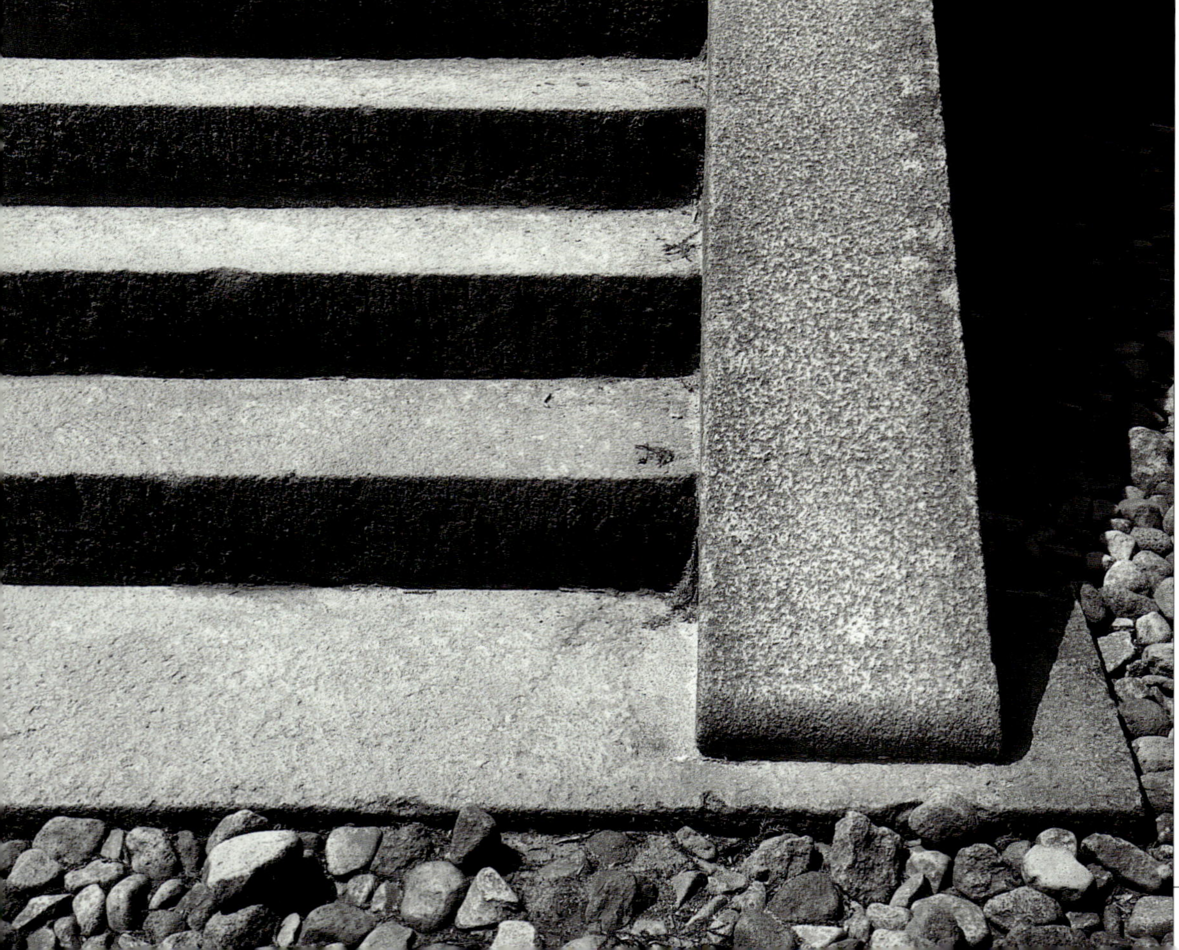

◀ Fact file 2 | Wynn White | Toshogu steps | Another image from my 'Umbra' project. It was late morning and the sun was strong. I was intrigued by the play of light and shadows on the ancient stone steps and decided to keep the composition uncluttered.

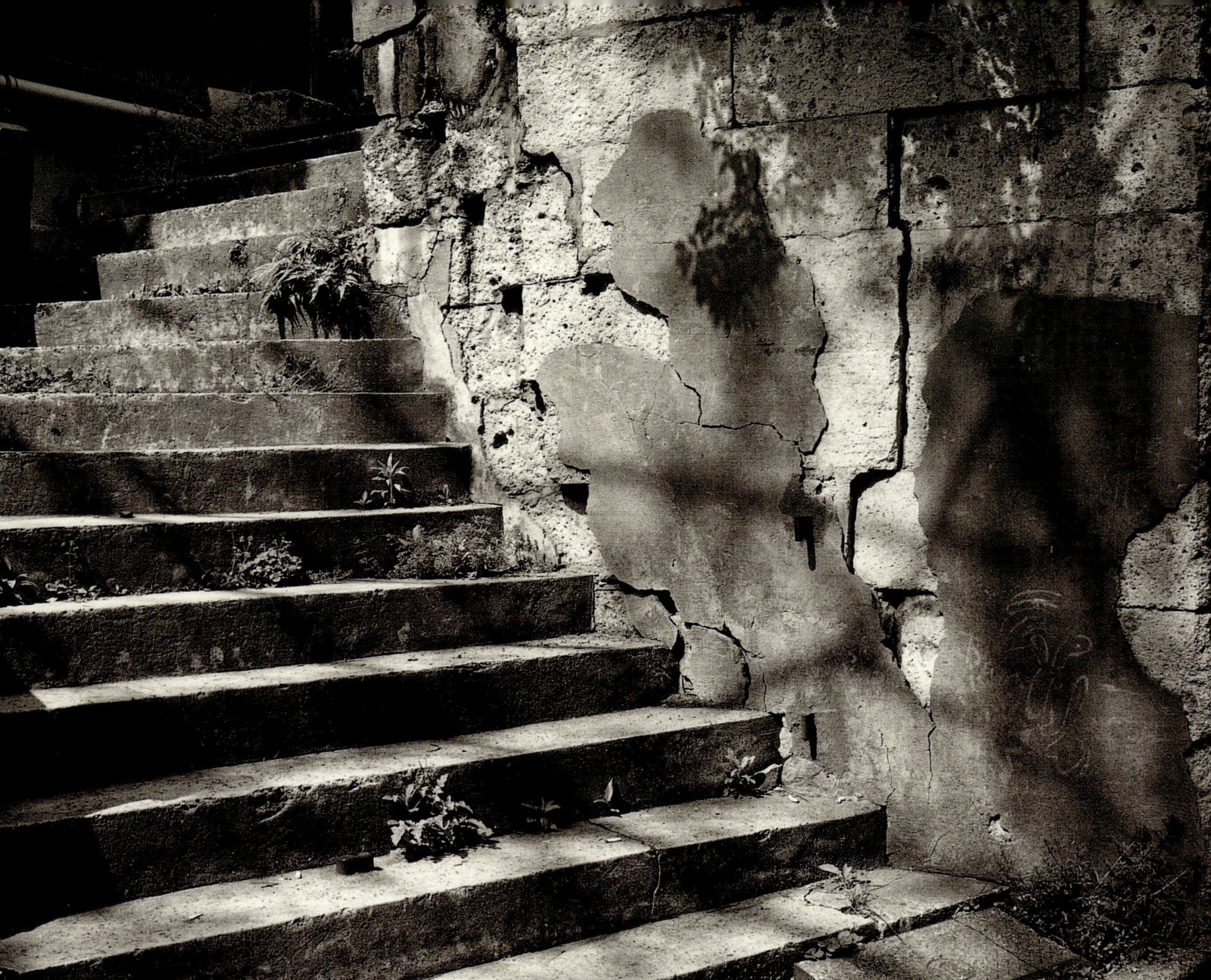

Technique

Metering with print film is important to ensure detail in the shadows. I took a step forward so that I could take a reading from the shadow areas with the camera meter, then went back to my original position to take the picture. It was quite straightforward really, although I did some burning in and dodging when I made the print.

Camera tip

Making notes of which camera settings such as aperture, shutter speed and focal length are used and relating them to the finished pictures is a great way to progress your skills. The most convenient and quickest way to do this is with a small tape recorder. Of course, the important thing is that you regularly transcribe the recordings, say after every shoot.

Fact file 1: Nancy

Photographer: Marco Girolami

Camera: Nikon F4s, lens: 80–200mm f/2.8, film: Kodak T-Max 100, exposure: 1/250sec at f/8, lighting: Elinchrom 1000 fitted with a 70x70cm softbox

Concept

The picture is from a personal beauty shoot. I was keen to explore the girl's face, which I found very photogenic and powerful at the same time. I was very happy with the resulting images.

shooting light in the studio

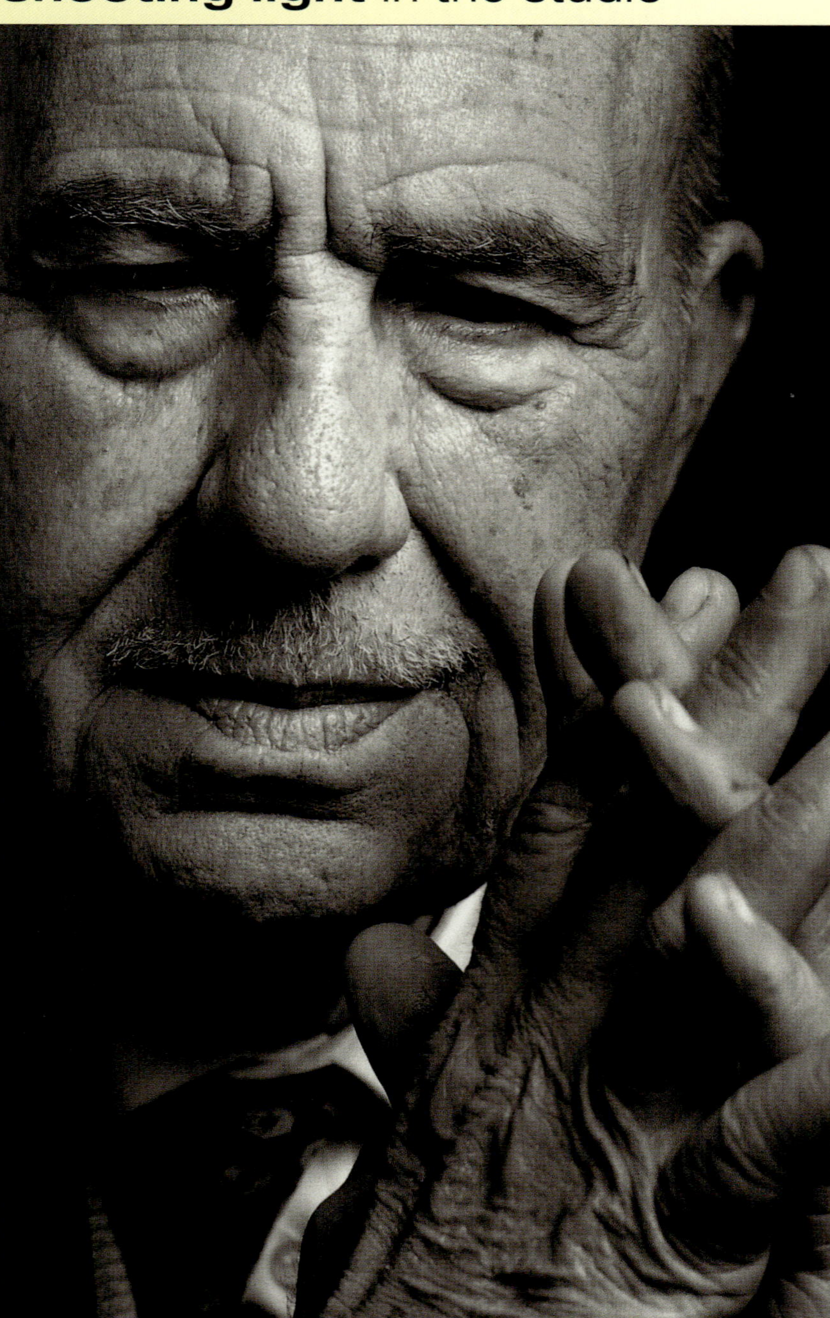

Composition

I like to experiment with the effect of different crops on the impact of the composition. Cropping really tightly as I have done here is a great way of giving a portrait impact but care should be taken because it can look like a mistake. Of course, focusing with a telephoto lens this close to the subject was critical so I took care to make sure the eye area was pin-sharp. I set a mid-lens aperture to give enough depth-of-field.

Technique

I had one main's flash fitted with a softbox which gave a very directional light. To soften any heavy shadows I placed a white reflector panel under her face to bounce light back up. White gives a soft, natural effect which is much more subtle than silver which can be very harsh and too directional. In colour photography, gold reflectors are worth trying because they imbue the scene with a pleasant warmth.

◀ Fact file 2 | Marco Girolami | Vangelli | My aim was to capture a really emotional portrait of this artist for his catalogue. I thought he had a great face for this sort of creative approach. In the studio, I mixed the output from one flash unit with daylight to get this very atmospheric lighting.

Camera tip

Deep shadows are dramatic and add extra modelling but on occasion the effect can be overpowering. The use of reflectors to throw light back into the shadows will help soften shadows and give a more balanced contrast within the image. Specially designed reflectors that fold up are very popular and portable too, but you can just use a sheet of white card or stick some silver kitchen foil onto a piece of hardboard. Careful positioning of the reflector is important so do make sure you check the effect back at the camera position and adjust it to suit the effect that you want.

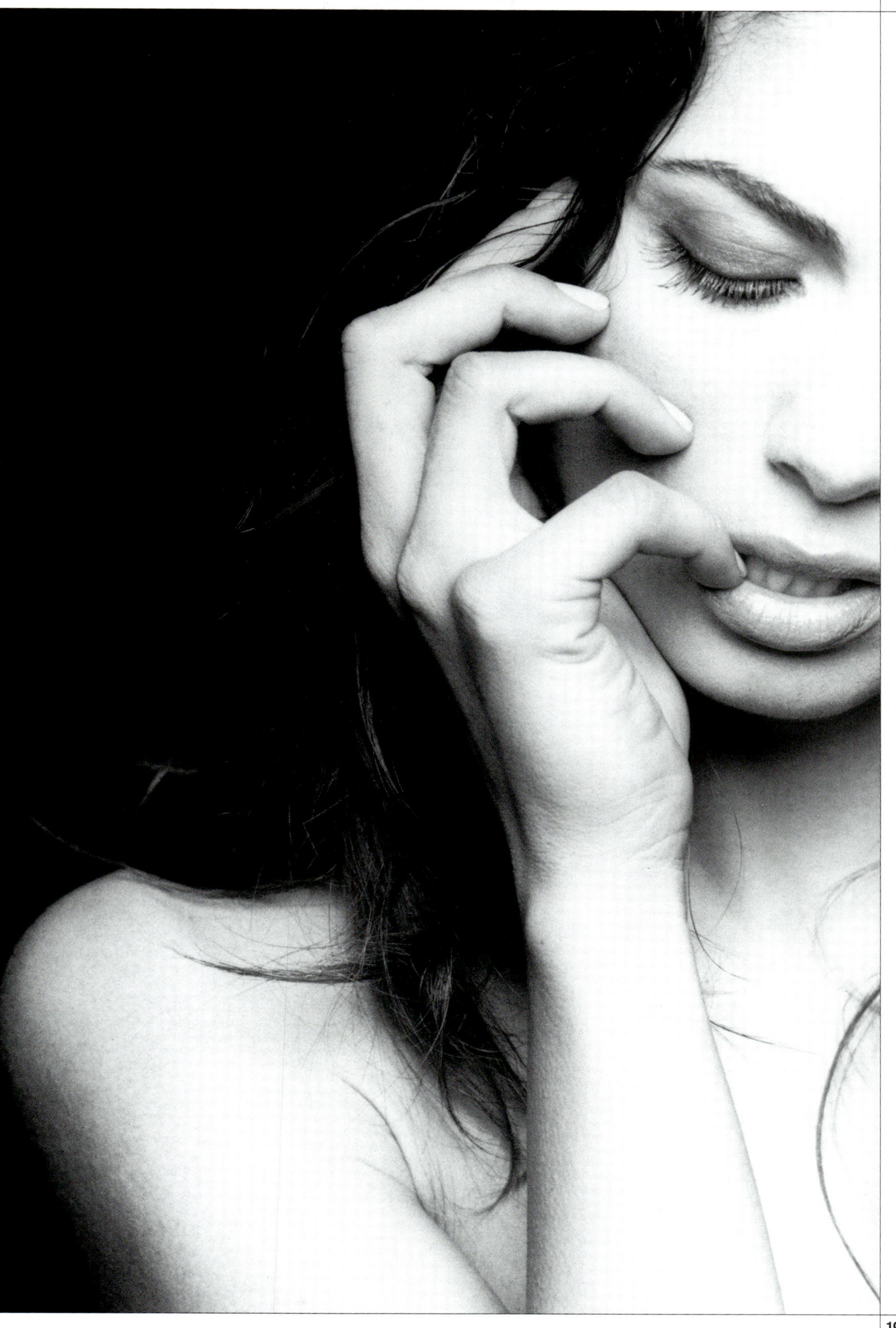

making prints

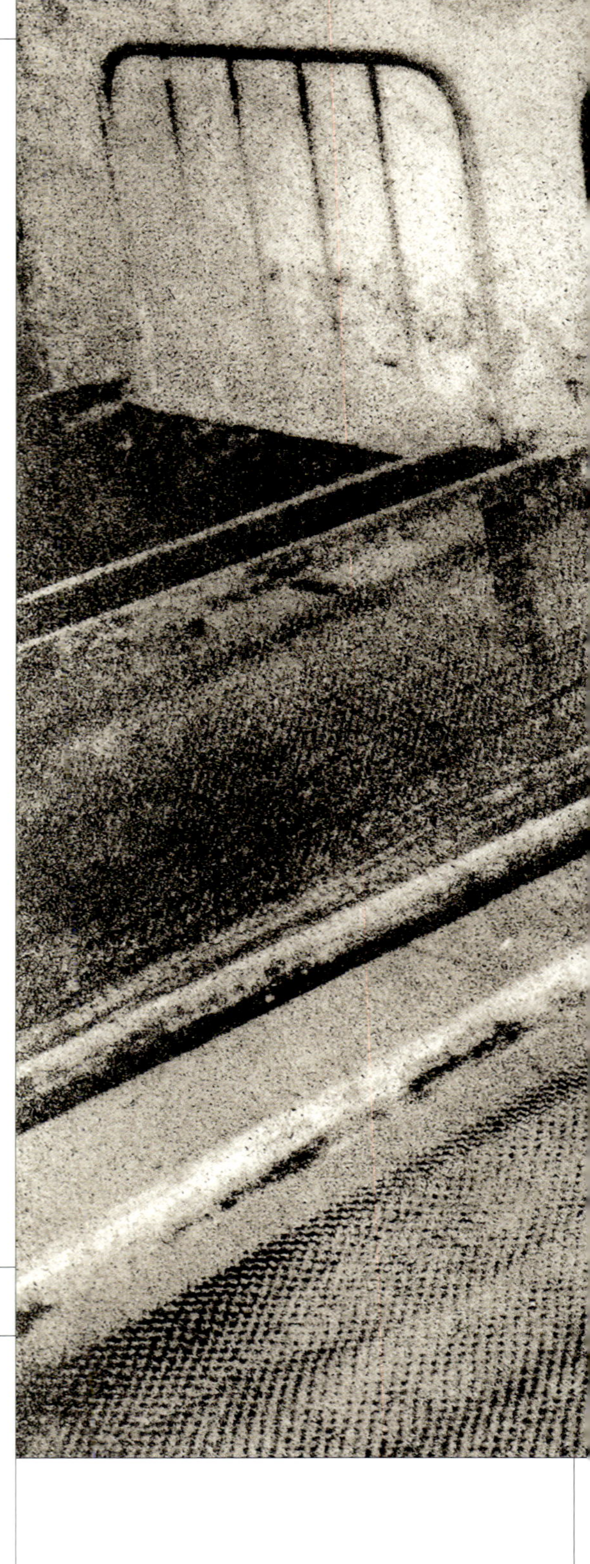

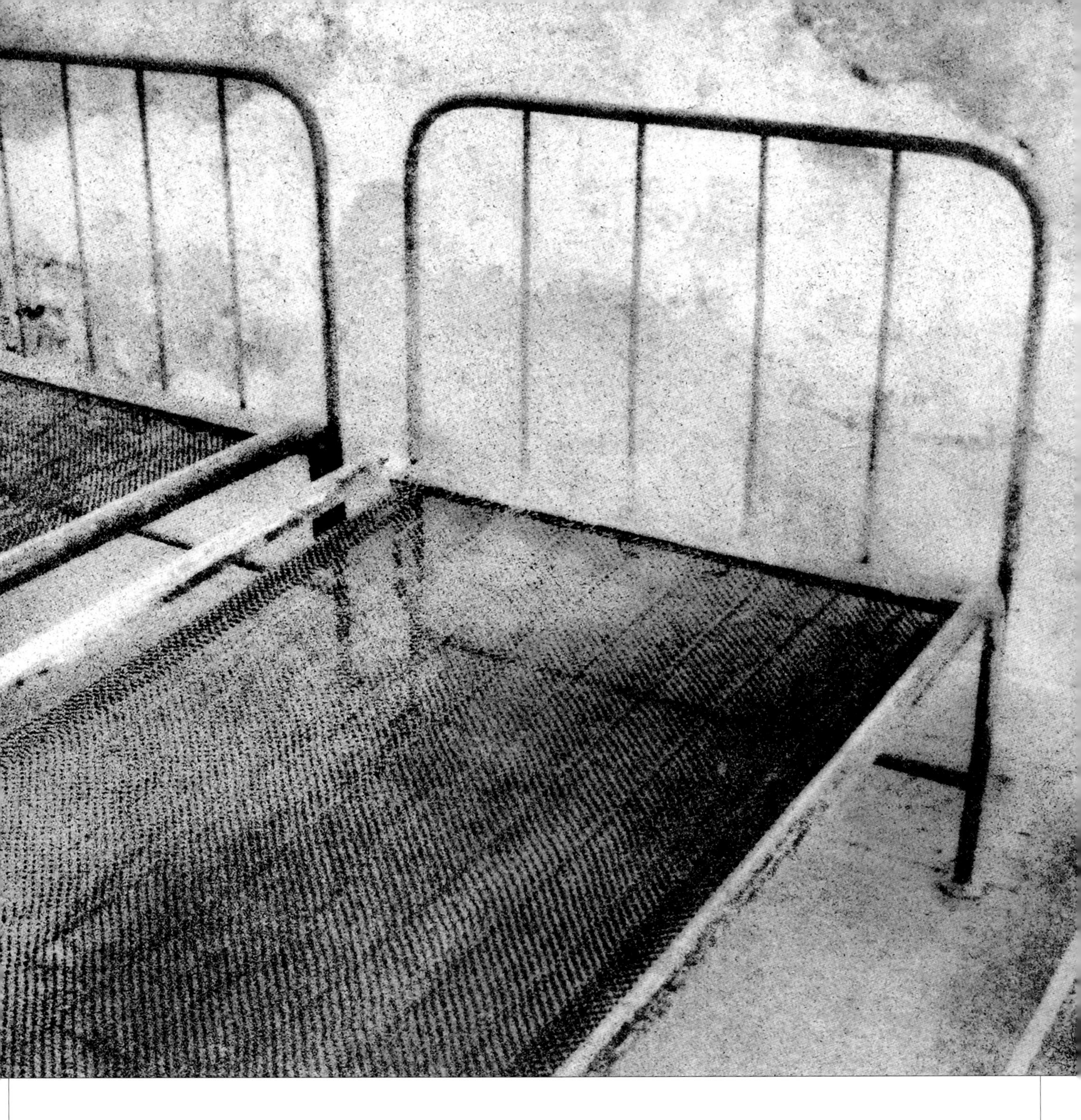

<table>
<tr><td>

</td><td>

</td></tr>
</table>

making prints dodging & burning

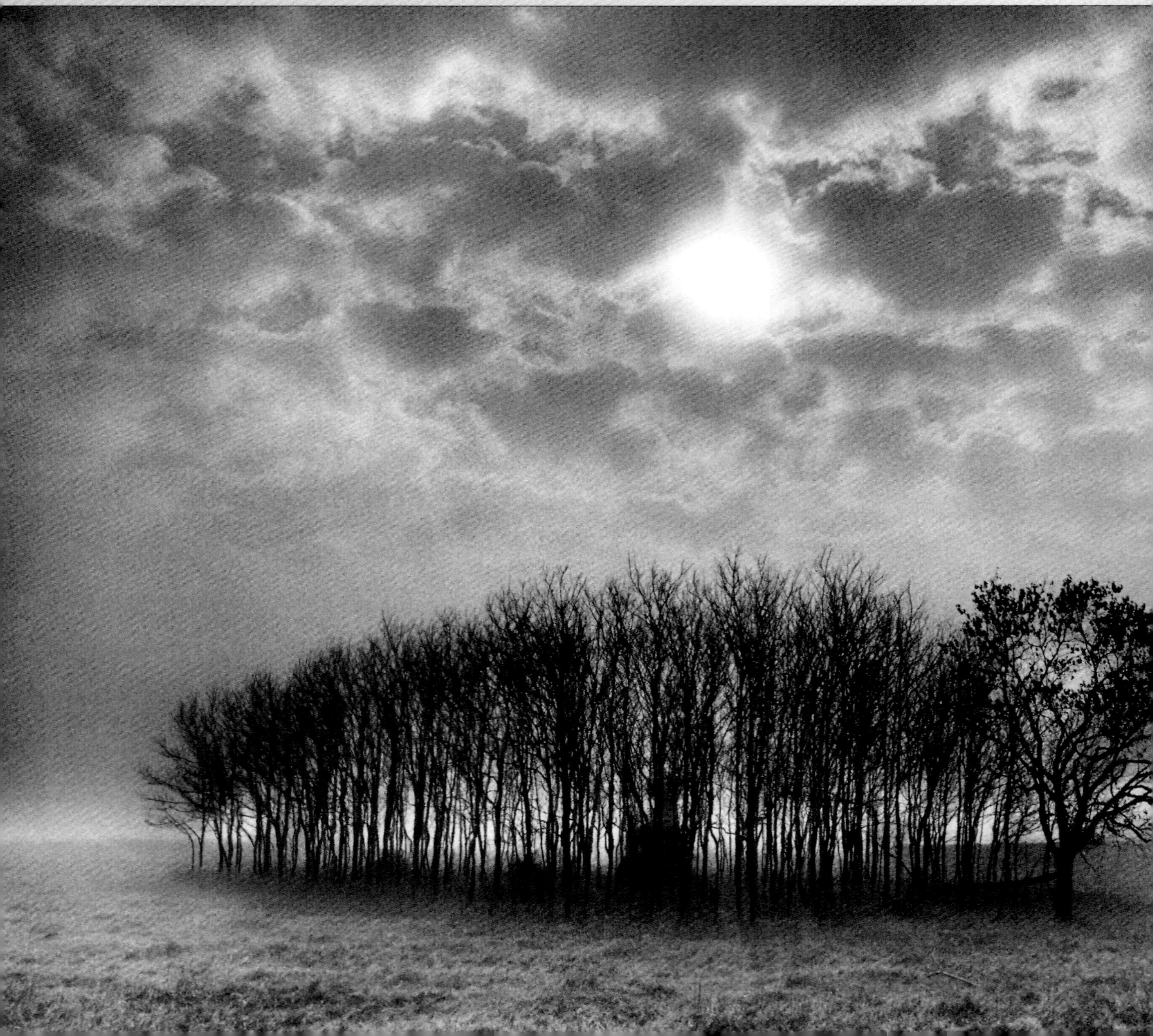

Composition

I am a sucker for symmetry in my images. Perhaps I overuse the centralised subject theme but it is a style that I find myself drawn to over and over. In this case I felt the stand of trees would be best placed low down in the frame which would let me use that wonderful sky to balance the composition.

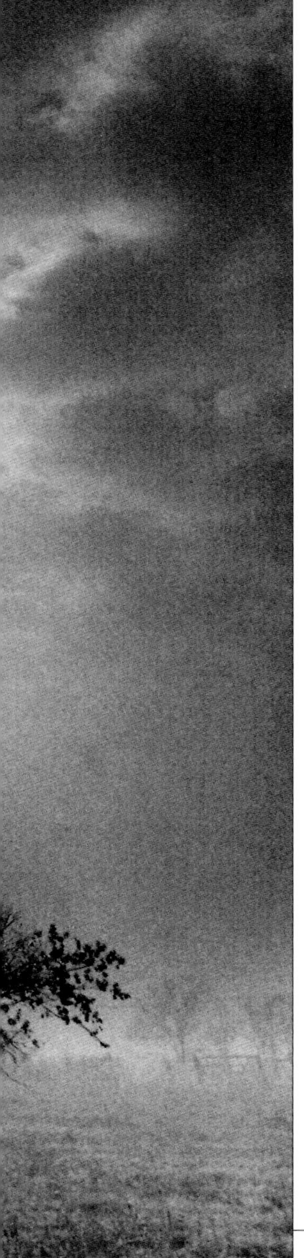

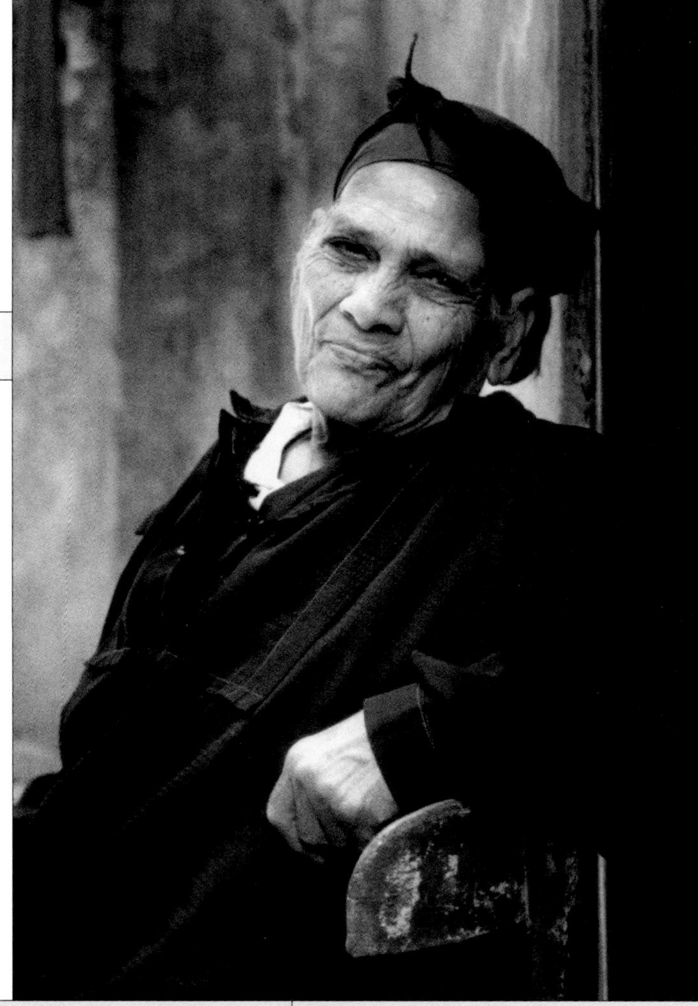

▶ Fact file 2 | Felix Tian | Cairo | This old woman sitting in the shadow of a wall blended in so well with the historic atmosphere of Cairo. I asked her permission and took the picture. I love the woman's aged face and her kind eyes. I gave the background wall extra exposure during printing.

Technique

I had the camera set to aperture-priority autoexposure but because the sun coming through the clouds was very bright in relation to the foreground I had to use exposure compensation to ensure that the negative had enough shadow density. I set it up an extra stop.

During printing, this image required complex on-easel masking to control the densities. The bright sky needed a great deal of extra exposure to reveal the beautiful detail and that had to be done without the foreground getting any more exposure.

I also bleached the tree line at the horizon to keep the feeling of lightness.

Camera tip

Not all black-and-white negatives print perfectly without any help in the way of exposure manipulation during printing. Giving extra exposure (burning-in) and giving less exposure (dodging) are incredibly useful printing techniques to help fulfil your previsualised effect. Hands, fingers, small pieces of Blu-tack held on wire, sheets of card, all can be used, depending on the shape of the area being manipulated.
Dodging and burning-in should not be obvious so using relatively long exposure times is advised for greater control. Of course, test strips are needed to determine how much the exposure should be adjusted by.

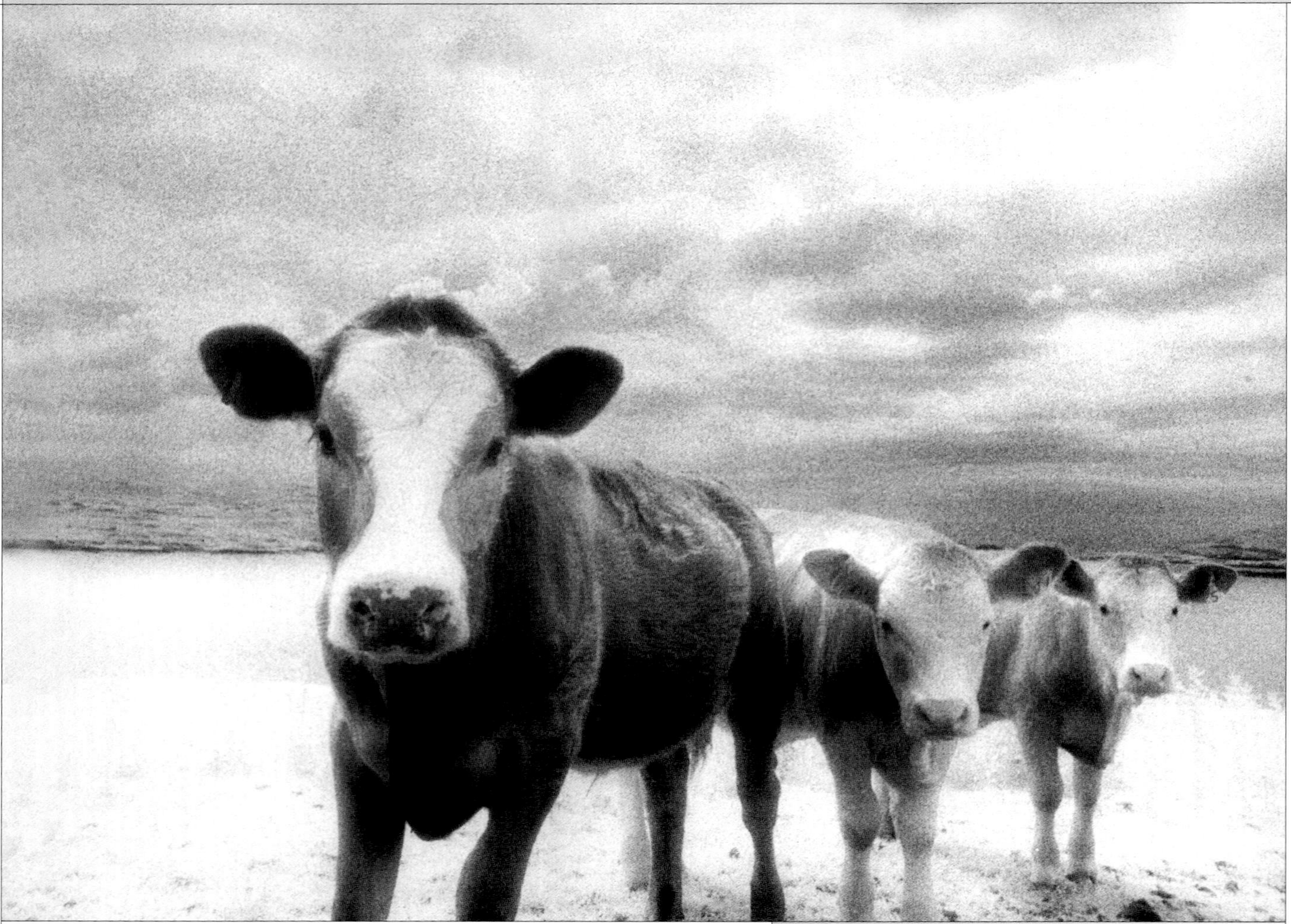

▲ Fact file 3 | William Cheung | Three cows | This photograph was taken on infrared film and because it was a cloudy day the sky did not go very dark which is typical with this film type. Consequently, a great deal of extra exposure during printing was needed to bring out the sky. A card mask was carefully cut out to shield the three cows while the sky was burnt in to bring out the tone. During the printing exposure the card mask was moved around and the height varied to avoid any obvious signs of burning-in.

Camera tip

For more accurate dodging and burning-in, cut a mask from stiff card. Support the card a few inches off the enlarger baseboard, focus the image on it, draw the area you want to manipulate and carefully cut out the mask. Re-focus the image and make the print exposure. To dodge and burn just hold the mask at about the original height and move it slowly around during the exposure to avoid any sharp, obvious edges. Do this right and you will get a tonally balanced print without any obvious signs of manipulation.

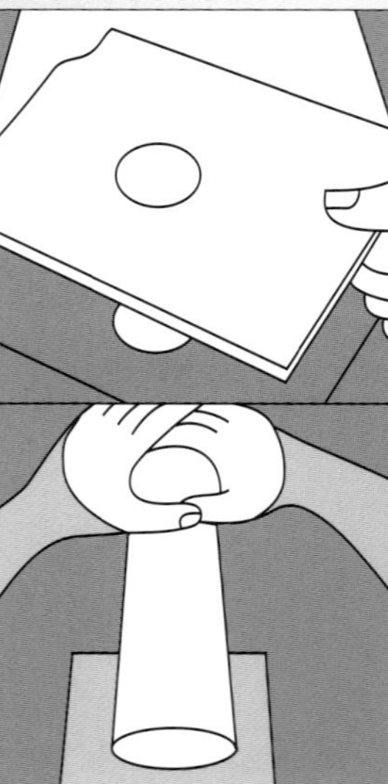

▶ Fact file 4 | Ian McFarlane | Amy in creek | I was trying to make some interesting shots of the model, focusing on her expressive eyes. I think this is a very good image, haunting and strange, helped by the shallow depth-of-field. To concentrate attention on her face I did burn-in all around her to darken everything down. Burning-in the top corners makes it appear as if she is coming into the light.

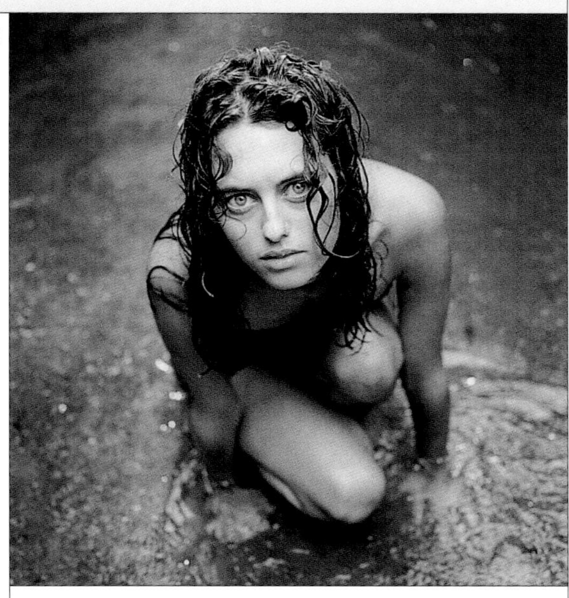

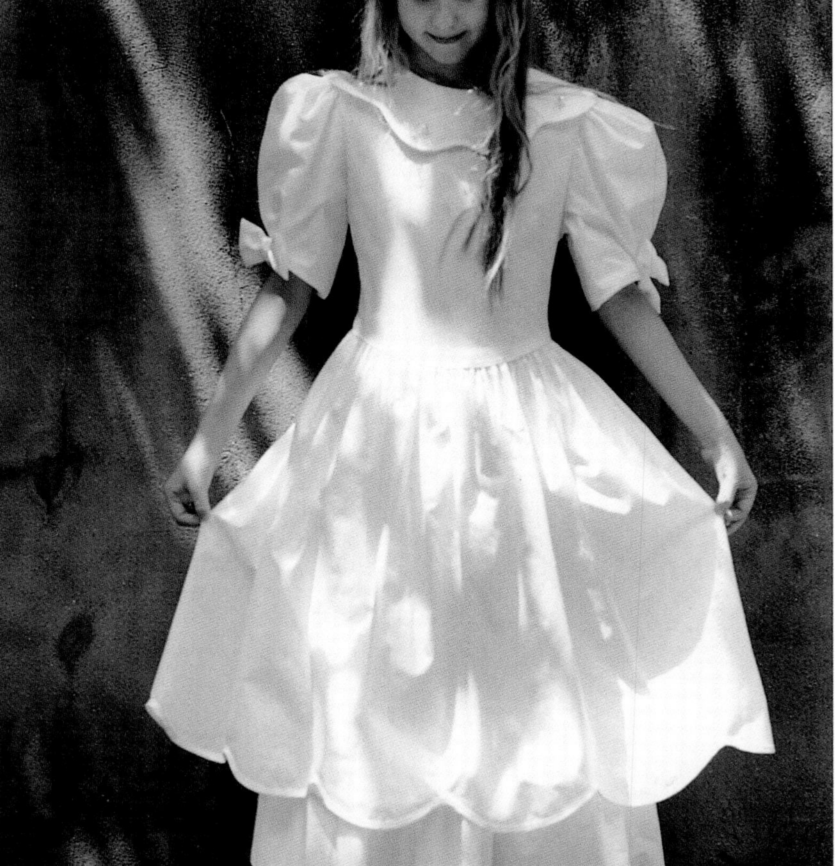

◀ Fact file 5 | Ian McFarlane | Claire's dress | This was a personal portrait of the girl taken late in the day but the contrast was still high, with light coming through the trees. I wanted a textured background but I had to burn-in all around the dress so that it would stand-out boldly against it. I used variable-contrast paper, with grade 2 for the girl's face and grade 3 to give the darker background more intensity.

Fact file 1: Tree by Vietnam Memorial

Photographer: Dan Burkholder

Camera: Nikon F4, lens: 28–85mm, film: Kodak T-Max 400 at ISO 400, developer: Kodak T-Max

making prints adding diffusion

Camera tip

Diffusion can be applied at the taking or the printing stage. In black and white photography, diffusing at the camera stage gives highlights spreading into the shadows, while diffusing at the printing stage has shadows spreading into the mid-tones. The effects are very different and both are worth trying.

A wide variety of materials can be used to add diffusion. The easiest way is to gently breathe on the lens and take the shot as the condensation evaporates. Obviously, this only works in cold days and is difficult to repeat identically time after time. Filters are the most common way to achieve diffused results. Different strengths and types of diffusion are possible so check with the filter manufacturers.

If you diffuse at the taking stage, slight overexposure is advised to give an attractive effect. Setting an extra half-a-stop at least is a good starting point.

Technique

Taking the photograph was straightforward. In normal daylight I used the camera's automatic exposure mode and because I wanted a silhouette no extra compensation was needed.

In the darkroom, I used a diffuser under the lens to add drama to the image. Diffusion at the printing stage causes the dark tones to spread into the lighter areas to give this moody effect. By contrast, diffusion at the taking stage works the opposite way with highlights spreading into the shadows.

There was also extensive burning and dodging to balance the tones in the print.

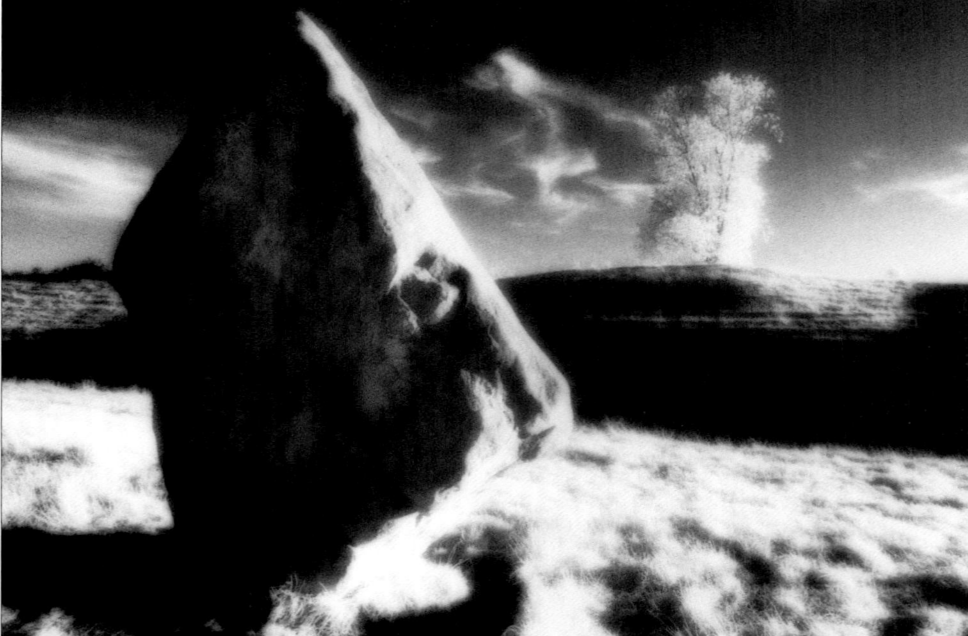

◀ Fact file 2 | William Cheung | Avebury Stone Circle | I wanted to enhance the mood of the ancient stones by diffusing the image during printing. Half of the exposure was made with no diffuser and the second half with. This resulted in a subtly diffused image.

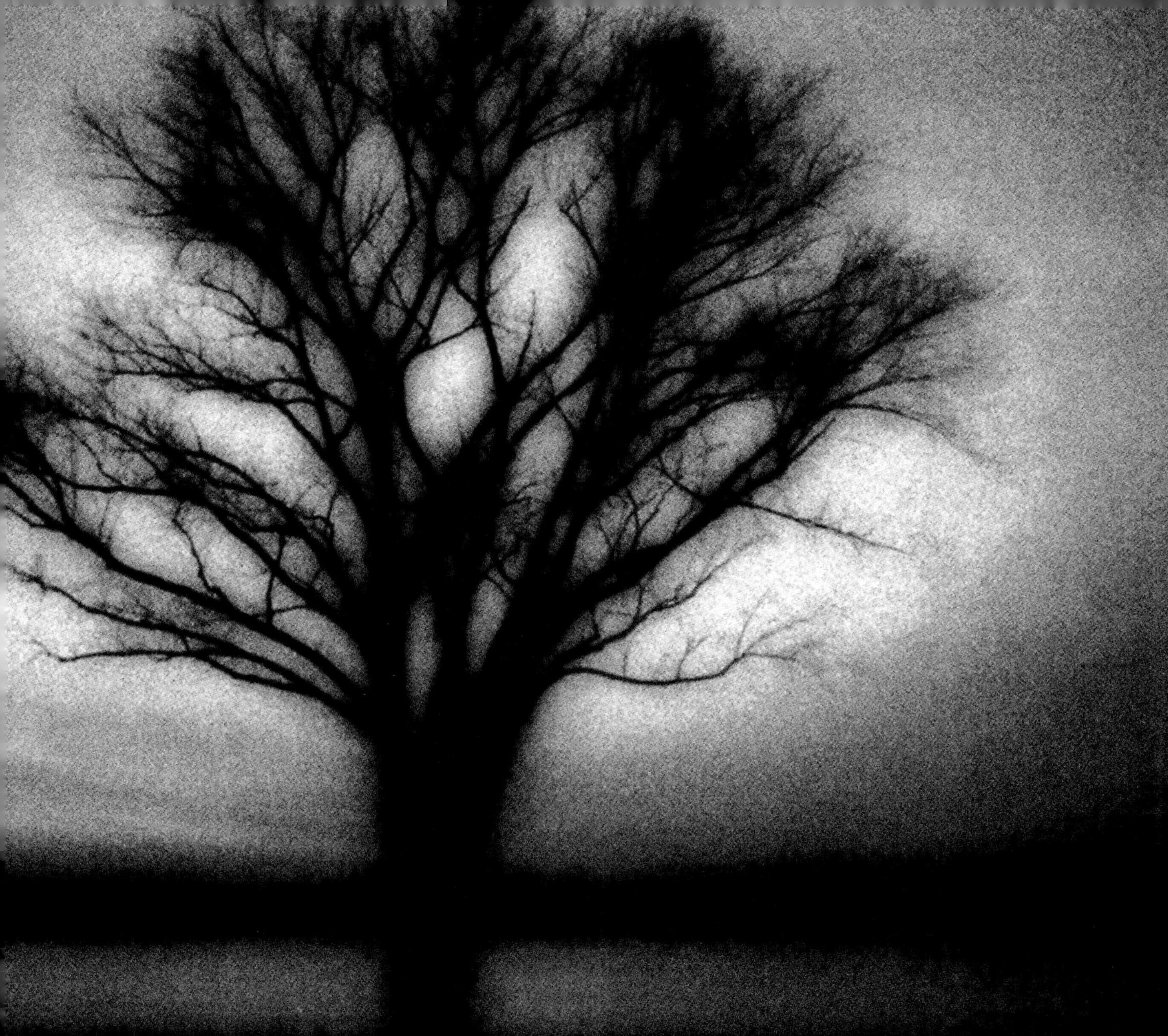

Composition	Concept		
I wanted the silhouetted tree to dominate the composition so placing it right in the middle and filling the frame with it was the obvious thing to do. This also meant it fulfilled my desire for a symmetrical composition.	My aim was to capture and reflect my feelings at the Vietnam Memorial in Washington DC. The mood of the image had to complement the subject matter and even the picture's title is important; it sets the stage for the viewer's response to the picture itself.		

Fact file 1: Mary

Photographer: Wojciech Gepner

Camera: Nikon F80, lens: 70–300mm, film: Fuji Sensia 100, flashgun: Nikon SB-28, software: Adobe Photoshop

▼ Fact file 2 | Wojciech Gepner | Clint | My aim was for a straight and simple composition, but perhaps I used too long a lens which made the face appear too flat. The harsh noon light of summer filtering through trees gave a very dramatic effect but using Adobe Photoshop helped to produce the desired effect.

making prints from colour originals

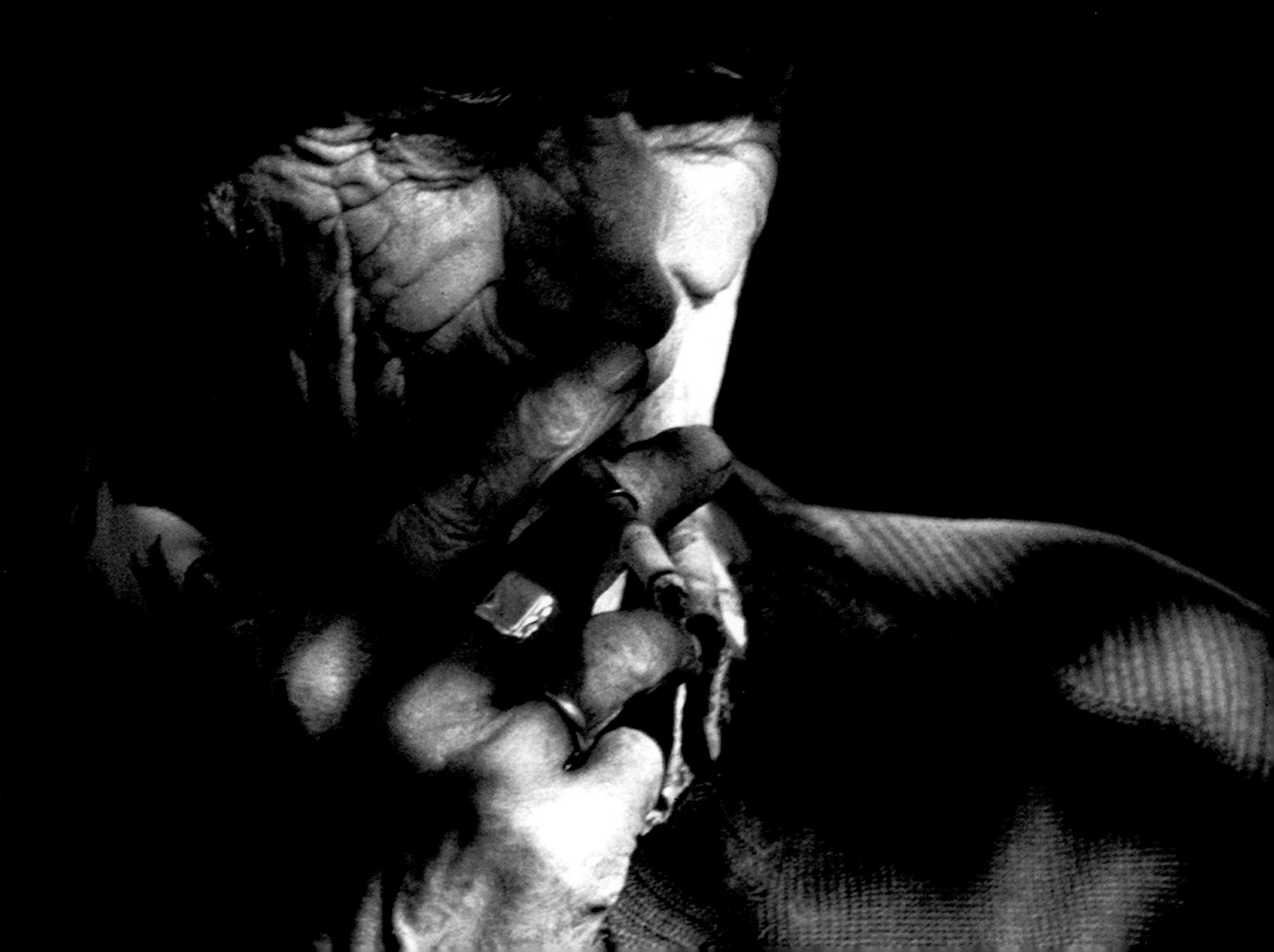

Concept

Positioning the woman against an area of darkness makes her stand out prominently in the composition.

I cropped down the rectangular 35mm format of the original slide to a square shape because I felt it suited this portrait much more effectively. I set her face slightly off-centre in the frame to add an extra element of intrigue to the dramatic portrait.

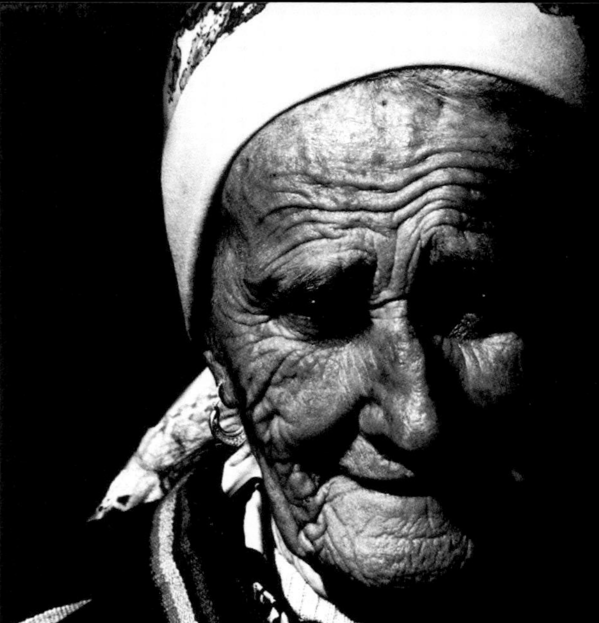

Camera tip

Many photographers only use a flashgun when there is not enough light. But flash can also be used in bright daylight, especially for portraits. This is called fill-in flash and helps to lower the picture's contrast by lightening any heavy shadows in the face. it also gives attractive catchlights to the eyes. The trick with fill-in flash is not to have too much, which can look unnatural. Experiment with your flash and see which output settings you prefer.

Technique

Very strong harsh summer light gave a very contrasty effect which is what I wanted. However, I did use a flashgun for fill-in flash to add catchlights to the eyes.

The colour slide was scanned as 256 shades of grey and I adjusted Levels in Adobe Photoshop. Because of the very high contrast, correction of the brightest highlights was very important.

Composition

Old faces tell stories and that is what I wanted to show in this picture. I wanted to show how much life and character this woman had. The strong lighting given by an almost overhead sun has really brought out the lines of the face to give a powerful portrait.

Photographer: James Webb

Camera: Hasselblad 503CX, lens: 80mm, film: Kodak T-Max 400 at ISO 400, exposure: 35secs at f/22, developer: Kodak T-Max

Concept

This was taken on a mild winter evening and the sky had an odd orange glow. It was that which attracted me. Whenever I perceive something that I connect with, I like to try to take a photograph of it to discover if that connection can be preserved in a picture.

making prints lith printing

Camera tip

Put simply, lith printing is processing the exposed printing paper in a lith developer. The success of this technique depends on several factors. First, is the choice of paper. Some types give more pleasant warm tones than others so it is worth trying different types. Second, the print has to be removed or 'snatched' from the developer and the development stopped with a fresh stop bath and the timing of this is critical. This is done by inspection under red safe-lighting. Lith development is 'infectious' so it builds up slowly before accelerating quickly, and removing the print when the effect looks just right is important.

Composition

I wanted to retain the feeling of depth within the scene and positioned myself so that this interesting tree ran down the centre of the composition. Its shape and the darker tones produced the desired effect and make for a strong focal point while taking the viewer into the fine details in the background.

Technique

A spot meter was used to take readings from the most important areas of the scene. I then overexposed by two stops to ensure adequate detail in the dark areas of the tree and to allow for a soft quality in the middle values of the negative. Film development, in Kodak T-Max developer, was reduced too.

In the darkroom I used Bergger Warmtone VC paper which was processed through Fotospeed LD lith developer. This combination gives good lith prints with an attractive tone and subtle details.

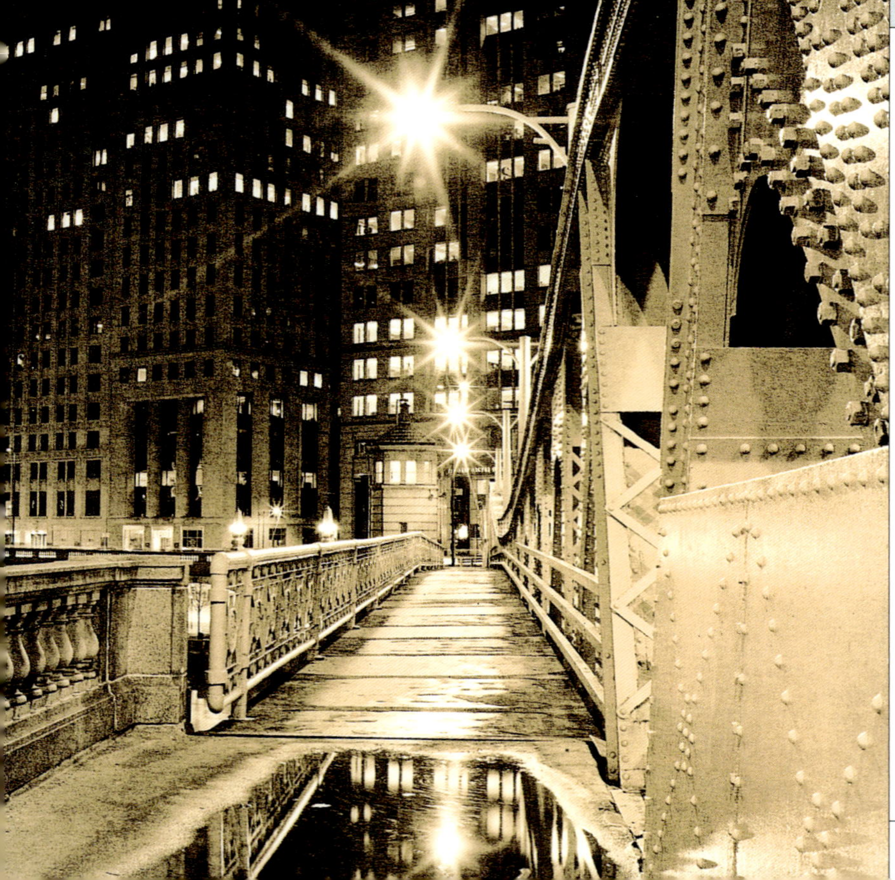

◀ Fact file 2 | James Webb | Orleans Street Bridge | It was a freezing evening and there were no people around. The cold moist air was saturating most of the things I was photographing and gave this scene an eye-catching sheen. Lith printing gave the effect I previsualised at the time.

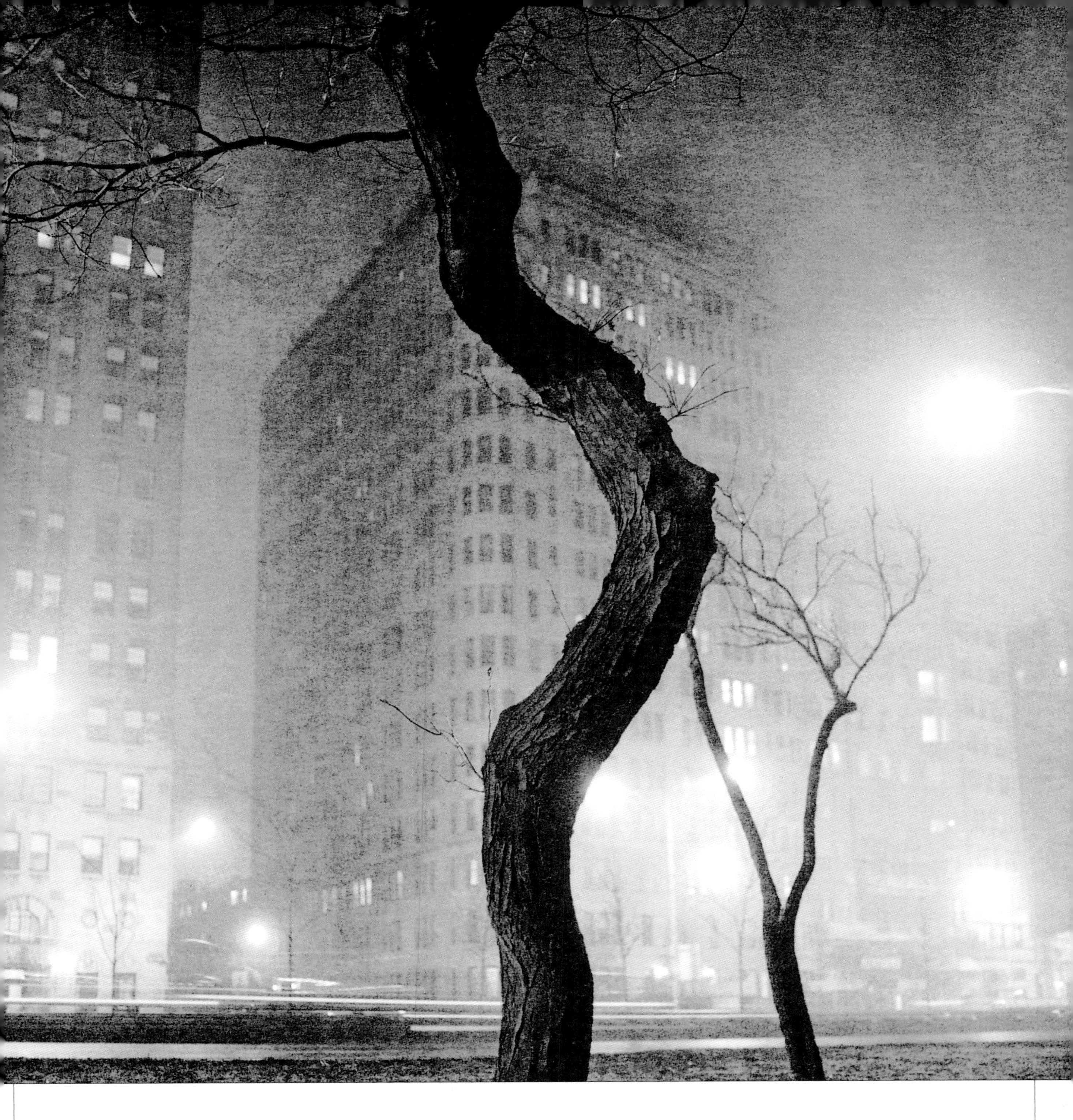

Photographer: Dan Burkholder

Camera: Nikon F4, lens: 20mm, film: Kodak T-Max 400 at ISO 400, developer: Kodak T-Max, paper: platinum/palladium, software: Adobe Photoshop

making prints multiple printing

Concept

I am more attracted to wide-angle shooting than using telephoto lenses. For example, I am magnetically attracted to the forced perspective caused by aiming an ultra-wide 20mm lens down. The mood of the river Ganges on this early morning was incredible and it was this I wanted to capture.

Technique

To enhance the atmosphere I decided to add a different sky. Actually, it's a sky which I photographed in Texas. In this instance I did the multiple print in the wet darkroom, though I would probably now do it on the computer.

I made test prints for both negatives before trying to combine the print. Once I knew the correct print exposure times, I exposed the Ganges negative while masking off the sky area. Next, I swapped negatives, masked the boat foreground then exposed the previously masked area with the moody sky. With some gentle movement of the mask during the two exposures I got a seamless join.

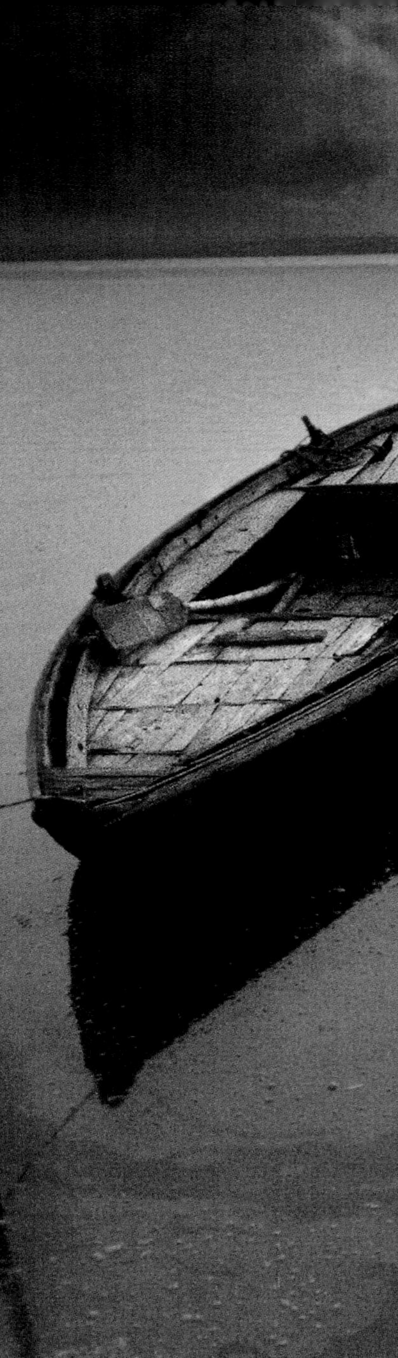

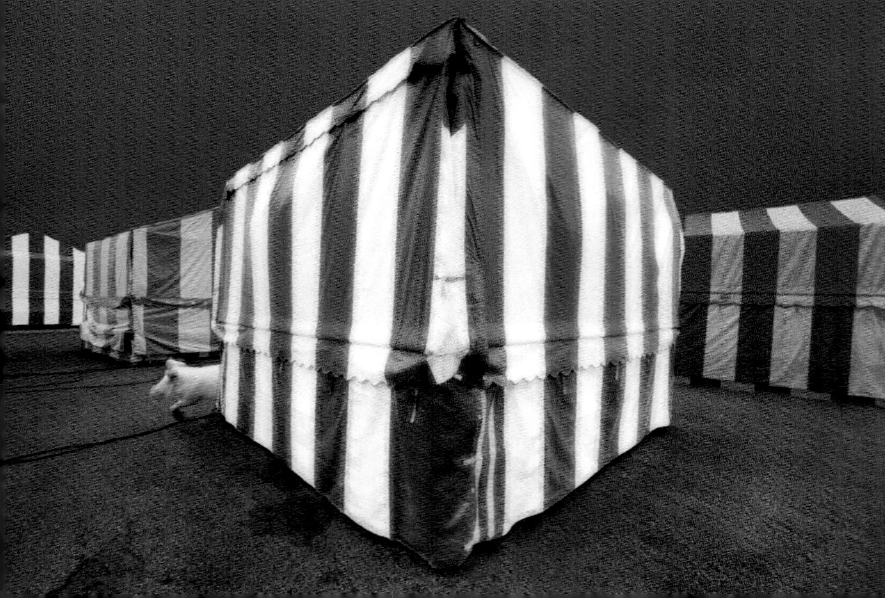

▼ Fact file 2 | Dan Burkholder | Tents with little pig | Whatever gets in front of my camera that has elements of beauty or visual intrigue, I take it. In this case I love the design of the tents and the surprise of the pig – you can also see my attraction for symmetry. The pig image started life as a colour slide and the tents were a black-and-white negative. I combined the two images in Adobe Photoshop and carefully controlled the contrast of each tent to get that receding effect. In the final result the pig is a strong visual magnet to attract the viewer.

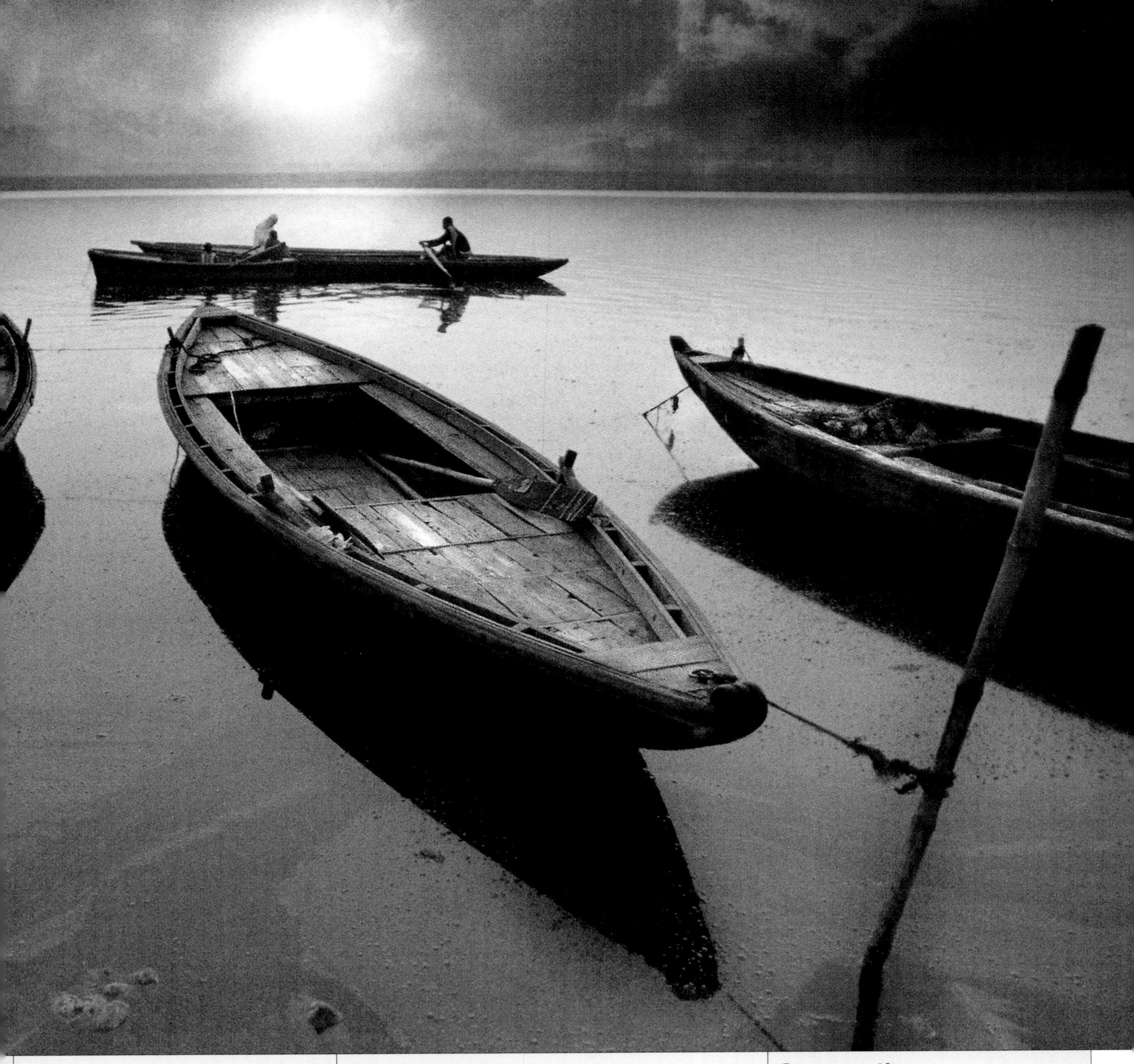

Composition

The angles of the boats rendered by the wide-angle lens helps to draw the viewer into the picture. Ultimately, I think it is that boat in the background that finishes off the composition extremely well.

Camera tip

The success of combining images, whether in the darkroom or on the computer, is largely dependent on the original images. The concept obviously has to be good, but it is also very important that the component images have similar lighting. If you start combining images featuring vastly different lighting conditions, the effect will be visually jarring.

making prints toning

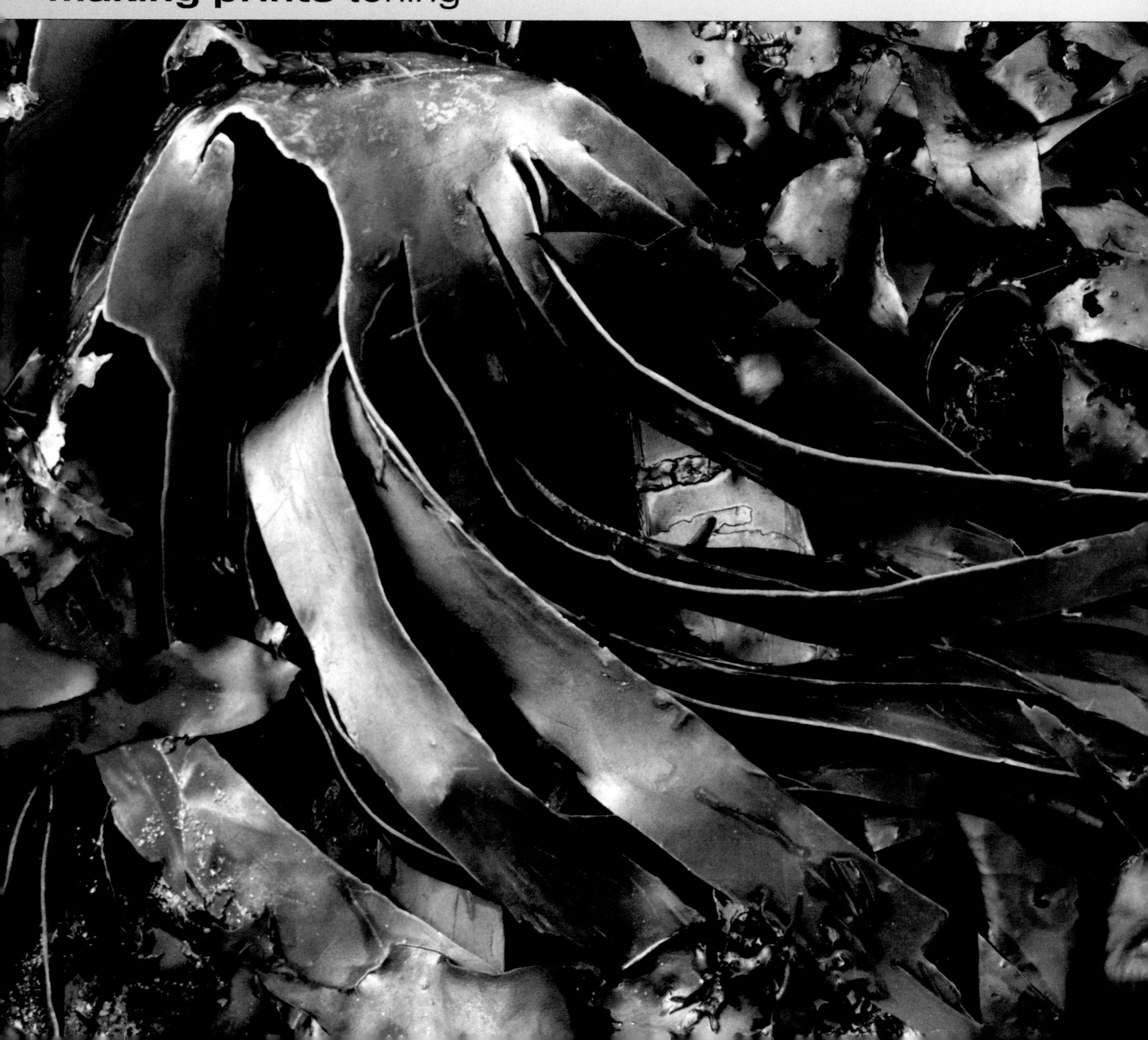

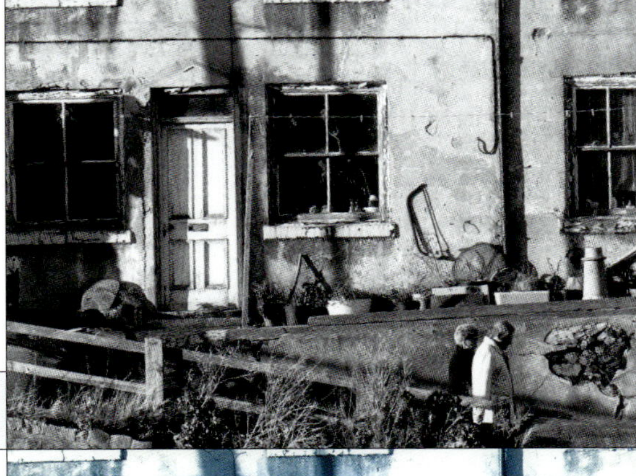

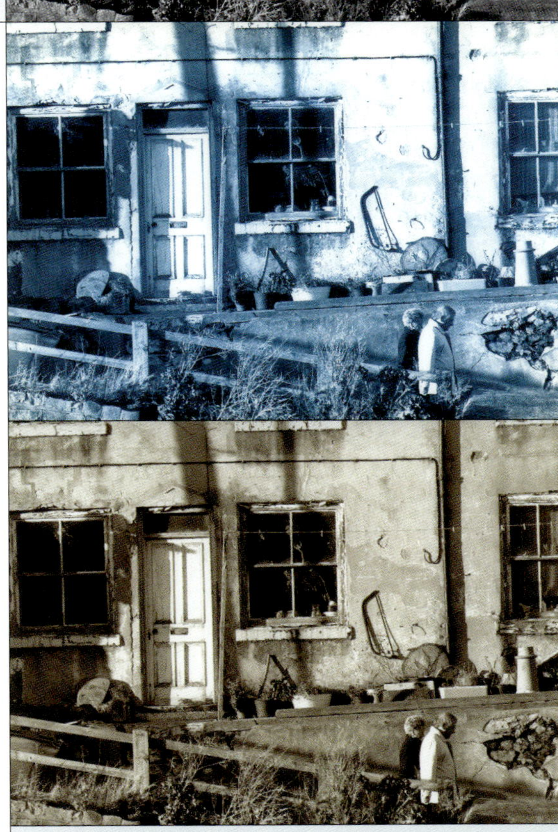

Concept

There were large clumps of photogenic seaweed washed up along the beach and I wanted to explore the textures and shapes within the weed. It was a cloudy day so there was no problem with high contrast, which is the result of strong sunlight. A macro lens was not needed but an 85mm short telephoto lens was used at its minimum focusing distance to allow tightly cropped photographs.

Composition

With so many good potential photographs it was important to explore options through the viewfinder to save wasting too much film. In this picture, it was the gentle sweeping curves of the seaweed fronds that attracted my lens. The scene was more or less as I found it, but a few bits of debris were moved for a cleaner composition. To my mind, this form of 'gardening' is perfectly acceptable if it enhances the final result.

Technique

The straight black-and-white print seemed to lack the depth and feeling that I felt at the time, which is why I resorted to a toning technique. I wanted a subtle effect that added a touch of realism to the print without making it too obvious that the picture was toned. Home-mixed thiocarbamide toner was used. The fibre-paper print was first bleached before being thoroughly washed and toned.

Camera tip

Toning is done to alter the image's tint but it can also enhance print stability. Selenium, for example, is a popular toner for giving better print permanence and it can do this with a subtle colour change. Black-and-white prints made on colour paper will not accept toning techniques, so if you want to try toning get prints made on silver-based black-and-white paper.

Fact file 1: Stairwell, Fort Popham

Photographer: David W Lewis

Camera: Hasselblad, lens: 150mm, film: Kodak Tri-X ISO 400 rated at ISO 320, exposure: 2secs at f/8 reading taken using a spot meter, developer: Amidol, paper: David Lewis's bromoil paper

Camera tip

Many cameras have a spot meter which lets you measure light from small parts of the scene. Photographers love them because they are so specific but they can cause problems for the inexperienced because it is important to meter from the right areas and then make adjustments should they be needed. With black-and-white print film the best place to take a reading is from a mid-tone.

Composition

▼ **Fact file 2 | David W Lewis | Charles Carr | The bromoil process has brought out stunning textures on this portrait and has added enormously to the mood of the image.**

I was attracted to the texture and strong lines of this stairwell. I knew that the image would work well with the bromoil process and produce a very effective composition. The square format of the camera suits the image well and I think it encourages the viewer to enter the picture and climb the stairs.

Concept

The bromoil process is an old one but serious collectors, galleries and museums worldwide consider the process a vital and important art form within photography. I have been working in the pigment process for over 30 years and my images have been widely exhibited throughout North America, Europe and Asia. Art galleries, museums, corporations as well as private collectors have acquired my work for their permanent collections.

making prints bromoil

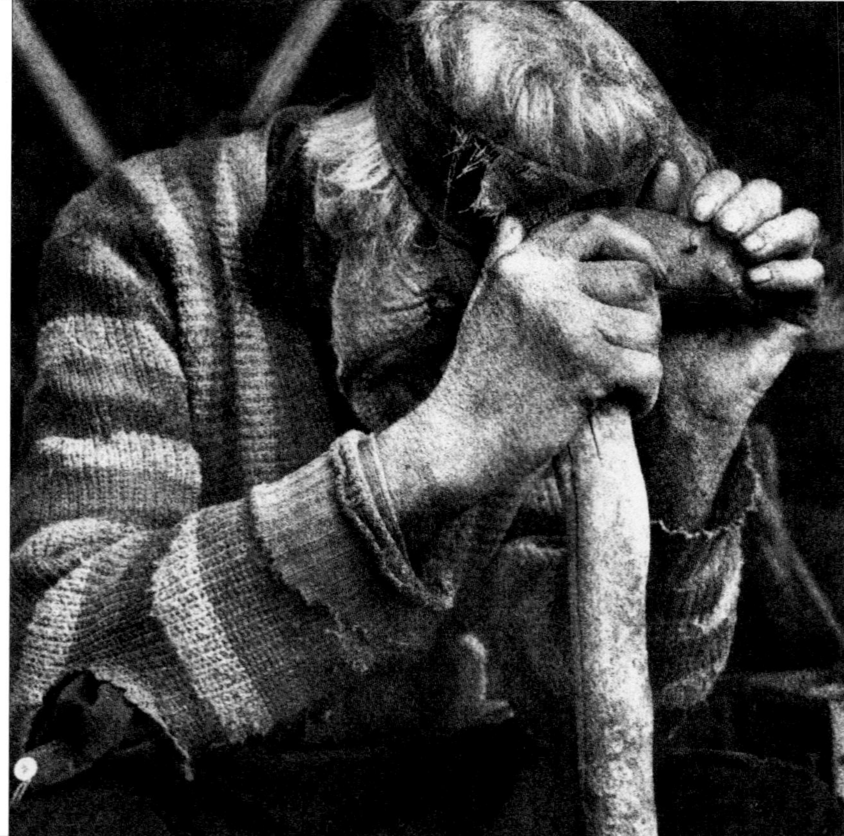

Technique

The bromoil process was invented in 1907 by Welbourne Piper. A bromoil print is a silver bromide or chlorobromide photograph which has had its silver removed and replaced by a stiff pigment. It is done by first immersing the print in a chemical solution which bleaches away the silver image and converts into degrees of insolubility the gelatin coating which held the silver. This print is now called the matrix and is soaked in warm water and here the gelatin swells in inverse proportion to the amount of silver originally in the emulsion. As a result, in the shadow areas the gelatin is very hard and thus swells very little. The highlights, on the other hand, swell considerably and go soft. The tonal values between the highlights and the shadows are hardened proportionally. When a stiff ink is applied with a bromoil brush to the damp gelatin surface, the ink is freely accepted in the darker tonal values.

A skilled bromoil worker has incredible control over the final appearance of the print. Tonal values can be enhanced with skilful manipulation of the brush while atmosphere and recession can be created by varying the amount of pigment added or removed from the matrix.

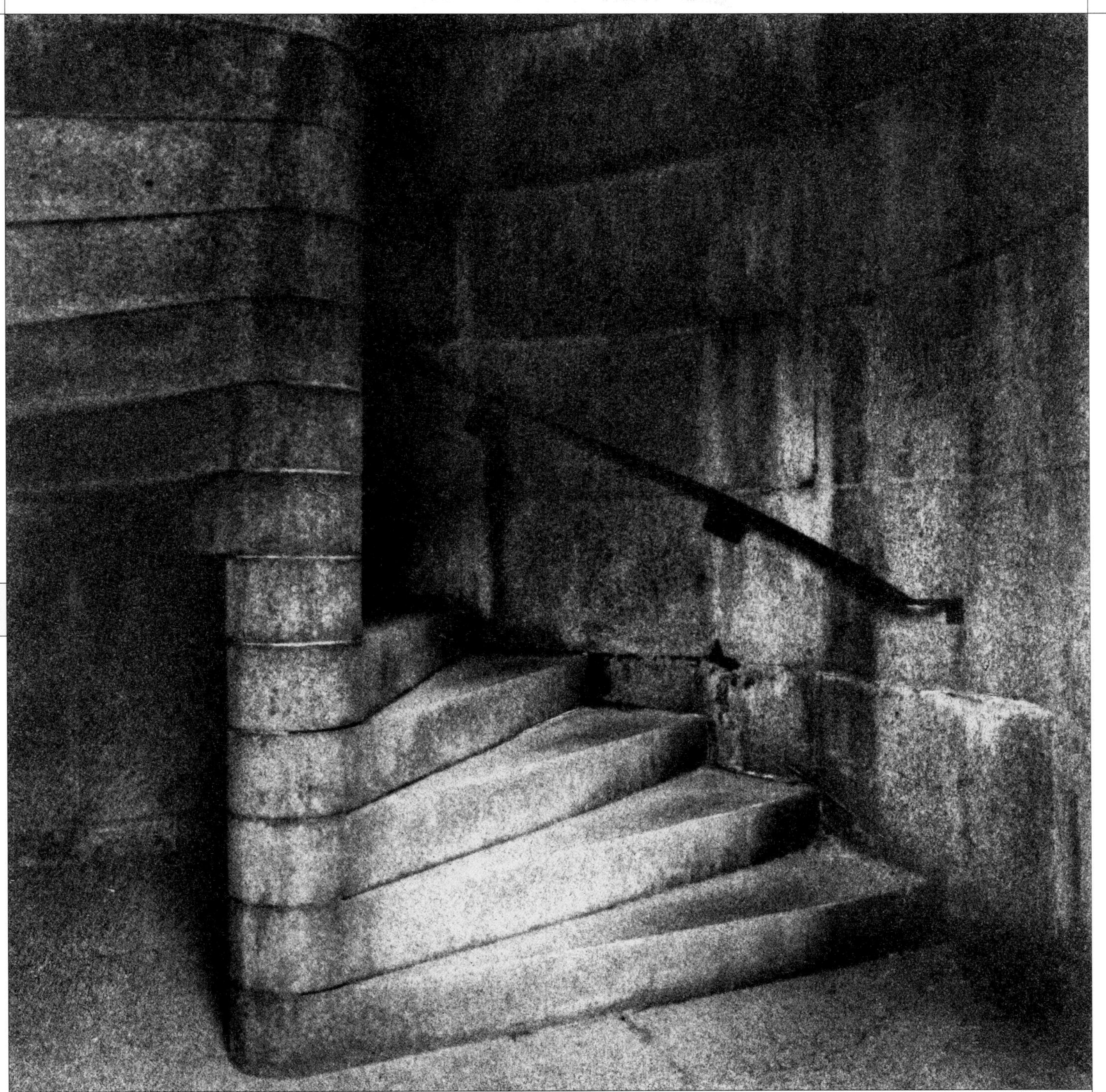

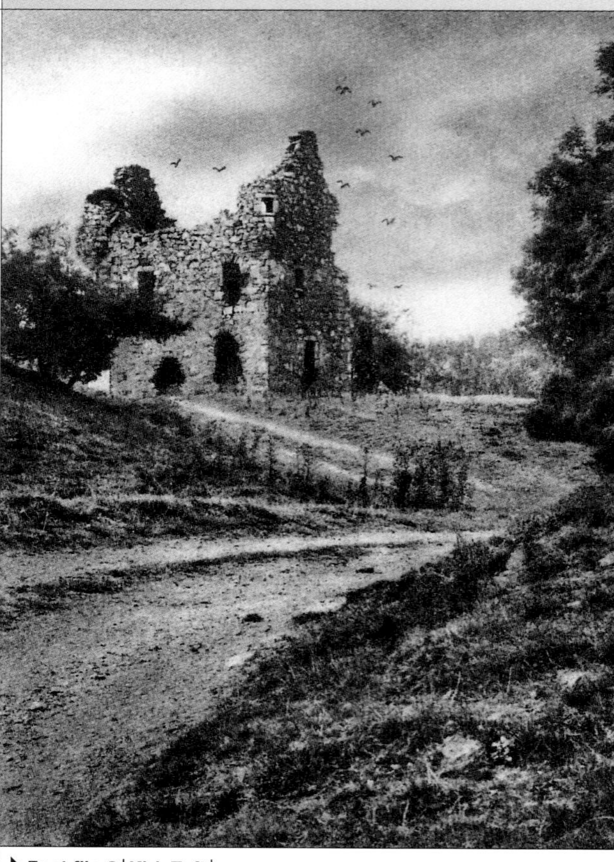

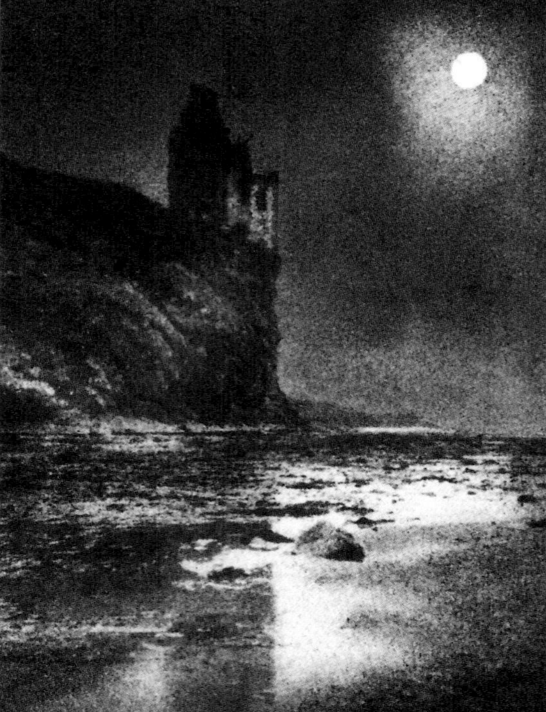

◀ Fact file 4 | Kirk Toft | Plunton Castle, north view | I looked for a camera viewpoint which would give a feeling of isolation in context with the castle's surroundings and with the track leading the viewer into the scene.
It was a hazy sunny day and because I want a negative with plenty of detail I overexposed by two stops and then underdeveloped the film.
Like Fact file 3, I made the print using the Oleobrom-Bromoil process.

▶ Fact file 3 | Kirk Toft | Greenan Castle, Moonlight | I took this picture on a very dull day, which I prefer because I want a low-contrast negative with plenty of detail in the highlights and shadows. There was actually no sky detail which is why I made it into a 'moonlit' scene.
I make a print that is low contrast so the shadows are more grey than black and the highlights are slightly veiled. This is because all my final prints are made using the Oleobrom-Bromoil process, although this image was transferred onto art paper using an etching process.

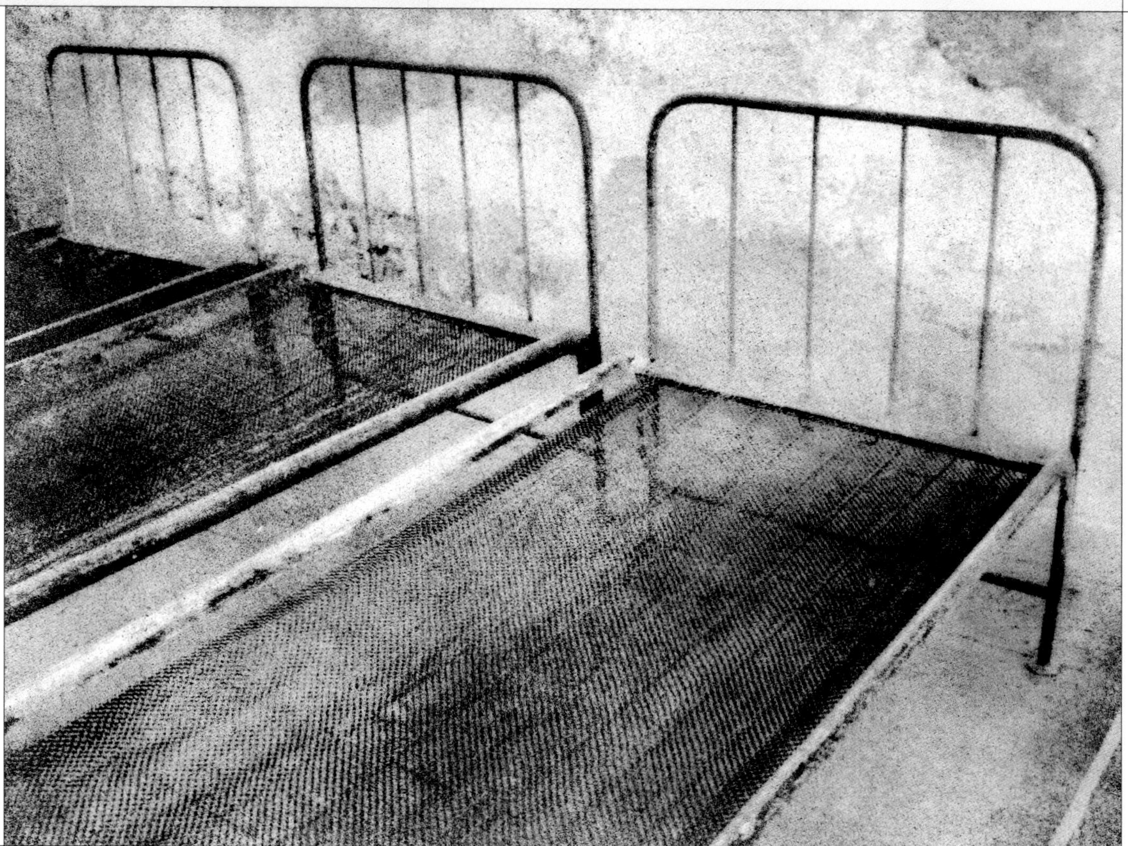

▲ Fact file 5 | Jill Skupin |
Three beds | This picture
was taken digitally in very
poor light and it is of
Terezin, near Prague in the
Czech Republic, which
served as a Gestapo prison
during World War II. I
wanted to capture the
haunting absence of people
and of the strong sense of
loss. From the file I made a
digital negative using Epson
Glossy film on an inkjet
printer and from that I
made a bromoil print. The
print started as a
conventional black-and-
white print, which I dried,
bleached and then soaked
before using brushes to
apply oil-based lithographic
inks to reconstruct the
image. These soaking and
inking steps were repeated
to give the final print its
richness and delicacy.

Camera tip

Most modern cameras are
wholly battery reliant so it
is worth checking the cell
regularly. Most cameras
display the battery's status
or have a check facility.
But whatever the battery's
condition have a spare
battery or two in the bag
just in case. When you do
change the battery, use a
cotton bud soaked in
alcohol to clean the
contacts before slipping
the new one in place.
Extreme cold affects
battery performance so in
the winter keep the
camera tucked inside the
front of your jacket and
have spares in a warm
pocket so you can
continue shooting.

making prints photograms

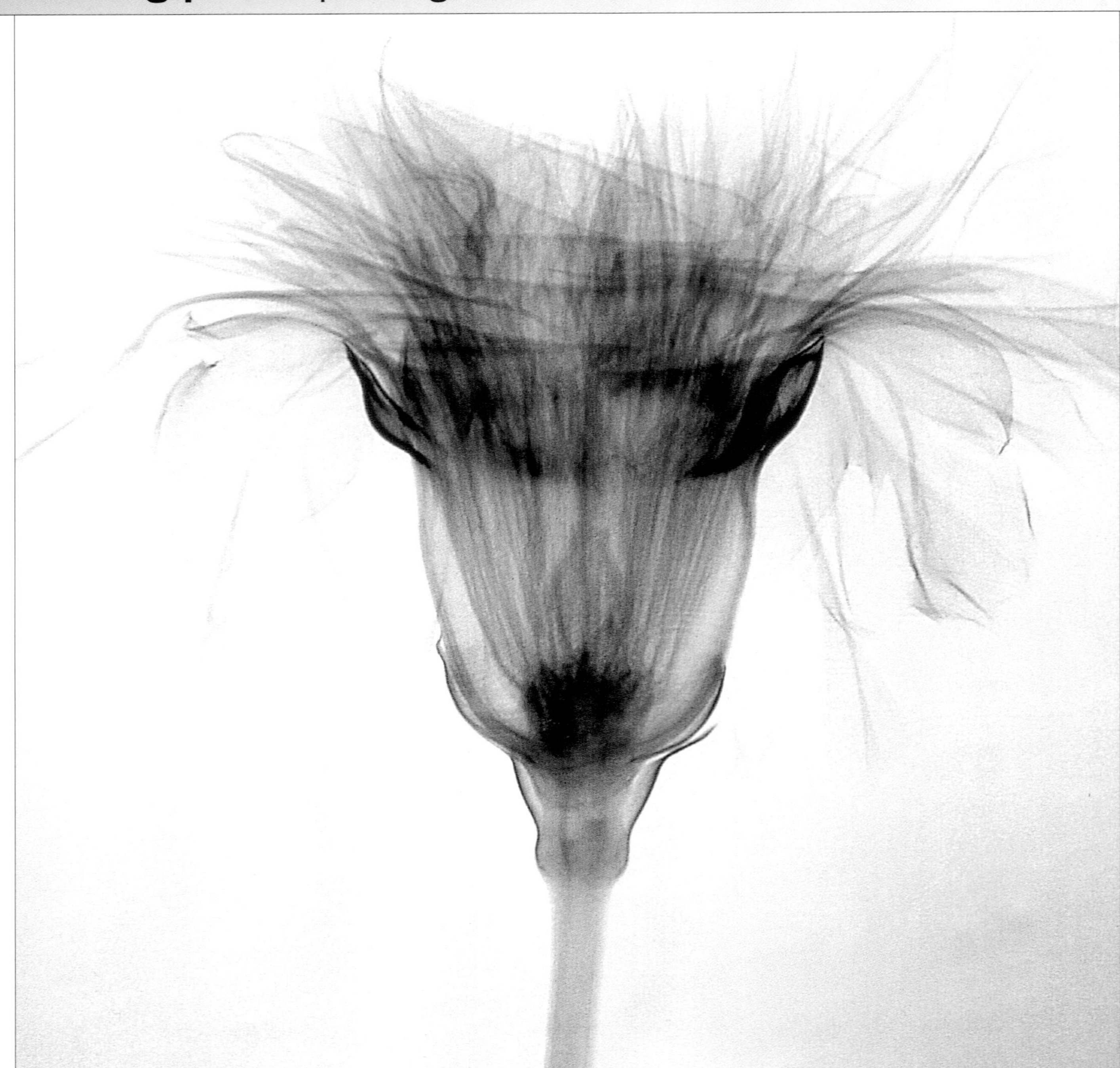

Concept

My goal in creating this series of images was to capture the simple beauty of these everyday objects that we normally take for granted. I felt that the simple lines and geometric patterns created with photograms would enhance their inner beauty.

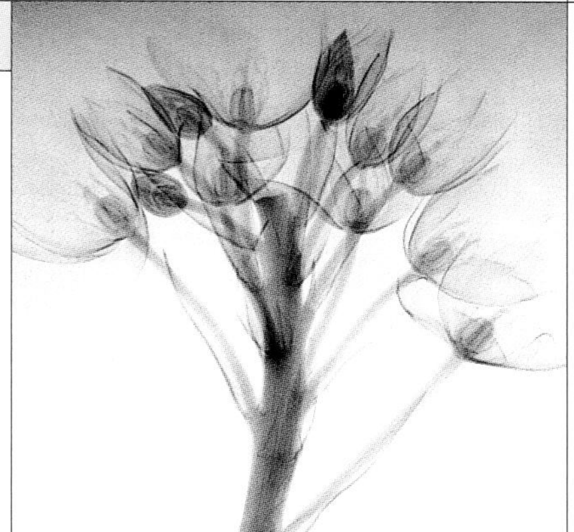

Composition

There is a marvellous delicacy which is possible with this technique. Under safe-lighting I took great care to place the flowers on the film surface, giving the desired compositions.

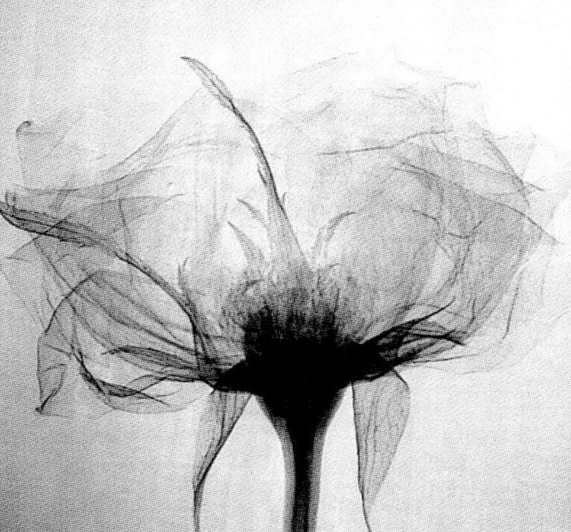

Technique

My photograms are produced by placing floral objects on orthochromatic film and then exposed using an intense light source. After exposure, the ortho film was developed in a very dilute lith developer. The film was agitated in the developer for 20 minutes and was then 'snatched' out as soon as the infectious development began. This kept the tones delicate. The images were than washed and dried before being scanned and printed out on archival quality inkjet materials.

▶ **Fact file 2｜3｜4｜5｜Cece Wheeler｜ ｜Bouquet｜Rose｜Dandelions｜Iris｜**

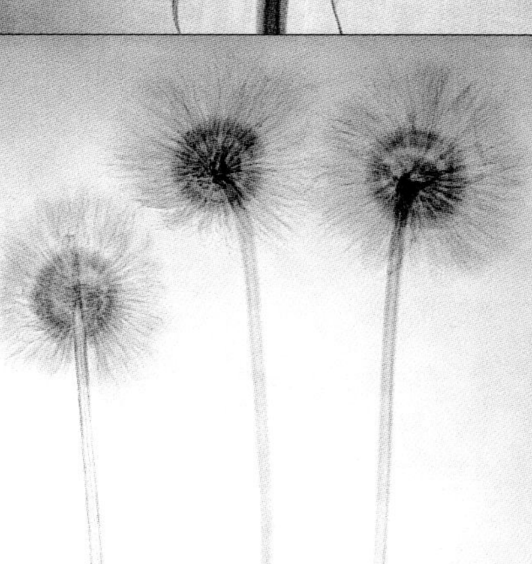

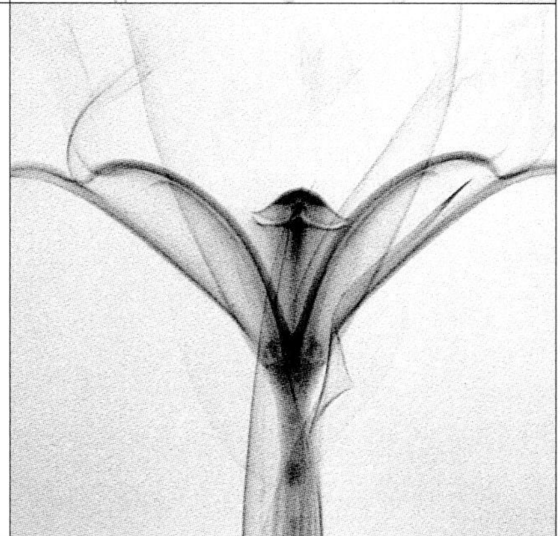

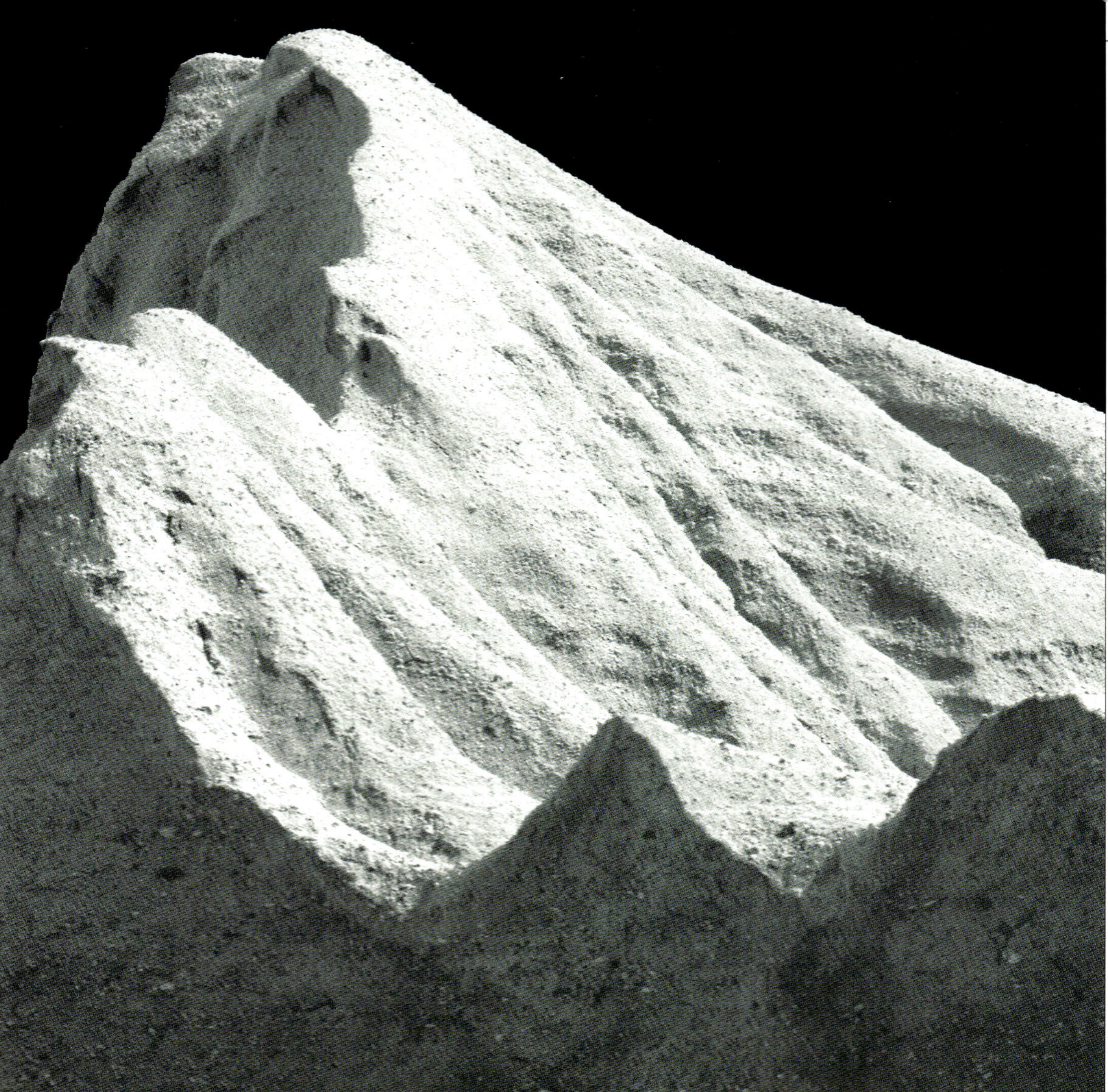

field. Extreme depth-of-field means everything from close to the camera to the far distance is sharp. Conversely, a shallow depth-of-field means the zone of sharpness is very limited. Depth-of-field is affected by lens focal length, the camera-to-subject distance and the lens aperture in use. (See also Depth-of-field preview.)

Depth-of-field preview
Most SLR cameras have a facility that allows the photographer to close down the lens aperture so that it is possible to see how much depth-of-field there is within a scene. Unless the lens is set to its widest aperture, operating the preview feature will darken the image in the viewfinder and it is possible to see, approximately, how much sharpness there is available. Because the viewing image is darker, allow the eye a few seconds to get used to it before making a judgement.

Digital cameras
Cameras that do not use sensitised film and are becoming more and more popular. Obviously, no film means no processing costs so digital is, potentially, a cheap way to take pictures. Instead of film, images are recorded to a storage or memory card and from here down-loaded onto a computer for manipulation, sending out via e-mail or for printing. Direct printing without a computer is also possible.

Digital darkroom
Of course, with digital

glossary

A brief explanation of many of the technical expressions used in this book.

▲ Fernando Redondo | On the moon | This black-and-white image started life as a colour slide which I scanned and converted on the computer. The picture is of an area of sand cliffs south of Lisbon, Portugal, and I was trying to convey the extreme harshness of the region.

Burning in
When extra exposure is given to an area of the print during the printing exposure. (Also see Dodging.)

C-41 process
Universal colour print film chemistry. Some black-and-white films use colour dye technology rather than silver halide and can be processed in this chemistry. This means photographers can enjoy black-and-white photography but with the convenience of fast commercial processing. (Also see Chromogenic film.)

Chromogenic film
A black-and-white film based

on colour film dye technology which means it can be processed in normal colour chemistry.

Darkroom
A blacked-out room set aside for developing prints. Usually, there is a dry bench for the enlarger, negatives and sensitised materials and a wet bench for the trays of processing chemicals. Red, orange or brown safe-lights means the printer can see what is going on.

Depth-of-field
The amount of front-to-back sharpness within a scene or picture is known as depth-of-

imaging there is no longer any need for a blacked-out room to make prints. The term 'darkroom' is still commonly used though, for a set-up comprising a computer, scanner and inkjet printer.

Dodging
Dodging is where less exposure is given to an area of the print during the printing exposure. Pieces of card held on thin wire, fingers or the hand can be used for dodging. (See also Burning in.)

DX coding
In 35mm cameras, electrical

contacts in the camera's film chamber automatically 'read' the film speed off the chequered pattern on the side of the cassette. Ensures correct ISO setting although most SLR cameras will allow manual override.

Enlarger
The centrepiece of the 'wet' darkroom. At its simplest, an enlarger is a light source with a lens and it is this that projects the image onto the sensitised printing paper. Enlargers are available in many types and to suit different film formats.

Colourhead enlargers are available and these have dial-in filtration (cyan, magenta and yellow) for colour and mono printing with variable-contrast materials.

Enlarger lens
It is through this that the image is projected onto the printing paper. It is important to buy the highest quality enlarging lens so that there is minimal quality loss.

Enlarging easel
A specially designed frame that keeps the printing paper flat under the enlarger. Can give borders or be borderless and two- and four-bladed easels are available. The latter are perfect for positioning an image in the middle of a sheet of paper with a wide surround.

Fibre-based papers
Traditional papers, favoured by fine art printers, because they give superior image quality compared with resin-coated papers. Because chemicals and water are absorbed by the paper base, handling is much slower with longer processing, washing and air-drying times. (See also Resin-coated papers.)

Film developer
An exposed film is processed in a film developer to bring up or amplify the latent image. Many different film developers are available promising different negative characteristics. An 'acutance' developer gives excellent edge sharpness while an ultra-fine grain developer gives negatives with near-invisible grain. There is such a wide choice and because the film developer has such a profound impact on the final image that if home developing appeals it is important to experiment with a variety to see which is preferred.

Filters
In black-and-white photography, filters are used on the camera lens and, often, under the enlarger lens, but the filters are different and have different purposes. On the camera lens, filters are often used to modify the tonal relationship of subjects. A single-colour filter transmits light of the same colour and blocks other wavelengths. For example, a red filter lets red light pass while keeping out blue and green light. The result is that red subjects come out lighter and blue and green subjects much darker. Filters such as the skylight, polariser and neutral density have no effect on tonality but are still very useful. The polariser, for example, reduces glare and cuts-down reflections. Filters under the enlarger lens are used for contrast grade selection. (See also Variable-contrast papers and Paper grades.)

Fixer
This is the final chemical bath in film and print development. It is used after the stop bath and before washing and fixes the developed image. Proper fixing and washing are crucial to ensure maximum image permanence.

Grain
The light-sensitive grains in the film's emulsion layer clump together to give a grain effect. Generally speaking, the slower the film the less visible the grain and, conversely, the faster the film the more obvious the grain.

Inkjet printer
Device for outputting high quality prints from the computer or digital camera's storage card. The latest printers give true photographic image quality although the lightfastness of the results vary according to the inks and paper used.

ISO
The film's ISO number indicates its 'speed' or its sensitivity to light. A slow film is ISO 50 or lower, a medium speed film is ISO 100–200, a fast film is ISO 400–800 and an ultra high-speed film is ISO 1600–3200. In bright light, a slow or medium speed film is fast enough to allow a high shutter speed or small aperture but when the light levels drop, a faster film is essential to ensure sharp pictures.

Lith printing
Developing exposed mono printing paper in a lith developer gives lovely peachy-fleshy toned black-and-white prints. However, not all papers respond well so it is worth trying different types. The key thing with lith printing is knowing when to remove or 'snatch' the print from the developer when it looks right. Leaving a print in the lith developer too long gives a contrasty print with none of the delicacy possible with this technique.

Paper grades
Papers are available with fixed contrast grades, but variable-contrast materials are much more popular nowadays. (See Variable-contrast papers and Split-grade printing.)

Generally, for contrasty, overexposed negatives a 'soft' or low paper grade such as grade 0 or 1 is used; for 'normal' negatives a grade of 2 or 3 is advised; and for underexposed negatives a 'hard' or high contrast grade such as 4 or 5 is needed. Paper grade selection is dependent on personal printing styles.

Print developer
Designed for bringing up the image on exposed printing paper. Different types are available depending on the paper type and the desired hue. Most developers will develop a resin-coated print to finality in 60 seconds and two minutes for fibre-based materials.

Push-processing
A very useful technique when the lighting levels are low and a faster film is not available. Many, but not all, films respond well to being underexposed slightly and then compensating for this by extending development time. Broadly speaking, increasing development time by 30% is about right for a film underexposed by one stop. Some film developers work better than others with this technique. (See also Uprating.)

Resin-coated papers
Very popular, RC printing papers have a 'plastic' coating so there is no absorption by the paper which helps speed up processing, especially washing and drying. The surface finish is usually more predictable too. (See also Fibre-based papers.)

Scanner
Computer peripheral for digitising images into a form readable by the computer. Two types are available. The film scanner gives high resolution files off the original negative or slide and is available in 35mm and medium-format versions. Consumer flatbed scanners are usually A4 size (21x29.7cm) and deal with artwork, documents and photographs but can be used to scan three-dimensional objects. Because of the high cost of medium-format film scanners many photographers use a flatbed scanner and the latest models are high resolution so the results are excellent.

Split-grade printing
A popular technique to maximise image quality and made possible with variable-contrast papers. A split-grade print can have one part of the print exposed with a high contrast filter and the rest exposed through a low contrast filter. Exposing the same areas using different contrast filters is another popular technique and with difficult images ensures deep blacks and sparkling highlights. Making test prints is vital to successful split-grade printing.

Split-toning
Magical effects are possible by putting prints through two or more chemical toners. For example, a print can be put through a blue toner, washed and followed with a gold one.

Stop bath
An intermediate acidic bath between the developer and the fixer used to immediately stop any further development. Developers are alkaline and fixed acidic and using a stop bath not only halts development instantly, it also prolongs fixer life.

Toning
The base colour of traditional black-and-white prints can be chemically modified with toners. Toning is often done for aesthetic reasons but many toners (selenium, sulphide, gold) also have benefits in terms of print lightfastness. Some toners (usually blue and green) have limited, if any, archival benefits and are used for aesthetic reasons only.

Uprating
This is exposing a film at a higher ISO speed than its nominal rating. For example, an ISO 100 film exposed at ISO 200 is uprating by one stop. The same film exposed at ISO 400 is uprating by two stops. This deliberate underexposure is compensated for by prolonging film development. Uprating and then push-processing a film increases contrast and grain and tones can look compressed. For the best image quality, have a selection of film available for different lighting situations. (See also Push-processing.)

Variable-contrast papers
Variable-contrast materials are very popular because of their convenience and versatility. One box provides all contrast grades to suit different negatives and are accessed with the use of colour filtration in the enlarger. This filtration can be provided by the enlarger's colourhead or by special printing filters that fit below or above the lens. As a guide, yellow filtration gives the 'softer' or lower grades (0, 1, 2) while magenta produces 'hard' or higher contrast (3, 4, 5) prints.

Zone System
A system of exposure, processing and printing devised by American landscape photographer Ansel Adams. Used by fine art photographers, especially those using large-format cameras, after superbly toned prints.

Mario Abbatepaolo
Italy/USA
www.marioabbatepaolo.com
info@marioabbatepaolo.com
Pages 61, 68, 69, 76

Daniel Bayer
Aspen, Colorado, USA
www.dbpix.com
dphotobayer@yahoo.com
Pages 38, 39

Vince Bevan
Penzance, UK
www.vincebevan.co.uk
contact@vincebevan.co.uk
Pages 4-5, 10-11, 43, 46,
47, 66-67, 86-87, 96, 97

John Braeckmans
Lier, Belgium
www.braeckmans.com
john@braeckmans.com
Pages 34, 74-75

Dan Burkholder
Carrollton, Texas, USA
www.danburkholder.com
danphoto@aol.com
Pages 13, 32-33, 70-71, 72,
73, 92, 104-105, 108-109,
114, 115

William Cheung
Peterborough, UK
www.williamcheung.co.uk
willtherooster@hotmail.com
Pages 17, 18, 20, 23, 25,
32, 48, 49, 56, 57, 62, 93,
106, 108, 116, 117, 128

Jamie Drouin
Victoria, British Columbia,
Canada
www.jamiedrouin.com
info@jamiedrouin.com
Page 91

Nökkvi Elíasson
Reykjavik, Iceland
www.islandia.is/~nokkvi
nokkvi@islandia.is
Pages 60-61

Wojciech Gepner
Kielce, Poland
wogep@poczta.onet.pl
Pages 44-45, 110, 111

Marco Girolami
Rome and Milan, Italy;
New York, USA
www.marcogirolami.it
info@marcogirolami.it
Pages 36, 80, 100, 101

Rene de Haan
Amsterdam, The Netherlands
www.renedehaan.com
rene@urcentral.com
Pages 14, 27, 35, 90

Bob Hudak
Coconut Creek, Florida, USA
www.bobhudak.com
bob@bobhudak.com
Pages 42, 58-59, 64, 84, 85

David W Lewis
Callender, Ontario, Canada
www.bromoil.com
dlewis@onlink.net
Pages 118, 119

Ian McFarlane
Athens, Georgia, USA
www.ismphotography.com
ian@ismphotography.com
Pages 50, 51, 107

Jacek Pomykalski
Krakow, Poland
pomykalski.com
jacek@pomykalski.com
Page 52

Lynn Radeka
Placentia, California, USA
www.radekaphotography.com
and
www.maskingkits.com
lynn@radekaphotography.com
Pages 30, 31, 41, 65

Fernando Redondo
Lisbon, Portugal
via www.photoblink.com
fredondo@netcabo.pt
Page 124

Jill Skupin
Dallas, Texas, USA
www.jillskupinburkholder.com
jillskupin@aol.com
Pages 102-03, 121

Éric Soulé
Montesquieu, near Toulouse,
France
http://ericsoule.free.fr
eric.soule@laposte.net
Pages 94, 95

Nana Sousa Dias
Lisbon, Portugal
www.photo.net/photodb/
folder?folder_id=219901
ousadias@netcabo.pt
Pages 7, 8-9, 28-29, 40, 42,
66, 76

Gorden Thye
Bochum, Germany
www.gordenthye.de
info@gordenthye.de
Pages 53, 81

Felix Tian
Fremont, California, USA
www.felixphoto.net
felix@felixphoto.net
Pages 54, 55, 57, 62, 105

Kirk Toft
Dewsbury, West Yorks, UK
www.alternativephotography.
com
KIRK@ktoft.freeserve.co.uk
Page 120

Nic Tucker
London, UK
www.nictucker.com
nic@nictucker.com
Page 63 and cover

**Aguinaldo Calheiros
Vera-Cruz**
Lisbon, Portugal
www.photoforum.ru/rate/us
er.php?u_id=1395
guivera-cruz@clix.pt or
guivera.cruz@netcabo.pt
Pages 77, 82, 83

James Webb
Urbana, Illinois, USA
www.prairienet.org/~jwebb66
jwebb66@yahoo.com
Pages 112, 113

Cece Wheeler
Hampton, Virginia, USA
http:/members.aol.com/
cecewheeler
wheelerc@tncc.vccs.edu
Pages 122, 123

Wynn White
Yotsukaido, Chiba, Tokyo
www.wynnwhitephoto.com
wynn@wynnwhitephoto.com
Pages 32, 37, 98, 99, 127

Zosia Zija
Warsaw, Poland
www.zija.net
zosia@zija.net
Pages 78, 79, 88, 89

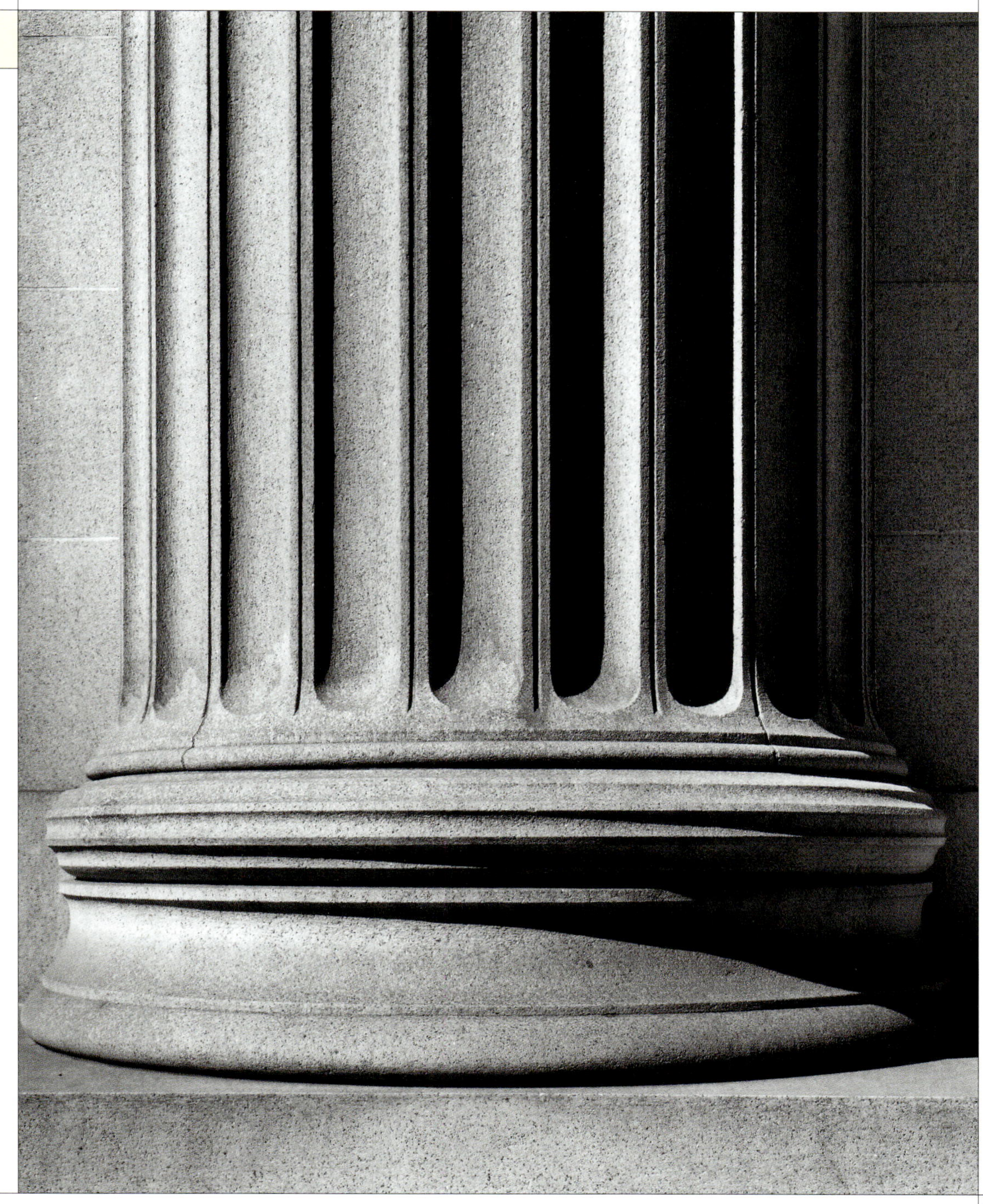

▶ **William Cheung** | In 30 years of photography 'Man and reeds' is my favourite single picture. I am not holding it up as an example of camera genius, but this image is simply packed full of wonderful memories and to me that is what photography is all about. True, photography is a creative medium but above all else it is absolutely ideal for capturing memories and so many people forget that. Sadly, it is their loss.

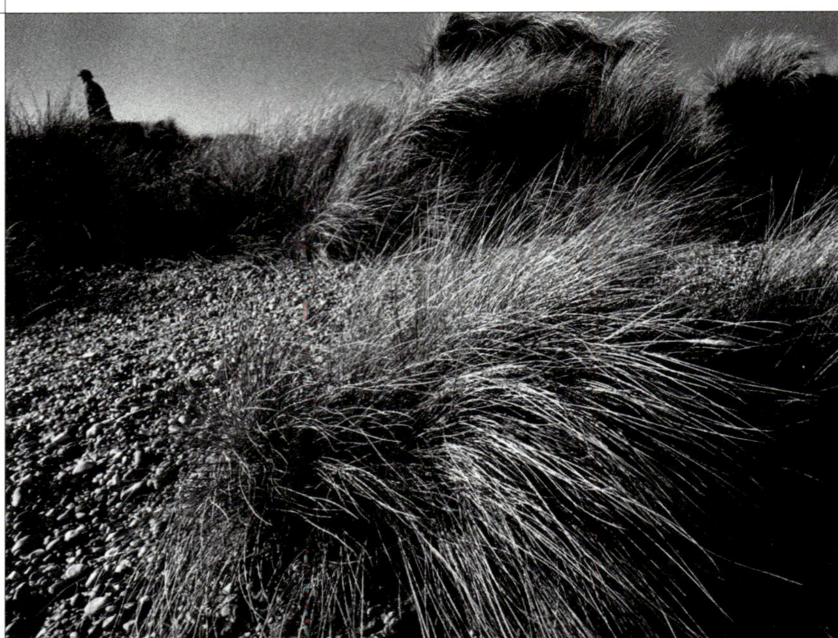

acknowledgements

Creating a book is very much a team effort and Camera Craft: Black & White is no exception. My thanks are due to many people for their creativity, unstinting support and commitment.

First of all to Brian Morris who commissioned me in the first instance, to Sarah Jameson who is responsible for finding the photographers featured and to Kate Stephens. It was Kate's skill and talent that has resulted in a beautiful book.

Of course, without pictures there would be no book in the first place so my gratitude also goes out to those wonderful photographers whose work is featured. Black-and-white photography is a challenging and incredibly creative medium and the people featured here are excellent ambassadors for the medium and deserve all the praise that they get for their works.

Finally, I want to thank my family and friends and a very special lady called Jo, all of whom have kept me motivated during the time this book has taken. Without them, none of this would have been possible. Thanks to them all and thank you for buying it. May it inspire you to a greater enjoyment of photography.